Happy Birth day Lee
from
Ed & Wilma
Taugenberg
1983

The Faith of the Church

A Reformed Perspective
on its
Historical Development   M. Eugene Osterhaven

WILLIAM B. EERDMANS
PUBLISHING COMPANY • GRAND RAPIDS, MICHIGAN

Library of Congress Cataloging in Publication Data

Osterhaven, M. Eugene (Maurice Eugene), 1915–
   The faith of the Church.

   Includes bibliographical references.
      1. Theology, Doctrinal. 2. Reformed Church—Doctrinal
and controversial works. I. Title.
BX9571.084   230'.57   82-5061
ISBN 0-8028-1916-8   AACR2

To My Students

Contents

x The Faith of the Church

Preface

In writing this manual on the faith of the church I have followed the method which most appeals to me when I reflect on Christian doctrine: to think of doctrine in terms of its historical development. The questions that arise are why a doctrine received attention at a particular time, what circumstances played a role in determining the shape that it took, what issues were at stake, and what settlement was formulated by the church.

I believe, with James Orr and others, that there has been a certain logical progression in the way in which the various items of faith have received attention. Those of a more fundamental nature became dogma first. Thus the doctrines of God and of the person of Christ required settlement before the doctrines of salvation or the sacraments. For the latter teachings rest on the former and cannot be formulated apart from them. That is why it is impossible to bypass history in a study of the beliefs of Christians.

Our main interest is not history, however, but theology. It is not the development but that which developed, the faith of God's people, that has prompted this study. Latent from the first, and implicit in Scripture, doctrine needed time for conceptualization and articulation. Once articulated, the statement was there to be rethought, rephrased, passed on to others. It might be forgotten for a time — as the doctrine of grace was forgotten in the late Middle Ages — but the earlier statement was there waiting to be reconsidered. One thinks of Luther reading Augustine on Pelagianism or of John Wesley reading Luther's exposition of *Romans*. The doctrine had already been developed; what was needed was understanding, perhaps rediscovery, and dissemination.

I treat each doctrine in the period in history when it received its most significant attention. If there were earlier attempts at statement which had lasting influence, these may be noted, and later additions are included where these seem to me to be important. Moreover, I indicate my own stance, and try to give each doctrine a normative rounding-off, either in the position of the theologian being discussed, or in squaring an idea with Scripture, or both.

The selection of doctrines studied is inevitably somewhat arbitrary.

However, I have chosen the major topics which have been mined from Scripture and wrought into the faith as I understand it. Certain items that might have been included, because of my own particular tradition, predilection, or whim perhaps, do not appear. What does appear is, to my mind, fundamental and necessary for a mature understanding of the Christian faith.

That faith belongs to the whole church. I believe in the oneness and catholicity of the church even while I am a member of a particular branch of it. There is no "ecumenical Christian" who does not have his own ecclesiastical roots. The subtitle of this study refers to it as "a Reformed perspective." That makes clear the tradition from which I write. I have expanded on what the word "Reformed" means to me in my book *The Spirit of the Reformed Tradition*. To me "Reformed" means having an appreciation for the faith of ancient Israel and the struggles of the early church; standing with Augustine and Luther for the doctrines of sin and sovereign grace; believing with the Wesleys and Kierkegaard in living for the Lord. It means yielding all of life to the lordship of Jesus Christ and acknowledging the Holy Spirit as the source of all gifts and graces.

This study is dedicated to my students past and present for two reasons: it expresses my indebtedness to them for their patience with me and for their love for the faith of the church; and it confirms the conviction I have tried to convey in the classroom that the best way to understand systematic theology is to learn how its major ideas developed. I would add that one cannot be a proficient theologian — and a minister is a theologian, or should be — apart from such learning. That knowledge is not only necessary for professional ministry, but also important for others in the church who desire a degree of sophistication in the handling of Christian doctrine. In order to appeal to such readers in this work I have avoided technical terms and foreign languages as much as possible.

I express appreciation to the Board of Theological Education of the Reformed Church in America for a sabbatical during which most of this writing was done. The reading that lies behind it was done then and earlier. To my wife Margaret, who typed the manuscript, I express my gratitude. To my colleagues Christopher B. Kaiser at Western Seminary and Paul K. Jewett at Fuller Seminary, and to Marlin Van Elderen and Jon Pott of the William B. Eerdmans Publishing Company, I am grateful for helpful counsel. The shortcomings are mine alone.

— *M. Eugene Osterhaven*

Abbreviations

NPNF   *The Nicene and Post-Nicene Fathers,* First Series. Edited by Philip Schaff, *et al.* Grand Rapids: Wm. B. Eerdmans Publishing Company, 1956.

ANF   *The Ante-Nicene Fathers.* Edited by Alexander Roberts and James Donaldson, *et al.* Grand Rapids: Wm. B. Eerdmans Publishing Company, 1953.

LCC   *The Library of Christian Classics.* Edited by John Baillie, John T. McNeill, and Henry P. Van Dusen. Philadelphia: The Westminster Press, 1953- .

TDNT   *Theological Dictionary of the New Testament.* Edited by Gerhard Kittel, translated and edited by Geoffrey W. Bromiley. Grand Rapids: Wm. B. Eerdmans Publishing Company, 1964-1976.

LW   *Luther's Works.* American Edition. Edited by Jaroslav Pelikan and Helmut T. Lehmann, *et al.* 55 vols.; Philadelphia: Muhlenberg Press and the Concordia Publishing House, 1955- .

CO   *Joannis Calvini Opera quae supersunt omnia.* Edited by G. Baum, E. Cunitz, E. Reuss, *et al.* 59 vols., "Corpus Reformatorum," vols. xxixff. Brunswigae: Schwetschke et Filium, 1863-1900.

Inst.   *Institutes of the Christian Religion.* Translated by Ford Lewis Battles and edited by John T. McNeill. 2 vols., "Library of Christian Classics"; Philadelphia: The Westminster Press, 1960. Vols. XX-XXI.

Tracts *Tracts Relating to the Reformation.* Translated by Henry Beveridge. 3 vols., Grand Rapids: Wm. B. Eerdmans Publishing Company, 1958.

The Faith of the Church

Chapter 1

Some Preliminary Considerations

1. THEOLOGY AS A FUNCTION OF THE CHURCH

By theology we mean the *deliberate and careful consideration of the Christian faith*. Theological activity may be carried on at a humble level or with great subtlety and sophistication. Sometimes it is done poorly, sometimes well. The professional theologian may be employed by a secular institution or by a seminary of the church. And not all theology is the work of professional theologians officially supervised by the church: often theology is done by lay people, and sometimes the intellectual pilgrimage of the theologian takes him or her outside the pale of the believing community.

But in spite of this diversity, we maintain that theology is a function of the church. It is within the bosom of the church that God comes to be known; it is within the covenant community that the faith has been articulated and believed; and it is through God's people that his work is carried out for the benefit of the world. Not that theology is the *only* task of the church. Evangelization, proclaiming and teaching the Christian faith, preserving and studying Scripture, writing of creeds and confessions, worship, faithfully administering the sacraments — all of these are important functions of the church. Yet all of these other functions require the use of theology.

The church, the New Testament form of the people of God (Rom. 2:29; Gal. 3:29), has been entrusted with "the oracles of God" (Rom. 3:2). Paul's image of the church as the "pillar and bulwark of truth" (1 Tim. 3:15) presupposes that the church can make theological judgments and engage in theological activity.

2. THE NEED FOR THEOLOGICAL REFLECTION ON THE FAITH OF THE CHURCH

Granted that the church *can* undertake deliberate and careful reflection on the Christian faith; does it have to do so? Isn't simple faith enough? Indeed, doesn't theology, with its definitions and distinctions, just confuse matters? Why is all this elaborate theological apparatus and training necessary anyway?

The mood reflected in such questions is a common one, and it requires a response. We can mention at least three reasons why theological reflection is indeed necessary. First, the faith which believes the gospel seeks understanding, as Anselm demonstrated long ago. Faith is not content to rest in ignorance. It wishes as far as possible to comprehend. Believers desire to love the Lord with the mind as well as the heart and soul, and theology helps them do so. Through its distinctions and definitions, linguistics and logic, its study of history and hermeneutics, theology helps clarify belief. Bearing in mind that Christians are "stewards of the mysteries of God" (1 Cor. 4:1), theology seeks to make those mysteries as meaningful as possible to the greater service of God.

A second reason theology is necessary is the rise of heresy. Throughout the history of the church false doctrine has had to be opposed. Paul's firm opposition to works righteousness in his letter to the Galatians, Irenaeus' denunciation of Gnosticism, Augustine's rebuttal of Pelagianism, the Reformation criticism of Roman Catholic error—all these and more have been cases in which theological discussion was necessary to preserve the faith of the church. Humans are prone to error. We tend unconsciously to substitute our own ideas for the Word of God. This danger of perverting the gospel makes reflection and definition, comparison and comprehension imperative. Simply quoting Scripture is not enough, for meanings must be determined and ideas related to each other. Sometimes entire systems of thought have to be set over against one another. And there is no way to do this competently apart from theological endeavor and theological understanding.

Third, theology is necessary for instruction. God's people need to think through their faith after they have been instructed in it. From the earliest days of the church, instructors have prepared manuals on the faith to help believers give a reason for the faith that was in them. The Apostles' Creed is one such writing—a short summary of certain articles of faith which needed emphasis in the second century. The instructional task of the church is perennial. As there can be no believers without knowledge, so there can be no knowledge apart from instruction in the faith. And instruction worthy of the name means involvement in ideas, in doctrine, in theology.

3. THE OBJECT OF THEOLOGY

When we say that the *object* of theology is God and his relations with humanity, we are using the word "object" as it is often used in philosophy to mean that of which the mind takes cognizance. Since all our knowledge of God comes from him, we might also speak of him as the "subject" of theology. The point is that theology is fundamentally and primarily interested in God. Its ultimate concern is not even the *knowledge* of God but God himself in his living, dynamic relationship to us.

John Calvin began the first edition of his *Institutes of the Christian Religion* with these words: "Nearly the whole of sacred doctrine consists in these two parts: knowledge of God and of ourselves."[1] For good reason, that statement was unchanged in later editions. Nothing else can compare in importance with knowledge of God and then of ourselves in the light of his Word. The prophet envisioned the day when "the earth shall be full of the knowledge of the Lord as the waters cover the sea" (Isa. 11:9); and Jesus said that the knowledge of God is eternal life (John 17:3).

One Reformed theologian has written that the idea of God is at the beginning and the end of Calvinistic theology. "In a particularly profound sense Calvinism is a theocentric theology. . . . For the Calvinist the doctrine of God is the doctrine of doctrines, in a sense the only doctrine."[2] But other Christian traditions make the same judgment,[3] so no one branch of the church has an exclusive claim to this central conception. Because theology seeks to know God and his relations to us, it has been called the "queen of the sciences" or the "highest science." An Anglican theologian has characterized systematic theology as "the most daring effort which the human mind has ever made, namely, the attempt to arrive at as near an approximation of absolute truth concerning ultimate reality as the human mind is capable of attaining."[4]

4. THE NORM OF THEOLOGY

What gives theology its authority is Scripture, the Word of God. Because God has spoken through prophets, apostles, and "in the fulness of time" through his Son, the record of that revelation is given a special place within the body of literature. That deference given to Scripture as norm is accentuated by the Bible's witness to itself. It claims to be the very Word of God, which ought to be received and which "cannot be broken" (2 Tim. 3:16; Heb. 1:1f.; 2 Pet. 1:20; John 10:35).[5] Little wonder then that the church from the first appealed to Scripture to settle differences, to learn God's will, and to ascertain the faith.

Sometimes, however, the church has set itself over Scripture, declaring that its own traditions are as revelatory and authoritative as the Word of God.[6] Claiming the sole right to teach the faith, it has drawn from its traditions and devotional practices in determining the content of the faith. In doing so (as, for example, in the doctrine of Mariology) it has wandered from the teaching and practice of the apostolic church. Forgetting that all its teaching and practice must be subjected to the scrutiny of the Word of God, the church — Protestant and Roman Catholic alike — has assimilated foreign elements and at times been hardly recognizable as the church of the living God.

In other periods the church, weakened by unbelief and cowed by the popularity of natural science, has allowed reason to usurp the Bible's place. Submission to Scripture as the rule of faith has been dismissed as credulity, and Christianity has been likened to the ripest fruit on the tree of human knowledge and achievement. The results have been predictable: cardinal doctrines were discarded, faith vilified, and the human mind made the measure of truth. The Barthian movement earlier in this century took aim at such theologies of self-realization, which weakened the sense of need for God and his grace. But as schools of theology come and go, the Barthian movement had largely run its course by the early 1960s, and new theological fads have followed one after another. Hence the question of norm or authority in theology continues to be a pressing one.

A generation ago Emil Brunner argued that Jesus Christ is the norm for theology.[7] But this position merely raises the further question of which Christ. The Christ of Scripture, or some other? One who accepts the apostolic witness concerning Jesus Christ is in agreement with the ancient tradition of the church and has in fact made Scripture the final court of appeal. One who rejects the testimony of Scripture, on the other hand, not only rejects that which Christ accepted, the criterion of a word from God, but embarks on a sea of subjectivism where it is hard to find any shore. The doctrinal storms that inevitably arise are bound to toss him about, and with no haven in sight or mind shipwreck is a real possibility.

The way to avoid this is to stay close to the Word. The Lord Jesus Christ, the Word incarnate who lived among us, was crucified, rose from the dead, and reigns as Lord of heaven and earth, told the Jews that their Scriptures bore witness to him (John 5:39; Luke 24:25-27). Moreover, the writers of the New Testament make it abundantly clear that their witness is to that same Christ (see John 20:31 and the opening verses of Luke, Acts, Romans, Hebrews, and Revelation). We know Christ through the Scriptures, and Scripture makes sense only when we see it as witnessing to him.

Jesus Christ, the reigning Lord, builds the church and makes his kingdom come. As Lord and King he makes his will known through the Bible, from which God's commandment

> rings out . . . in the power of the Holy Spirit with an ever fresh note, and demands to be heard and obeyed in faith. The Bible has therefore no mechanical authority for the right ordering of . . . life set out in paragraphs like a legal code, but a spiritual and religious authority. It tells us how Christ wishes to make his Kingship prevail here and now.[8]

5. THE METHOD OF THEOLOGY

Like other sciences, theology gives itself wholly to the object of its inquiry and allows that object to determine the method of its investigation. Theology differs from other sciences in that its object, God, is not a part of the natural order.

Since theological investigation is a task of the church, which owes its existence to God's self-disclosure, theology's first assignment is to listen to the record of that self-disclosure as given in the books of the Old and New Testament.[9] To gain knowledge of the living God and not of some idol, theology must come to God on his terms. First, if it "would draw near to God [it] must believe that he exists and that he rewards those who seek him" (Heb. 11:6). Then it must seek him in his Word, "living and active, sharper than any two-edged sword" (Heb. 4:12), which is where it pleases him to address us.

Theology pursues its task of trying to understand the faith God has given not haphazardly, but in a scientific manner, using all the assistance other areas of human understanding can render. History, philosophy, the study of ancient languages, archaeology are among the organized bodies of knowledge important to theology. Its investigation is carried on in the full light of day.

Theology must further demonstrate its scientific character by carefully analyzing its subject matter and being fully aware of how reason, authority, and faith function in achieving understanding. Since theology claims an understanding of reality as a whole, theologians must be particularly aware of the presuppositions they bring to their task and indeed eager to discuss these presuppositions — convinced that the more profound such a discussion is, the better the case for persuading others that we live in a universe designed by God. Among the theologian's presuppositions are the reality of the world, the reality and validity of mental experience, the coherence of data, knowledge as part of experience, the partiality of knowledge, the compatibility of the human mind and nature around us, the objectivity of truth, the reality of moral and spiritual values.[10] An awareness of presuppositions is often absent from other sciences, especially the natural sciences, which tend uncritically to assume a whole host of details.

6. SYSTEM IN THEOLOGY

If the object of theology is God and his relations to humanity, theology itself is the organization of that knowledge into a meaningful pattern. It may be defined as *systematized* knowledge of God and his relations to us.

We live in an age when "system" is often disparaged, and systematic theology in particular has come in for considerable criticism. But the underlying conviction supporting the claim that it is *ordered* knowledge of God with which theology concerns itself is that the human mind is so created that it seeks to relate whatever material is given it into an intelligible pattern. It cannot rest with particulars but seeks to organize or arrange them into a meaningful scheme. "If we know so much as two facts concerning God," it has been said, "the human mind is incapable of holding these facts apart; it must contemplate them in relation to one another. Systematization is only a part of the irrepressible effort of the intelligence to comprehend the facts presented to it, an effort which the intelligence can escape only by ceasing to be intelligence."[11]

The philosopher Brand Blanshard concludes the first volume of his major work on the theory of knowledge by stating that thought cannot be satisfied until it introduces order and system in its handling of data.[12] Building a ship or an airplane illustrates that thesis, as do cooking oatmeal and getting dressed in the morning. So does the writing of a book on theology, even by a scholar who would stigmatize the position taken here as "rationalistic."[13] The charge that the organization of knowledge is rationalistic is no new phenomenon. Nor is the use of reason to disparage reason. In his arguments with the Puritans, Richard Hooker once said that his opponents "never use reason so willingly as to disgrace reason."[14] Whatever the details of their argument, both Hooker and his adversaries were right in their appreciation of reason's ability to organize ideas.

Beginning with the attempt to make the experience of apprehending

God rationally meaningful, the theological enterprise grows into an endeavor to do intellectual justice to whatever we may know about God and his relations to the world he has made. Included within the scope of theology is every discipline and department of activity needed to make the message from God meaningful. In the history of the church the departments of theology which have developed are exegetical, historical, systematic, and practical. Each has its own subdivisions and fields of specializations. In each department the mind brings its powers to bear on the body of information furnished it in order to perform its own work. No one department of theology is self-sufficient and, given the total task, none is more important than any other. Each is essential and each depends on the others.

7. THEOLOGY AND EXPERIENCE

The faith of the church has not been hammered out in a vacuum. It comes out of the experience of God's people struggling to hear his Word in the context of life. That means that theology is conditioned by psychological and sociological factors which affect human understanding and interpretation of the Word. Some people are reluctant to admit this, preferring to fancy that their own interpretations and formulations of doctrine are in complete harmony with the Word of God.

The truth is, however, that our interpretations are always imperfect. No system of doctrine is ever in complete harmony with Scripture. Human reason, like all the rest of our existence, has been affected by sin. Moreover, the writing of creeds and manuals of doctrine is not accomplished by reason alone. Human existence is larger than reason. Reason or understanding is only one aspect of existence, and it is conditioned by experience in various ways.

The way a person is constituted psychologically may result in a greater emphasis on certain aspects of faith than on others. For example, a person highly sensitive to the difference between right and wrong may have a deeper appreciation for the doctrine of atonement than someone else. Appalled by her awareness of the fact of sin and guilt — more particularly, of *her sin* and guilt — before the face of God, she may reflect that in her theological formulations. Similarly, a well-disciplined person may have a sharper awareness of obligation grounded in the reality of the law of God than someone who "hangs loose" in these matters. He will disagree doctrinally with those who incline towards permissiveness.

What is true of individuals is true of societies. Social environment affects our attitudes, our ideas, and our ability to apprehend truth. Understanding varies from person to person and from society to society, even while both read the same Bible. This is true of central concerns as well as peripheral ones. We see it in the different interpretations of salvation in Jesus Christ worked out by churches in eastern and western Europe. The eastern church has understood salvation primarily as Christ's infusion of new life into humanity and his victory over the powers of darkness. The western church has believed Christ's work to be primarily atonement, seen as a sacrifice and penal satisfaction for sin. Such western ideas as guilt, penance, propitiatory sacrifice, and redemption did not develop in the eastern church. Another example of variation in doctrine is the way in which attitudes towards sin and the devil in the Middle Ages differ from those of today.

Personal, psychological, and social factors inevitably affect understanding and the theology that is produced by it. Diligently as we strive to be faithful to the Word of God, tradition and other influences will still be operative. If we do not recognize this, we are naive or self-deceptive. The ideal is to make our formulations of doctrine conform to the Word of God, but we always fall short of perfection. As Tennyson wrote:

Our little systems have their day;
They have their day and cease to be;
They are but broken lights of Thee,
And Thou, O Lord, art more than they.

These nontheological factors lurking in the background are not always given due credit. Until the beginning of the nineteenth century, only two faculties were seen in the life of the soul, the intellectual and the moral. Feeling or emotion was disregarded almost entirely. What exceptions there were—the Heidelberg Catechism, the experiential theology of early Dutch Calvinism,[15] the Great Awakening of the eighteenth century, and the strain of pietism ever to be found in the church—were regarded as mystical aberrations, hardly worthy of serious *theological* consideration, by those in the mainstream of orthodoxy.

The publication in 1799 of Friedrich Schleiermacher's addresses *On Religion* marked a change in this attitude. A religious expression of the Romanticism of the time, these addresses spoke directly to a generation starved by an inadequate theological and spiritual diet.

The eighteenth century had seen a religious philosophy develop which the subjective religiosity of scholastic psychology was willing to allow to assert itself, but the end result was that "religion" could be nothing other than *knowledge* of the eternal truths of reason, and *doing* the immutable demands of the moral law. With that development only a caricature of religion remained against which the Schleiermacher of the addresses *On Religion* directed his attack while he sought to bring to light new points of view. A new depth of the spirit had to be discovered if religion were really to be allowed to flourish, and that new profundity was shown to be *feeling*. . . . Little wonder that the rumor of the new romantic religiosity spread itself over many lands as the rumor of a new springtime.[16]

Theology has not been the same since Schleiermacher. Although his romantic adulation of experience was sometimes at the expense of the normativity of Scripture, theology has greatly benefited from the realization that experience is important in doing theology as well as in other aspects of the church's life.

Theology is not arid ratiocination removed from everyday life. It is an exceedingly practical concern, directly related to and coming from the whole of human existence in a world governed by God. Such recent emphases as liberation theology, the demand for "contextual theology," and the call for orthopraxis (right behavior) to be given as great an emphasis as orthodoxy (right teaching) suffice as reminders of that. Theology comes out of experience, to be sure, and it must be *seen* as having this broader relationship if it is to be done adequately. Furthermore, it must issue in new experiences of obedience and faith. William Ames, the English emigré to the Netherlands who was the most widely read Puritan in New England, had this in mind when he defined theology as "the teaching of living for God" and divided his major book *The Marrow of Theology* into two parts: faith and observance (this theme is developed further in Chapter 15 below).[17]

8. FAITH AND THEOLOGY

We have not yet said anything about the relation of theology to faith. Having defined theology as deliberate and careful consideration of Christian faith and, with Anselm, as faith seeking understanding, we note that faith may be defined as trust in the God who speaks in Scripture. This "faith" by which one embraces the gospel is distinguished from "faith" as used in the title of this book, which refers to the faith which is believed. The first (sometimes called by its Latin name *fides qua creditur*) is an attitude; the second (Latin, *fides quae creditur*) is a body of doctrine. In this section we are concerned with the former meaning.

The relation between faith and theology has often been a problem in the church. Sometimes theology has been unpopular, and faith alone has been extolled as sufficient for the church and for the life of the Christian in the world. Faith is its own certainty, it is said, and needs no further argumentation or confirmation. From time to time philosophy is out of fashion and a wedge is driven between learning and faith.

The late Middle Ages was one such period. Scholastic theology had in effect dug its own grave. Aversion to its method of correlating faith and life was widespread. The times were ready for something new, and the Reformation helped fill the void. Seeing scholasticism as a mixture of Scripture and philosophy, Luther denounced it as "nothing else than ignorance of the truth and scandal placed side by side with Scripture."[18] He grieved over how many Christians had been "deluded and made fools of" by Aristotle, "this damned, conceited, rascally heathen," most of whose works ought to be "completely discarded . . . [since] nothing can be learned from them, either about nature or the Spirit." Yet Luther acknowledged that Aristotle's books on logic, rhetoric, and poetry should be retained, and he was a strong advocate of schools that would advance true learning and piety.[19] Unlike many in the radical wing of the Reformation movement, Luther did not condemn learning as such. But he felt that the learning in which he had been trained was false, filled with idle speculation, and thus detrimental to faith. In spite of his bombastic reaction to the use of Aristotle's physics, metaphysics, psychology, and ethics in the schools, he favored intelligent inquiry and a close relationship between faith and theology.

Luther's younger friend and collaborator Philip Melanchthon, whose humanist sympathies, incredible learning in various fields, and genius in educational organization earned him the epithet "teacher of Germany," had a passion for clear and scientific apprehension of any subject to which he gave his attention. Among Melanchthon's many interests theology was first, and he more than anyone else gave the emerging evangelical theology a new method. In it he sought to combine the best of the past with new insights from the learning of his day and from Scripture. Melanchthon thus restored the close relationship between faith and theology which had prevailed in the early history of the church.

Almost from the first, Bavinck remarks, the church was not satisfied with faith in itself, but strove for an understanding of its faith in the context of culture.[20] The reason for this was not any insufficiency on the side of faith, but the relation of faith to the rest of human existence. Faith does not live in isolation from human learning and the world around it. This has been the error of some sects which, because of their isolation, have lost the possibility of influencing their age. Rather, faith desires to be related to the world around it. Faith and theology belong together just as the Christian is an integral part of his world.

To think otherwise, Bavinck comments, would mean that the believing community and the world, the church and the school, religion and science would fall apart in some dualistic fashion.

> Theology has the glorious calling of keeping all these in union with each other so that, on the one hand, Christian living may be preserved from the diverse spiritual ills of mysticism and separatism, and, on the other, scientific thought may be liberated from error and deceit. Theology's right is grounded in the very essence of the Christian religion. Revelation directs itself at the entire human person and has all the world as its object. In every field it struggles against dishonesty and deceit. It offers food for the profoundest thought and establishes the knowledge of God on scientific ground alongside of and in organic union with that of mankind and the world.[21]

Faith and theology are born from the same mother, the church; they are fixed on the same object, the Word of God; their purpose is the same, the service of God; and they are motivated by the same Spirit. Moreover, theology stands on the foundation of faith and beholds Scripture and the rest of reality from that perspective. Faith has priority as the believer's fundamental attitude towards the Word of God. Theology follows as faith seeks to make intelligible to itself its own meaning as faith and that which it embraces as God's revelation.

The differences between faith and theology are not so much matters of essence as degree. Faith is simple acceptance of the Word of God; theology is a scientific inquiry concerning faith and its content. Theology knows that a divinely given faith is more desirable than a brilliant mind and that an unsophisticated believer is better off than an infidel with a dazzling intellect. Theology knows itself to be a human attempt to present in intelligible form a coherent statement of all that God has revealed to us about himself and our relation to him. Faith is the openness to God, brought about by his Spirit, which makes our relationship to God possible and maintains it from day to day.

Theology recognizes its limitations and its possibility of error. Faith acknowledges no limits, no possibility of error in its commitment. Theology is aware that it is unable to describe its object adequately;

faith embraces its object and rejoices in it. Theology, faced with problems, wrestles against darkness. Faith, aware of problems, scorns the darkness knowing that "God is light . . . , in him is no darkness at all" (1 John 1:5); and it is content to rest in that light. Optimistic about both present and future, faith sustains the Christian when theology is no help. Only faith can affirm, in the face of contrary evidence, "Though he slay me, yet will I trust in him" (Job 13:15, KJV). To theology is given the task of trying to make such apparently irrational statements meaningful. Bavinck uses an analogy to illuminate the distinction between the common experiential knowledge of faith and the more scientific knowledge of theology:

> Every man has some empirical knowledge of the sun, moon, stars, etc., but this knowledge is as far as heaven is from earth from the scientific knowledge of astronomy. The first knows only the facts, the latter the reasons. The man of science does not despise the common, empirical knowledge; nor does he reject "natural certainty." But he has the calling to illumine the common knowledge, to analyse it, and to clarify and improve as necessary. It is not otherwise in theology. Faith stands by the facts; theology seeks to press through to the idea. Faith has enough on the *that*; theology asks about the *why* and the *how*.[22]

9. THE WITNESS OF THE HOLY SPIRIT

Before the faith of the church can become real to a person an internal work of grace is necessary. Running through the Bible is the theme that no one can hear, see, understand, or believe the good news of the gospel apart from the grace of God. Christian faith is a gift of God (Eph. 2:8). It is he who opens the ear, removes the veil and gives sight to the blind, illumines the understanding, changes the heart. Sovereign grace is etched deeply into Scripture. The agent who effects the change is God himself in the person of the Holy Spirit.

> What person knows a man's thoughts except the spirit of the man which is in him? So also no one comprehends the thoughts of God except the Spirit of God. Now we have received not the spirit of the world, but the Spirit which is from God, that we might understand the gifts bestowed on us by God. And we impart this in words not taught by human wisdom but taught by the Spirit, interpreting spiritual truths to those who possess the Spirit (1 Cor. 2:11-13).

The doctrine of the internal witness of the Holy Spirit is a gift of John Calvin to the church. Other writers had seen it but none wrote about it so effectively as he.[23] Since his time this doctrine has become the possession of the whole church. An acute problem in Calvin's day was the question: by what authority does one believe the Bible to be the Word of God? Prior to the Reformation the answer had been: the church. Through its teaching office the church claimed to possess the right to give certainty in matters of faith. The definition of the content of faith was the prerogative of the church, and the faithful were to believe what the church defined, *because the church defined it*. Once that authority was challenged, the question of the ground for religious belief became urgent. Following the example of the early church in its struggle with heresy, the Reformers appealed to Scripture. Here one could stand, for here God speaks with the voice of authority.

> Daily oracles are not sent from heaven, for it pleased the Lord to hallow his truth to everlasting remembrance in the Scriptures alone. Hence the Scriptures obtain full authority among believers only when men regard them as having sprung from heaven, as if there the living words of God were heard (*Inst.*, I, vii, 1).

Yet, Scripture in itself is insufficient, for "the Word will not find acceptance in men's hearts before it is sealed by the inward testimony of the Spirit. The same Spirit, therefore, who has spoken through the mouths of the prophets must penetrate into our hearts to persuade us that they faithfully proclaimed what had been divinely commanded" (*Inst.*, I, vii, 4).

This, then, is the answer of the church to the question of religious authority. Its objective ground is the word of prophets and apostles, who spoke and wrote as instruments of God. Its subjective ground is the Holy Spirit, who gave the message to those prophets and apostles and who uses that same message to accomplish his work in the world today. Holy Scripture is his book and "our full persuasion and assurance of the infallible truth and divine authority thereof is from the inward work of the Holy Spirit, bearing witness by and with the Word in our hearts," as the Westminster Confession says. The external Word must be internalized; the Word outside must be experienced inwardly if one is to become convinced that it is the very Word of God. Once he has become convinced, further proof is unnecessary.

> Illumined by his power, we believe neither by our own nor by anyone else's judgment that Scripture is from God; but above human judgment we affirm with utter certainty (just as if we were gazing upon the majesty of God himself) that it has flowed to us from the very mouth of God by the ministry of men. We seek no proofs, no marks of genuineness upon which our judgment may lean, but we subject our judgment and wit to it as to a thing far beyond any guesswork (*Inst.*, I, vii, 5).

The Reformers who developed the doctrine of the internal witness of the Holy Spirit did not mean it as an escape from other considerations, such as those of history. They themselves appealed to history when settling questions concerning the canon of Scripture. Rather, the doctrine of the internal witness of the Spirit is meant to point out to believers the true ground on which religious certainty must be based — namely, God himself speaking in his Word — and to assure us that it is indeed God whom we hear and not just the voice of the prophet.

The witness of the Spirit is to Scripture as a whole. This must be said lest Scripture be dismembered and questions raised about the authority of disconnected, or even isolated, parts. The Bible is an organism, the witness of chosen persons to the salvation which God has brought to pass in history. The canon of Scripture is closed and a proper investigation of its contents takes into account God's one purpose in instigating and carrying to completion his program for the salvation of the world. That purpose was to unite all things in Jesus Christ (Eph. 1:10; Col. 1:16ff.). He is the key to a proper understanding of the Bible.[24]

10. FAITH AND HISTORY

The Scripture to which the Spirit witnesses is a thoroughly historical book, and Christianity is a religion grounded in history. Unlike religions which seek to transcend history, considering it an inferior, earthbound category of thought, Christianity sees history as second only to God in importance. For it is the stage on which God works out his mighty acts of redemption, the arena in which he wrestles with us as we work out our destinies. Little wonder then that the Old Testament sees God's hand in everything that happened to Israel and that the marvel of the New Testament is that the eternal God became a man to dwell with humanity in its history. The one characterization of God that runs throughout the entire Bible is that he is the God of history. The ancient world knew nature gods and nature worship, forms of idolatry into which Israel occasionally lapsed, but those who followed the leadership of Moses and listened to the prophets knew that it is the living God — not just deified powers and potentialities of nature — who encounters men and women in their daily life, calling them to repentance and faith and service, working with them and through them in the creation of history.

The ancients had no conception of the meaning of history and little interest in it. Even the greatest of the Greek thinkers considered history unworthy of philosophical interest. Like contemporary existentialist philosophers, they dismissed the past as unimportant. The covenant community, however, came to know the importance of history in its experiences with God as he revealed the everlasting significance of interpersonal relationships. Although they seemed to be mere pawns of empires like Egypt and Assyria, the Hebrew people received an interpretation of human history of which the great powers were unaware. The meaning of that drama came out of the struggle and suffering of the Hebrew people, often at the hands of those powers. Herbert Butterfield remarks that it cannot have been an accident that the tragedy which befell the Hebrews coincided with the age of the great prophets, whose message came out of their profound experiences and "so often took the form of historical interpretation itself." In them, he says, we see a search

> for an interpretation of history which would embrace catastrophe itself and transcend the immediate spectacle of tragedy. Altogether we have here the greatest and most deliberate attempts ever made to wrestle with destiny and interpret history and discover meaning in the human drama; above all to grapple with the moral difficulties that history presents to the religious mind.[25]

The great importance Scripture ascribes to history is not being forgotten today. On the contrary. The accent on history in contemporary theology is so great that there is danger of doing injustice to the doctrine of God. Wolfhart Pannenberg and process theology are cases in point, to which we shall give more complete attention in Chapter 16 below.

Pannenberg objects strongly to any denigration of history as if it were the realm of the relative and transient, above which God reigns in sovereign majesty. History for him is not just a stage to which God condescends to effect redemption and to govern the nations. Rather it is a mode of the divine existence, which brings into completion the very fulness of God himself.

Pannenberg's obsession with history leads him to reject traditional doctrines of Christ in favor of doing Christology "from below." What he means is that we should not speak of a pre-existent Logos coming to dwell on earth but of a man, Jesus, who revealed himself to be also God. Because in history God is working out his predestined purposes for himself as well as for humankind, it can be said that "God's being is still in the process of coming to be."[26]

Pannenberg does not wish to compromise the sovereignty of God;

his intention rather is to point out that God's eternity and power are not fully revealed and that only at the end will they be seen as complete. Yet it is fair to question whether Pannenberg's "eschatological ontology" adequately states the truth revealed, even while appreciating his insight into how crucial the events of history are.

More extreme in its deviation from what the church has understood to be its faith is contemporary process theology. A. N. Whitehead and Charles Hartshorne reject historical talk of God as "immutable being" as unreal, meaningless abstraction. Hartshorne writes that "the divine reality in its concreteness is the eminent form of becoming."[27] Because events are the stuff of reality, Hartshorne identifies God with them.

That kind of process theology falls short of the Christian conception of God because it fails to distinguish God from the process. We mention it here only to illustrate that some current interest in history is so severely one-sided that it cannot see God as he is, the high and holy one inhabiting eternity. Even though he condescends to live in the midst of his people, he remains the sovereign Lord.

Today's exaggeration of and one-sided emphasis on history are a far cry from the marginal attention given history in an earlier day. Perhaps the most often cited indication of that philosophical mood was Lessing's statement that "the accidental truths of history can never become the proof of necessary truths of reason." A proper orientation for theology is neither Lessing's extreme of short-changing history in the interest of rationalistic idealism nor the extremes of history-obsessed philosophers and theologians today. Both God and history are prime categories of thought in the biblical faith of the church; neither should be emphasized at the expense of the other.

Christian theology needs a strong doctrine of God, and it is important today to maintain the doctrine of God's lordship over history. While God is within history, he also remains its Lord. This understanding of God is even more fundamental than a correct understanding of history, for God creates and sustains history, gives it meaning, and enables us to understand it. Infinitely transcending the world he made, God yet inhabits it, so that what happens in its history happens also to him (Matt. 25:40, 45).

Christian faith — in the sense of what Christians believe — is thus bound up with history. The events narrated in Scripture happened and cannot be undone. The church's body of doctrine is grounded in that which has come to pass. Moreover, Christian faith — in the sense of the attitude by which we embrace the gospel — is related to history. Our believing rests on Scripture's testimony concerning God's great deeds for our salvation. So important is the history of that salvation that, if it were shown to be false, faith would disappear. Paul made this clear to the Corinthians. Discussing the relation of faith to the resurrection of Christ, he writes: "If Christ has not been raised, then our preaching is in vain and your faith is in vain" (1 Cor. 15:14). The idea that faith need not rest on objective historical fact is false from the point of view of the Bible. The faith about which Scripture speaks as necessary for salvation is not mere self-understanding or any other kind of inverted subjectivism. It is a wholehearted trust that what God says he has done for us has actually happened and that the biblical interpretation of those events is true. Modern subjectivism not only casts doubt on the authenticity of the history of salvation but, much worse, hardly seems to care about that history, declaring it unimportant for faith, which is alleged to be independent of historical events. From Friedrich Schleiermacher to Rudolf Bultmann the emphasis in certain circles has been on one's own inner religious state of consciousness rather than on the external historical event.[28] The church by contrast affirms that faith depends on the reality of God's grace as narrated and witnessed to in his Word. There is wisdom for today in Mackintosh's criticism of Schleiermacher:

> You can only speak of standing where there is ground to stand upon, and you can only speak of faith where there is a Word of God on which faith rests. Schleiermacher's eye—though not always nor exclusively—was bent on inward facts, as though the soul could feed on its own vitals. It was because the Reformers looked unflinchingly to God as self-unveiled in his Word that they escaped from the deceptive self-absorption and immanentism of the essential mystic, whose experience moves only within itself.[29]

11. THE DEVELOPMENT OF DOCTRINE

To say that the faith which the church professes has had a long development in history may strike some as a dangerous contradiction of Jude's reference to "the faith once for all delivered to the saints" (vs. 3). How could that which was delivered "once for all" need development? But what was revealed and set down in Scripture had to be thought through and worked out in the life of the church so that it could be understood and appropriated as the faith of the believing community. There has been a development of official church doctrine, even though the special revelation given through prophets, apostles, and Christ was completed by the end of the first century.

Later we shall discuss the completeness of special revelation; our concern here is to note that the giving of that revelation did not eliminate the need to articulate and formulate what was believed. Indeed the church had to think through its own understanding of its faith so that it could be taught to others, transmitted to generations following, and defended against attacks from inside and outside the church.

Not all would agree with this. Some Christians have argued that development means change and change means falsification of what has been committed to the faithful once for all. Moreover, it has been said, it would be a betrayal of the Giver who "is the same yesterday, today, and forever" (Heb. 13:8). Perhaps the most noted advocate of this position was the seventeenth-century Roman Catholic apologist Bossuet, who held that the faith of the church is "*semper eadem*: always the same." Any alteration in understanding or definition is heresy. Bossuet attempted to demonstrate that Protestantism was apostate because it departed from the teaching and jurisdiction of the one church which had held the Christian faith over the centuries unchanged and intact.

> The Church's doctrine is always the same. . . . The Gospel is never different from what it was before. Hence, if at any time someone says that the faith includes something which yesterday was not said to be of the faith, it is always *heterodoxy*, which is any doctrine different from *orthodoxy*. There is no difficulty about recognizing false doctrine: There is no argument about it: it is recognized at once, whenever it appears, merely because it is new.[30]

Bossuet believed that there had been progress but not development of doctrine. Progress did not mean greater understanding, but referred to the fact that Christian doctrine "had spread like a mustard-seed," from village to hamlet and throughout the world. In defining doctrine the church receives no new insight or understanding on the general question at stake but applies its mind to the particular question.

> In no sense would Bossuet have said that the church needed to "make up her mind." She never makes "new" articles of faith. She only declares what she has always believed — explicitly, consciously, and continuously believed. . . . The church knows what she believes. The heretics help her to find new language to express that belief.[31]

Improved historical understanding has made it impossible for the church to maintain Bossuet's rigid position. There is more to defining doctrine than clarifying and unfolding anew the same articles of faith. Development also takes place in the sense of new insights, deeper understanding, and clearer perception of the teachings of Scripture. John Henry Cardinal Newman, struggling with the discrepancy between the faith of the early church and that of nineteenth-century Roman Catholicism, and influenced by the quasi-evolutionary theories of contemporary German Protestantism, propounded a theory which revolutionized Roman Catholic thinking on the subject and influenced other theology as well.[32]

In his landmark *Essay on the Development of Christian Doctrine* Newman describes the faith of the church as first of all an idea.[33] By this he does not mean the mere notion of an object but, as Chadwick shows, "the object itself as it is capable of being apprehended in various notions. An idea will in this sense be more complex and many-sided than the individual notions about it, and perhaps never fully 'perceptible' in such notions as human language is capable of expressing."[34] Time is required to bring out various aspects of the idea in concrete historical situations, but its complexity is such that its full meaning will never be exhausted.

Heresy provides an occasion for the church to bring out meanings and definitions which it may have felt earlier without expressing them in words.[35] New understanding thus arises, new definitions emerge, new development takes place. Faith had existed before, even though only felt and unexpressed. But since there had not previously been the understanding, the definition of doctrine that later came to be also was lacking. In the course of time, the faith of the church—implicit, unrefined, and unarticulated at first—came to be explicit, refined, and articulated. More than that, what had not been known, understood, or defined came to be known, understood, and defined as the church reflected on the sacred deposit of faith God had given it.

Newman was correct that development in understanding and definition has occurred within the articles of faith, but he complicated and compromised his position by including within the corpus of the Christian faith doctrines for which there is no scriptural warrant, such as the "dignity" of Mary and the saints, "devotion to the Blessed Virgin," and "papal supremacy." Christian doctrine arises from the interaction of the Christian community of faith with Scripture, and it is limited to what is explicitly given in Scripture or derived from it by good and necessary inference. Since Mariology, veneration of saints, and papal supremacy, as developed within the medieval church, do not meet this test, they do not merit the status of articles of faith, nor should they become church dogma.[36]

Newman also erred in stating that when doctrine is officially defined, thus becoming dogma, it is irreformable. This notion, based on belief in the infallibility of the church, had a long history before the solemn and shocking declaration of the First Vatican Council (1870) that papal pronouncements on doctrine "are irreformable of themselves, and not from the consent of the church." Since the Second Vatican Council, however, the doctrines of papal and ecclesiastical infallibility have been challenged by some of their former advocates.[37] Roman Catholic theologians have shown a new willingness to acknowledge the wisdom of Luther's observation that church councils have erred and do err. Infallibility should thus not be attributed to their doctrinal utterances, nor should dogma be considered irreformable. Dogma should rather be seen for what it is: a human attempt to articulate the teaching of the Word of God.[38] Faith is thus driven back to Scripture as its one infallible guide. As the original witness to the self-disclosure of God, Scripture constitutes the apostolic tradition; and that tradition is not to be confused with the later ecclesiastical tradition which stems from it.

In affirming that the apostolic tradition, as distinct from later church tradition, is normative, we are saying that all doctrinal development is to be judged by Scripture. Although the doctrine of Scripture will be discussed more fully in a later chapter, we mention it here because of its importance in doctrinal development. Its uniqueness and superiority become evident when one measures later thinking against the Word of God. Patent examples are the doctrines of grace, the work of Christ, and justification by faith. Who can fail to appreciate the vast difference between what is set forth in Scripture on these subjects and what one reads in church fathers two or three centuries later?[39] Why, with Scripture before them, did Christian thinkers fail to see what was seen later?

When we ask questions like that, we should not forget that we have the advantage of the experiences of the centuries. Doctrinal development was a long, slow process. The scarce copies of biblical writings were limited to those few who could read and get hold of them. Moreover, certain ideas had to be worked through before other ideas could be considered. In theology, as in other sciences, the simpler had to precede the more complex. Fundamental concepts had to be understood before others could be contemplated. James Orr pointed out that doctrinal development "is not arbitrary but is shaped by the inner reason and necessity of the case."[40] There is an order of "logical dependence" in an arrangement of doctrine, or dogma, in which "one forms the presupposition of the other." He illustrates his point:

> The doctrine of redemption presupposes that of the Person of the Redeemer, and, prior to that, the doctrine of sin; the doctrine of sin, again, throws us back on the general doctrine of man, and also on the character, law, and moral administration of God; the doctrine of God, on the other

hand, underlies everything—the doctrine of man, of sin, of Christ, of salvation, of the purpose of the world, of human destiny. It is possible, no doubt, to alter or invert this order—. . . , yet in the logical order of dependence the sequence is as I have stated it. Just as in nature it would be found impossible to expound chemistry adequately without some antecedent knowledge of physics, or biology without some knowledge of both chemistry and physics; so in theology the derivative doctrine cannot be exhaustively expounded till those which it presupposes have, at least in some measure, been explained.[41]

To Orr the progress of dogma was "simply the system of theology spread out through the centuries."[42] Though some might suspect him of Hegelianism for trying to force history into systematic categories, Orr held to his thesis. No rhyme or reason may be apparent in the way in which some ideas have found a place in the teaching of the church, but Orr found both in the way legitimate dogma has evolved in history. There is similarity of pattern between the development of dogma and the "system" in which it is usually comprehended. Neither the development nor the "system" can be understood properly unless studied in relationship to each other. The history of dogma is a meaningless inquiry unless its end-product is envisioned, and the system of theology hangs in midair unless the many connections of its doctrines with their historical origins are indicated. Christian doctrine comes out of Scripture, but Scripture as it has come alive in the life of the church—that is, in history. And some knowledge of history is necessary if the mistakes of the past are to be avoided in the future.

Our intention is the chapters which follow is to discuss the faith of the church. The order in which various subjects are considered will be the order of their development in history—which is the order in which they are often found in theology handbooks. Each doctrine will first be discussed in the historical context out of which it arose to assume a place of prominence in the life of the church. We shall note its biblical base and set forth its meaning in relation to other doctrines. From time to time we shall also emphasize practical consequences of faith, in keeping with the overriding intention of this entire book to aid understanding for the strengthening of faith and the greater glory of God.

Chapter 2

The Faith of Israel

The faith of the church is a development of the faith that God had first given Israel as recorded in the Old Testament. To the Israelites, said St. Paul, "belong the sonship, the glory, the covenants, the giving of the law, the worship, and the promises; to them belong the patriarchs, and of their race, according to the flesh, is the Christ" (Rom. 9:4f.). No other nation had been so favored; only they had been made "a people holy to the Lord" (Deut. 7:6).

For centuries Israel was being prepared for its mission to humanity. During these years many fell away from the community; others were added to it. Always there was at least "a remnant chosen by grace" (Rom. 11:5). Finally Israel fulfilled its mission to the world when Jesus Christ came and the Christian church was established. The foundation of the church was "the apostles and prophets, Christ Jesus himself being the chief cornerstone, in whom the whole structure is joined together" (Eph. 2:20). Since the entire course of Israel's history pointed to Jesus Christ (Luke 24:27; John 5:39), he is the seed, or offspring, of Abraham in a unique sense (Gal. 3:16), for all the promises of God to his people are bound up in him (2 Cor. 1:20). Those who believe in him, Jew or Gentile, are likewise children of Abraham (Gal. 3:28f.).

"Historically and spiritually," one Old Testament theologian observes, "Christianity stands upon the shoulders of Judaism."[1] To God's earlier revelation to the Jews, Christianity adds his fuller revelation of himself in Jesus Christ. The new covenant in Christ completed the disclosure of himself which God began with the patriarchs and enlarged in subsequent Hebrew history. It was a literal fulfilment of the Psalmist's supplication that God would bow his heavens and come down (Ps. 144:5).

It is with the faith of Israel, then, that we begin our historical survey. And when we examine the later faith of the church, we find several doctrines from the Old Testament which are especially prominent. We shall look in turn at the fact of God, God's revelation of himself to a covenant community, the rise of that covenant community, the creation and preservation of the world by God, and salvation by the grace of God.

1. THE FACT OF GOD

God's disclosure of himself to Israel distinguished Israel's religion from all others on the face of the earth. Others wandered in darkness; Israel had the light of life. Others fashioned gods according to their own fancies; the highest heaven could not contain the God of Abraham, Isaac, and Jacob (2 Chron. 6:18). The Israelites' scorn when they thought of the vanity of heathen idols is expressed eloquently in the psalms and the prophets:

> Our God is in the heavens;
> he does whatever he pleases.
> Their idols are silver and gold,
> the work of men's hands. . . .
> Those who make them are like them;
>   so are all who trust in them (Ps. 115:3f., 8; cf. Isa. 40:18-20; 46:1f.,
>   5-7).

Israel's constant claim, over against all false gods who did not exist, was that its Lord was the living God. The source and giver of life, he was no less alive than the rest of his creation. To compare God with idols was improper to the pious Hebrew in view of God's sovereign majesty (cf. Isa. 40:22-26).

God's revelation of himself as God is the fundamental teaching in the Old Testament. Strictly speaking, however, God's existence is more assumed than taught. All people should know that he is God and give him the honor due his name (Pss. 48:10; 72:17). He is El-Shaddai, God Almighty, who will not and cannot give his glory to another (Isa. 42:8; 48:11). The Apostle Paul, who had drunk deeply at the wells of Hebrew religion, told an audience in Athens who did not know the Lord: "The God who made the world and everything in it, being Lord of heaven and earth, does not live in shrines made by man, nor is he served by human hands, as though he needed anything, since he himself gives to all men life and breath and everything" (Acts 17:24f.). When Israel rendered him formal worship while its heart was far from him, God declared:

> I am God, your God. . . .
> I will accept no bull from your house,
>   nor he-goat from your folds.
> For every beast of the forest is mine,
>   the cattle on a thousand hills.
> I know all the birds of the air,
>   and all that moves in the field is mine (Ps. 50:7, 9-11).

In a sense, because God is God, he can never be known, even by his covenant people. He reveals himself to them and speaks to Moses, their leader, "face to face, as a man speaks to his friend" (Exod. 33:11). Abraham, the father of all the faithful, is called a friend of God (2 Chron. 20:7; James 2:23). David is said to be a man after God's own heart (1 Sam. 13:14). Yet Moses is told that he cannot see God (Exod. 33:20), and Job asks whether anyone can find God by searching (Job 11:7). Isaiah inquires whether anyone can measure God's Spirit (Isa. 40:13) and declares that God is a God who hides himself (45:15). John states categorically that no one has ever seen God (John 1:18; 1 John 4:12). Paul's doxology voices the belief of the pious Jews: God "dwells in unapproachable light," and "no man has ever seen or can see" him (1 Tim. 6:16).

Scripture does not try to resolve these apparently contradictory portrayals of God as dwelling with his people, yet remaining eternal and transcendent. Sufficient unto himself, even while he creates a world and sustains it — so identifying himself with it in love that he becomes a part of his own creation — he remains "the King of the ages" whose deeds are "great and wonderful" and whose ways are "just and true" (Rev. 15:3).

This conception of a God so exalted that it is impossible to conceive of any other alongside him (Isa. 45:5, 6, 14, 21) is the first lesson to be learned in a study of Israel's religion. According to Vriezen, God's transcendence is the primary meaning of the attribute "holy," the perfection most commonly ascribed to him in the Old Testament.

> The idea of holiness is the one most typical for the Old Testament faith. The word qadosh is used in Israel especially of God and has acquired a quite distinct meaning. ... Qadosh is God as the "Wholly Other One," as appears from Hosea 11:9: "I am God and not man; the Holy One in the midst of thee."[2]

Because of who God is, even while he is in the midst of his people, he cannot deny his transcendent holiness but remains the Lord God, almighty in power and alone in mysterious majesty.

2. REVELATION

The next great teaching in the faith of Israel is God's giving of himself to his people. The one who could not be compared with any others revealed himself to Israel. Having made himself known through various media, he declared himself to be the high and holy one inhabiting eternity who yet condescends to be in fellowship with his creation.[3] Although those made in his likeness have sinned against him, he remains merciful. At a high moment in Israel's history he proclaimed to Moses: "The Lord, the Lord, a God merciful and gracious, slow to anger and abounding in steadfast love and faithfulness, keeping steadfast love for thousands, forgiving iniquity and transgression and sin, but who will by no means clear the guilty" (Exod. 34:6f.).

Thus Israel developed an appreciation for God's revelation and his perfections which entered later Christian teaching. God was seen to be sovereign Lord, dependent on no one, eternal, everywhere present, and unchangeable. But he is also compassionate and motivated by love, righteous in his judgments and altogether true. Although his eyes are too pure to behold evil (Hab. 1:13), his love and grace draw him to humanity in its helpless plight, and he provides atonement and whatever else is necessary for communion with him. It is his will that all whom he has chosen shall see and share his glory forever (John 17:24). Because he is mighty in power not one fails (Isa. 40:26; John 10:27ff.). In his eternal purpose he created the world and has determined to reconcile the whole creation to himself through Jesus Christ, in whom it pleased the Father that all fulness should dwell. Having made peace through the blood of his cross, Christ has returned to heaven. From there he will come to earth again at the end of this age to destroy all opposition and to give the kingdom to the Father, so that God may be everything to everyone (Col. 1:19f.; 1 Cor. 15:24ff.).

To be sure, not all of this is recorded in the Old Testament. The message of redemption in Christ could not be written until it had been achieved. But the God who revealed himself in Jesus Christ was the very same one who had been making himself known to Israel during the preceding centuries. "In many and various ways God spoke of old to our fathers by the prophets; but in these last days he has spoken to us by a son" (Heb. 1:1f.).

It was through the Son that the revelation had come to Israel. He was the mediator of revelation as well as of redemption. He was the Word of the Lord through whom the prophets had spoken. In the fulness of time the Word *himself* would appear. The revelation of God in Jesus Christ cannot be believed apart from the earlier disclosure through the prophets, who prepared a people and raised their hopes for the future. While other eastern religions had prophets, the phenomenon in Israel was unique, for in Israel the prophet was called by God to reveal a specific message in his name: that, unlike the idols, God "does not depend upon his people or upon the worship he receives. He punishes his people as well as the other nations of the world; he is not dominated by the cultic ceremonies offered by his servants. Yahweh is supra-national, supra-cultic, for he is holy, but also merciful and just. And for his name's sake he also expects these two qualities in his people."[4]

The prophets who brought this message of judgment and mercy often stood as solitary figures in the life of their people. Sometimes obeying God's call meant ministering against their own wills. As they struggled to lead their people out of sin into submission to God's will, they became personifications of their own message. Driven by the Spirit of God, the prophet often appeared as a tragic figure, while in reality he was an instrument of the Eternal One who was accomplishing his purpose through the prophet's ministry. Vriezen sees revealed in the activity of the prophets, which manifested their love for God and for their people, the very essence of Israel's religion and of Israel's God who desires the salvation of his people. "Thus the prophets as the servants of God are the image of Jesus Christ, the Son who gave himself completely to restore the communion between God and man."[5]

Prophetism is the dominant phenomenon in Israel's spiritual development, and it is evident throughout the Old Testament. Moses' promise that God would raise up another prophet to lead the people was fulfilled in Christ (Deut. 18:15; Acts 3:22). Malachi's prediction of the coming of one to prepare the way of the Lord was fulfilled by the last of the prophets of the old covenant, John the Baptist (Mal. 3:1; Matt. 11:9ff.). All that had been written "in the law of Moses and the prophets and the psalms" was fulfilled in Christ (Luke 24:44; cf. Acts 3:21). For "the Word became flesh and dwelt among us" (John 1:14) and thus became the key to the understanding of the whole revelation of God in both the Old and the New Testaments.

3. THE COVENANT COMMUNITY

In setting forth revelation as a concept which Christian thought took over from Judaism, we have of course made some mention of the people who received God's revelation. It was in order to constitute them as the people of God that the Word had come. The purpose of the revelation was the creation of a covenant community. The Christian church looks back to Israel as its prototype and sees itself as serving God in this age in much the same way Israel served him earlier.

This notion of a covenant community is at the center of Israel's religion, as Eichrodt has shown.[6] "I will be your God, and you shall be my people" is a theme of both Testaments, but it is a particularly constant refrain under the old covenant, when the special relationship of Israel to God was being established and had to be impressed on the minds of the people (Lev. 26:12; Deut. 14:2). Thus we read that God wanted a tabernacle built so that he might dwell among his people (Exod. 25:8). As his relationship with them became more personal, he demanded nothing less than the heart (Deut. 6:5). This theme became the summary of the law of God (Mark 12:30). To leave him was to play the harlot; but, as the book of Hosea so vividly shows, even then God's love was so great that his heart yearned for his unfaithful spouse, whom he would bring back to himself at any cost.

Yahweh's great desire was a people on whom he could lavish the abundance of his grace, so that cleansed from sin and dedicated to him it might enjoy his fellowship. Thus it could be said later that Christ came to "purify for himself a people of his own" (Titus 2:14). In a celebrated statement Peter declared to Christians scattered abroad:

> You are a chosen race, a royal priesthood, a holy nation, God's own people, that you may declare the wonderful deeds of him who called you out of darkness into his marvelous light. Once you were no people but now you are God's people; once you had not received mercy but now you have received mercy (1 Pet. 2:9f.).

The establishment of a covenant community teaches us something about the nature of God and ourselves. As a trinity of persons, Father, Son, and Holy Spirit, God had always known the joy of fellowship, but he desired to go outside himself, to create something, someone with whom he could be in personal correspondence. So he made a world in which there would be people with whom he could share his thoughts and who could enjoy fellowship with him and with one another. Thus it was that Abraham became "a friend of God" and that God spoke to Moses "as a man speaks to his friend." These are not isolated incidents in the history of the covenant community but the very norm of the relationship that the eternal God desires to have with his children.

God desires this relationship with his people as individuals as well as with the group, for only as individuals respond does the group as a whole live in fellowship with its God. Hence the Old Testament emphasis that individuals were to love him. The whole community was his possession—his vineyard, his bride, his people—but his eye was on the individual as well. The garment of the high priest bore the names of the twelve tribes of Israel on engraved stones as a "remembrance for the sons of Israel" so that Aaron could "bear their names before the Lord upon his two shoulders for remembrance" (Exod. 28:9ff.; cf. Isa. 49:15f.).

The teaching in the New Testament is no less personal. Jesus' parables of the lost sheep, the lost coin, and the lost son (Luke 15) emphasize God's love for individuals, as does his teaching about God's care for birds (Matt. 6:26; 10:29f.; Luke 12:6f.). The thought is that God does not lose sight of the individual within the community, but rather that his love and concern are without parallel in nature or in human society.

The establishment of the covenant community also speaks to the relations of human beings to each other. God's people are related to each other by common bonds of faith, commitments, and loyalties. Both the legislation in the Pentateuch and Jesus' definition of the neighbor as any person with whom one has to do (Luke 10:25ff.) point to the obligation of God's people to love and assist one another. Jesus goes so far as to require that which seems impossible—love for one's enemy (Matt. 5:44). But that which is impossible in a world of sin becomes possible through the gift of the Holy Spirit, who is given to all those who ask (Luke 11:5-13). The fruit of the Spirit is observed in human relationships, so that God is glorified (Matt. 5:16; 7:17ff.; Gal. 5:22ff.).

The covenant community then becomes a model or paradigm of what all human society should be. That is why Jesus told his disciples that they were the salt of the earth, leaven, and the light of the world (Matt. 5:13ff.; 13:33). Although many of the details of this instruction were given later, it was there in essence from the first. God had told his people through Moses that they were to love the Lord their God with all their heart, and with all their soul, and with all their strength, and with all their mind, and their neighbor as themselves (Deut. 6:5; Lev. 19:18). Jesus' teaching was simply an elaboration of that fundamental message.

The covenant was established with the patriarchs (Gen. 17:1-7; 26:3f.; 28:13ff.), expounded by the prophets (e.g., Isa. 54:10; 55:3; 56; Jer. 31:31ff.), and extolled by the Psalmists (e.g., Pss. 78, 89, 103, 105, 106, 111, 132). Jesus and his apostles enriched the doctrine and showed that it attained its ultimate meaning in the death of the Son of God, who gave his disciples the bread and cup "of the new covenant" (Matt. 26:28; Luke 22:20; Heb. 8:6; 10:29; 12:24), a memorial which is to last until he and they are gathered into the Father's eternal kingdom. One would think therefore that the doctrine of the covenant would have been at the center of the faith of the church just as it was in Israel and in the experience of the first disciples. In fact it was centuries before the covenant received the emphasis in the church that it had had earlier among the people of God. To be sure, the fathers of the early and medieval church occasionally mention the covenant, and certain monastic and other communities sought to embody its ideals, but nowhere did it receive due emphasis until the Reformation of the sixteenth century. Even then it was limited at first to a few representatives of one Reformation tradition. Zwingli and Bullinger dug it out of Scripture in their encounter with Anabaptists in and around Zurich. From them it passed to Calvin and other Reformers and came to play a dominant role in much of the Reformed theology of the seventeenth and later centuries.[7] (Later we shall see its importance to Reformed theology in the understanding of infant baptism.)

4. THE WORLD CREATED AND GOVERNED BY GOD

The creation and preservation of the world by God was an article of faith unknown outside of Israel. Other ancient peoples supposed the world to have no beginning and primal matter always to have existed.[8] Israel came to know, however, that nothing exists of itself except God. Everything else that exists was fashioned by God out of nothing and is preserved and governed by him from day to day (Ps. 33:6f.).

The story of creation in Genesis is not a scientific description of how the universe came into being, though that beautiful narrative does not violate scientific sensitivity. It is a religious and theological statement of how God is related to it all. He is God the creator; all else is creation. This teaching, recapitulated in the first article of the Apostles' Creed, is philosophically the most important, for it acknowledges God as God and saves us from the pantheistic error of identifying God with nature, which would undermine every other article of faith.

The Heidelberg Catechism explains the first article of the creed as expressing our belief that:

> the eternal Father of our Lord Jesus Christ, who out of nothing created heaven and earth with all that is in them, who also upholds and governs them by his eternal counsel and providence, is for the sake of Christ his Son my God and my Father. . . .

Note in particular the expression "out of nothing." The doctrine of creation means that God made *out of nothing* heaven and earth and all that is in them. Even though they are extra-scriptural, the words "out of nothing" are of the very essence of this doctrine. The following illustration shows their importance:

> If Mrs. Smith goes downtown, buys herself a few yards of material and a printed pattern and runs up a dress on her sewing machine, you would say that she had *made* a dress. If Mrs. Brown goes downtown and buys herself a fifteen dollar dress off the rack, you might ask her where it was *manufactured*, in Toronto or Montreal or New York. But if Mrs. Jones spends two hundred dollars on a gown that came from Christian Dior's salon in Paris, it would be more than your life is worth to ask where it was manufactured or who made it. You would have to say, "Oh, my dear, what a stunning creation!"
>
> Why do we say this about reputed works of art? Why do we talk about artistic creations? Because we feel that something really new has come into being. If a painter paints the front room you can calculate the cost at so much for paint and so much for labour, but you would be insulting an artist who had painted your portrait if you paid him so much for paints, so much for the canvas, and so much for his time. The artist is supposed to be in a small way a creator; he creates something that was not there before, something that could not happen naturally or by accident, something quite new.
>
> Now, strictly and theologically speaking, not even the greatest artist is really a creator. He has to use something to express himself — paint or pencil, human words or musical notes. Even the most creative artist is also from one point of view a humble craftsman, a mere maker of things. But this is not so of God. He is a pure creator. His work is a pure creative act. He alone really creates out of nothing. He alone achieves pure and perfect expression of his purpose.[9]

The doctrine of creation means further the exclusion of all forms of polytheism and systems of philosophical dualism. The ancient world was full of these and the Old Testament leans over backwards to guard against such error. To emphasize the sole sovereignty of God and to militate against the idea that the forces of evil work outside his control, evil and evil spirits are said to come from him (1 Sam. 18:10; 19:9; Isa. 45:7). The intention is to teach not that sin and evil are from God but that he alone is the Lord God Almighty and that nothing is outside his sovereign rule. Even evil serves his purpose. Once this conviction is compromised something else — some principle, some power, some god — is placed alongside Yahweh in a position comparable to his own. He is then no longer the only God but he has to share his glory with another, and from the biblical point of view this is intolerable. Heaven and hell, good and evil are under his control. He alone is God the Father Almighty, maker of heaven and earth.

The mention of evil suggests that within creation God has given his creatures certain freedom, so that both obedience to God and rebellion against him are possible. Thus the problem of "free will" in a world ruled by God arises. The Old Testament is very aware of this problem even while it does not seek to solve it. It sets forth God as the sovereign Lord whose purposes will surely stand; men and women are creatures "in whose nostrils is breath" (Isa. 2:22), frail creatures who easily die. Yet God made them just a little lower than himself and crowned them with glory and honor (Ps. 8:5). A part of that glory is the freedom which was given them. The human person is no automaton but God's special creation made to rule the earth. God "has put eternity into man's mind" (Eccl. 3:11) even though he may live "like the beasts that perish" (Ps. 49:12).

The question of the relation of the human will to the divine will, of sin, grace, and predestination, was bound to become a major doctrinal problem to the people of God later. Here we only note it in connection with the doctrine of the creation and the preservation of the world by God. Preservation includes government, and government includes the problems of God's sovereignty in relation to human freedom and evil.

We noted above that, since God is the Lord, even evil will serve his purpose. This may not be evident here and now, but it will be apparent in the future. The presence of evil in the world contradicts God's goodness and sovereignty. However, that contradiction will not last forever. In his own time God will deal with it finally and bring to completion the redemption he has already achieved in Jesus Christ (Acts 3:21; Rom. 8:18-25; 1 Pet. 1:5). His "eternal purpose which he has realized in Christ Jesus our Lord" (Eph. 3:11) will be brought to a consummation. Evil will receive its deserved judgment whereas all that is a part of God's new creation will live and reign with him forever (Matt. 25:34, 41; Rev. 20:11–21:8).

The doctrines of creation and providence have remained a part of the faith of God's people in spite of ancient and modern challenges. Already by the end of the apostolic age the first of those challenges was offered. The Gnostics, who believed that spirit must oppose matter, denied the very possibility of a real creation and consequently that matter was sustained by God. The cosmos was fashioned by a second-rate divinity in their hierarchy of beings, far removed from the supreme God revealed in the coming of Christ. The response of the church to this teaching is evident in the first article of the Apostles' Creed.

But if the fundamental importance of this teaching has been acknowledged since then, the church, at least in its theological enterprise, has not given to the world God created and sustains the attention that Scripture gives and that it deserves. Christians have tended to focus on God, humanity, society, and salvation, and to leave nature out. Although Scripture frequently includes the earth in the divine saving activity, theology, in its preoccupation with these other themes, has neglected this aspect of redemption. Modern science by contrast has been very much aware of the natural world, drawing attention to its wonders and multiplying our understanding of its operation. Thus over the last two or three centuries nature has been abandoned to the scientists and the gap between the scientific community and the theology of the church has widened. Increasingly those who study the universe explain its phenomena with no thought of the Creator. It is not so much that God is denied; he has simply been forgotten. In Hendry's words, he has been allowed to retain the role of "honorary chairman" while the ordinary operation of the universe goes on without him.[10]

Fortunately, theology has more recently shown new interest in creation. Influenced by the widely discussed problems of energy, pollution, and conservation, Christian thinkers have begun to recover the regard for the natural environment evident in the Old Testament Psalms. Nature, as well as nature's God, has become a respectable subject for theological discussion. Such interest comes none too soon, for with the present rate of population growth, greater longevity, and increasing exploitation of earth's natural resources, the study of nature may become one of the most important theological concerns in the days ahead, a matter literally of life and death.

5. SALVATION BY GRACE

The last great teaching from the Old Testament that we shall mention is salvation by the grace of God. Although God's grace became more evident in Jesus Christ (John 1:17), it was as operative under the old covenant as under the new. Grace—the unmerited favor and mercy of God—is the motivating factor in the call of Abraham, the life of Moses and the exodus from Egypt, in the institution of levitical worship and the office of prophet, in chastisement and the promise of the Messiah. So pervasive and strong a motif is it in all of God's dealings with his people that it underlies even the giving of the law: "I am the Lord your God who brought you out of the land of Egypt, out of the house of bondage" (Exod. 20:2). By divine grace Israel left Egypt, was sustained in the wilderness, was led to the land of promise, and was enabled to fulfil its predestined mission to the nations.

That same grace is manifest in the Savior and in the ministry of the early church. Throughout the book of Acts it is Christ who is still active in the midst of his people. By his grace the apostles are illumined and energized so that they may do his work. Grace is the major theme of the New Testament epistles. This was no new concept that entered the life of the first-century church, but a reality which had become familiar to God's people centuries earlier. As they lived in fellowship with their God, the meaning of grace became ever fuller. In the literature of the old covenant this is perhaps seen most clearly in penitential psalms like Psalm 51:

> Have mercy on me, O God,
> according to thy steadfast love;
> according to thy abundant mercy blot out my transgressions.
> Wash me thoroughly from my iniquity,
> and cleanse me from my sin!
>
> For I know my transgressions,
> and my sin is ever before me.
> Against thee, thee only, have I sinned,
> and done that which is evil in thy sight,
> so that thou art justified in thy sentence
> and blameless in thy judgment. . . .
>
> Behold, thou desirest truth in the inward being;
> therefore teach me wisdom in my secret heart.
> Purge me with hyssop, and I shall be clean;
> wash me, and I shall be whiter than snow.
> Fill me with joy and gladness;
> let the bones which thou hast broken rejoice.
> Hide thy face from my sins,
> and blot out all my iniquities.
> Create in me a clean heart, O God,
> and put a new and right spirit within me.
> Cast me not away from thy presence,
> and take not thy holy Spirit from me.
> Restore to me the joy of thy salvation,
> and uphold me with a willing spirit. . . .

The Psalmist depends utterly on God's grace and mercy for forgiveness and for help along life's way. He ought to live uprightly and perfectly before the Lord but he does not. His only recourse is to plead for mercy. As this was true of the Psalmist and all Israel, it was true for all who were a part of the church. "There is none that is righteous, no, not one" (Ps. 14; Rom. 3:10). "All have sinned and fall short of the glory of God" (Rom. 3:23). But, in the face of this bleak fact, the happy reminder is that "God has consigned all men to disobedience, that he may have mercy upon all" (Rom. 11:32).

6. THE HOPE OF ISRAEL

The revelation given Israel was the foundation of the faith of the church. That foundation was no static set of ideas, however, but a living, pulsating faith which grew in content and depth as the people lived in fellowship with God, struggled to discern or resist his will, and heard the message of the prophets sent to them. When in the "fulness of time" revelation became complete with the advent and ministry of Christ, a new appreciation developed for what God had done earlier. The message of the Old Testament became more luminous with the realization that Jesus of Nazareth was its fulfilment (Matt. 5:17), the long-expected Messiah (John 1:41; 4:26), the hope of Israel (Acts 28:20).

What was that "hope of Israel" which persisted through the centuries despite captivity and apostasy, suffering and sorrow? It was that God would redeem his people. This theme runs through the Old Testament, from Israel's deliverance out of Egypt (Exod. 6:6) to the solemn journey back to Emmaus by the two perplexed disciples who "had hoped that [Jesus] was the one to redeem Israel" (Luke 24:21). Psalmists longed for Israel's redemption (Pss. 25:22; 34:22; 77:1-15); prophets envisioned the day that it would be accomplished (Isa. 1:27; 35:9; 43:1; 44:6ff.; 47:4ff.; 48:20; 52:3; 54:8; 59:20; Jer. 50:34). The gospels open with a portrait of pious Jews waiting for the redemption of Jerusalem (Luke 2:38) and the father of John the Baptist saw its realization as about to take place. Filled with the Holy Spirit, Zechariah "prophesied":

> Blessed be the Lord God of Israel,
> for he has visited and redeemed his people,
> and has raised up a horn of salvation for us
> in the house of his servant David,
> as he spoke by the mouth of his holy prophets from of old,
> that we should be saved from our enemies,
> and from the hand of all who hate us . . . (Luke 1:68-71).

After redemption had been accomplished through the blood of the cross (Rom. 3:24; 1 Cor. 1:30; Eph. 1:7; Heb. 9:12) the believing community was "born anew to a living hope through the resurrection of Jesus Christ from the dead" (1 Pet. 1:3). The resurrection was proof positive that the Redeemer was indeed Lord and Christ (Acts 2:36; Rom. 1:4). Having accomplished the work his Father had given him (John 17:4), he would come again at the end of present history when his redemption would be fully revealed and brought to its consummation (Luke 21:28; 1 Pet. 1:3-5). We will explore this theme in detail later; here we are interested in the continuity between the old and new covenants. We have seen that the faith of Israel was the foundation of the faith of the early church. That faith was enlarged and its details became sharper in the coming of the Redeemer, Jesus Christ.

Chapter 3

God: The Enlarged Conception

The most striking change in the transition from the old covenant to the new is the enlarged conception of God. Since the new covenant was instituted by the Son of God become man, Jesus Christ, God could no longer be thought of as *one* God in the old sense. "Hear, O Israel: The Lord our God is one Lord" (Deut. 6:4) had been the core of Israel's religion. God is one; there is none other besides him. To a Jew the worst blasphemy was polytheism, the admission of any other god alongside Yahweh. To be sure, the Word and the Spirit of God and the Angel of Yahweh appear as agents of God in the Old Testament, perhaps personal agents, executing his will. And the God of the Old Testament is not a simple monad; in the fulness of his being there is the highest variety. But the oneness of God is the fundamental conception.

Israel's conception of God was rich. Dedicating the temple Solomon had prayed: "Heaven and the highest heaven cannot contain thee; how much less this house which I have built!" (2 Chron. 6:18). Yahweh was conceived to be "fulness of being," "an ocean of infinity," as theologians later were to describe him in feeble attempts to say something meaningful. All perfection, all power was his. To try to limit him in any way was intolerable. Yet, with all his vastness of being, wisdom, and might, he was *one*. Especially after the struggle with the Baal-worship of the neighboring Canaanites, Israel's feeling on this point of the absolute oneness of God was intense. It became the hallmark of orthodoxy, the "starting-point for Hebrew dogmatics," as Vriezen calls it.

> Owing to this strict monotheism the Jews in the days of Jesus could not help being offended by Christ who knew that he was one with the Father. And on this ground the Jews could not but consider the Christian doctrine concerning God as tritheism and as the rejection of true monotheism.[1]

1. THE DOCTRINE OF THE TRINITY

The coming of Jesus Christ and the subsequent gift of the Holy Spirit enlarged the conception of God within the covenant community. Because the first disciples believed that God was in their midst in the person of Jesus, they had to make room for this astounding conviction in their thinking about God. Remarkably, they did so. Pious, monotheistic Jews who knew that Jesus was a man among them, were convinced after being with him for three years that he was also God. As believers reflected on this, the doctrine of the Trinity developed, though the word itself was not to be used until two centuries after the incarnation. "There is nothing more wonderful in the history of human thought than the silent and imperceptible way in which this doctrine [of the plurality of persons in the Godhead], to us so difficult, took its place without struggle — and without controversy — among accepted Christian truths."[2]

Within the bosom of the church the conviction was born that within the one God — this belief was retained — there is, alongside the Father and in communion with him, the Son; and both Father and Son are from eternity. Moreover, on the basis of their experience with Christ and the gift of the promised Holy Spirit, the early Christians confessed that there are *three* within the Godhead — Father, Son, and Holy Spirit. In this way the doctrine of the Trinity came into being. It did not emerge merely from the study of some church father, or because of a pronouncement from a church council; it arose in the experience of the people when God had made himself manifest in a new way.

The doctrine of the Trinity *as such* is not found in the New Testament. But the conviction which gave rise to that doctrine lies behind the New Testament in the experience of the people; and the New Testament is the record of that experience, a record which enabled the early church in its struggles over the faith to work out, state, and embrace the doctrine of the Trinity just as that New Testament record presupposes the belief.

And what was that belief? As has been stated: God is Father, Son, and Holy Spirit, tri-personal, yet one God. With a personal characteristic of his own which distinguishes him from each of the other persons, the Father is the Father and is not the Son or the Holy Spirit. The same can be said of the other persons in the Godhead; each has his characteristic or special property. Yet, all share the divine essence; all are one God. Being objective to each other, as those sharing the same divine nature, they exist "in, through, and unto each other," as the ancient fathers declared. Thus Jesus said that he was in the Father and that the Father was in him (John 10:38; 14:10), and Paul declared that all the fulness of deity dwells bodily in Jesus (Col. 2:9). It is thus improper to think of God as somehow divisible, or to suppose that any one of the persons is, say, one-third of God, or to imagine that the essence of God is constituted by adding each of the persons to the others.

The church took these positions, even though it could not clear up all the mystery, because on the basis of the New Testament alternatives were unbiblical and hence inadmissible. These alternatives forced the church to declare its faith. Two forms of Unitarianism (or Monarchianism, as the movement was called) were pushing for acceptance. Dynamic monarchianism, led by the Bishop of Antioch, Paul of Samosata, held that Father, Son, and Holy Spirit are one person, with the latter two being mere qualities within God and not persons. The person Jesus Christ is not eternal but he began in time. The other school, modalistic monarchianism, held that the three persons were simply different modes, manifestations, or "faces" of the one God. Their Trinity was a successive Trinity, therefore, rather than one in which the three persons exist simultaneously.[3]

Unlike these aberrations, the orthodox doctrine that God is one in being and three in personal subsistences was the only one which could stand up under scriptural scrutiny. For beside the undisputed teaching about the deity of the Father, the New Testament sets forth Christ as divine. In a unique sense, he is the "Son" of the Father, for "no one knows the Son except the Father, and no one knows the Father except the Son and any one to whom the Son chooses to reveal him" (Matt. 11:27). The Son does nothing on his own but only that which the Father does; and whatever the Father does, the Son does too. As the Father raises the dead and gives them life, the Son does likewise. The Father "has given all judgment to the Son, that all may honor the Son, even as they honor the Father. He who does not honor the Son does not honor the Father who sent him" (John 5:22f.). Everyone who hears Christ's word and believes on him who sent him has eternal life. The dead hear the voice of the Son of God and live, for "as the Father has life in himself, so he has granted the Son also to have life in himself, and has given him authority to execute judgment" (John 5:19ff.). Jesus' opponents sought to kill him for blasphemy, because he called himself God (John 10:33) and called God his Father, "making himself equal with God" (John 5:18).

Besides possessing God's attributes of life and self-existence, Christ is immutable (Heb. 13:8). He is the truth (John 14:6). He possesses God's love (1 John 3:16), holiness (Luke 1:35; John 6:69; Heb. 7:26), eternity (John 1:1; 8:58; Col. 1:17; Rev. 21:6), omniscience (Matt. 9:4; John 2:25; 16:30; Acts 1:24; 1 Cor. 4:5; Col. 2:3), omnipresence (Matt. 28:20; Eph. 1:23), and omnipotence (Matt. 27:18; Rev. 1:8).

In addition to raising the dead and judging the world, Jesus is credited with other works of God—like creation (John 1:3; 1 Cor. 8:6; Col. 1:16; Heb. 1:10; Rev. 3:14) and the upholding of all things (Col. 1:17; Heb. 1:3). He receives the honor and worship usually reserved for God (John 5:23; 14:14; 20:28; Acts 7:59; Rom. 10:9, 13; 1 Cor. 11:24f.; Heb. 1:6; 13:21; Phil. 2:10; 1 Pet. 3:15; 2 Pet. 3:18; Eph. 5:21; Rev. 5:12-14). His name is associated with the name of God on a footing of equality with him (Matt. 28:19; Acts 2:38; Rom. 6:3; 1 Cor. 1:3; 12:4-6; 2 Cor. 12:14; John 5:23; 14:1). Christ bestows spiritual gifts (Rom. 10:17; Col. 3:15; 2 Thess. 2:16f.) and shares the throne and the kingdom with God the Father (Eph. 5:5; Rev. 22:3).

In addition to the above, Christ is expressly called God in Scripture (John 1:1; 20:28; Rom. 9:5; Titus 2:13; Heb. 1:8; 1 John 5:20), and Old Testament descriptions of God are applied to him. Chief among these is the name "Lord," the name for the covenant God of Israel. The Hebrew equivalent "Yahweh" was so sacred that the Hebrews did not pronounce it but substituted instead the word "Adonai." When the Hebrew Scriptures were translated into Greek before the Christian era, this sacred name for the God of Israel—used over five thousand times in the Old Testament—was translated *Kyrios*. This is the name Jesus' disciples gave him; he was called "Lord." As in our language, this title sometimes meant "master" or "sir," but that may not have been the intent when the disciples addressed Jesus before the resurrection, and it is certain that this was not the meaning after that event.

That the disciples called Jesus Lord in the exalted sense is evident from a comparison of Matthew 3:3 with Isaiah 40:3, or Philippians 2:6-11 with Isaiah 45:20-25. In both Isaiah passages Yahweh, the Lord God of Israel, is the subject of the discussion. In the New Testament usage of these passages the reference is to Christ. Thus in the latter passage, it is "at the name of Jesus" that "every knee should bow, in heaven and on earth and under the earth, and every tongue confess that Jesus Christ is Lord." "Lord" here means nothing less than God, for Christ's conquest of sin and death and his accomplishment of redemption were things which, to the Hebrew mind, only God could bring to pass.

John 12:40 quotes the description from Isaiah 6 of the prophet's encounter with Yahweh in the temple. In the next verse the Apostle remarks: "Isaiah said this because he saw his [Christ's] glory and spoke of him." Similarly, Ephesians 4:7f. applies to Christ what is said of Yahweh in Psalm 68:18. In Luke 6:5 Jesus calls himself Lord of the Sabbath, meaning that he can dispose of the holy day, a prerogative of God. Paul declares that only by the Holy Spirit can one call Jesus Lord (1 Cor. 12:3); that is, without special revelation no one can discern Christ's true nature as God. That "Lord" and "God" are synonymous when used of Jesus after the disciples had come to a clear understanding of his mission is evident in Thomas' salutation to the risen Christ, "My Lord and my God" (John 20:28).

The early church also received the gift of the Holy Spirit. On one of his missionary journeys Paul asked some disciples in Ephesus whether they had received the Holy Spirit. They replied that they had "never even heard that there is a Holy Spirit." When Paul inquired about their baptism, he learned that they had received the baptism of John the Baptist for repentance as a preparation for the coming of Christ. On hearing this, Paul baptized them in the name of the Lord Jesus, laid his hands on them, and they received the Holy Spirit (Acts 19:1ff.).

This emphasis on the importance of the gift of the Spirit is no isolated incident. It is consistent with the general New Testament teaching, which continues and enlarges upon what the Old Testament taught about the Spirit of God. In Israel's religion, as B. B. Warfield has shown, the Spirit is related to the cosmos or first creation, to the theocracy, where individuals and the nation as a whole receive special gifts for purposes of Israel's mission, and to individuals to equip them for service as children of God.[4] Throughout Scripture the Spirit is the one who gives life (Gen. 1:3; Ps. 104:30; Luke 1:35; John 3:5f.), power (Judges 13:25; 14:19; Micah 3:8; Acts 1:8), guidance (John 16:13; Acts 8:29, 39; 13:4; 15:28; 16:7), comfort (Acts 9:31), joy (1 Thess. 1:6), renewal (Titus 3:5), skills (Exod. 31:3, 6; 35:31ff.; 1 Sam. 11:6; 16:13f.), faith (1 Cor. 10:44ff.; 12:9), hope (Rom. 15:13), love (1 John 4:7, 13), and a wide variety of spiritual gifts (Rom. 12:6ff.; 1 Cor. 12; 14; Eph. 4:11). Finally, it is the Holy Spirit who gave Scripture (1 Pet. 1:11f.; 2 Pet. 1:21; 1 Cor. 2:13), built the church (Eph. 2:22; 12:4ff.), and leads it into truth as Jesus promised (John 14:26; 15:26; 16:13f.; Acts 5:32; Heb. 10:15; 1 John 2:27).

These functions of the Holy Spirit are not the work of an impersonal force but of one who has intelligence, feeling (Eph. 4:30), power, and an objective relationship to Christ and the apostles (John 16:14; Acts 15:28). The Holy Spirit can be sinned against (Acts 5:3; 1 Cor. 6:19). He witnesses to and prays for the saints (Rom. 8:16, 26). Jesus calls him by the masculine pronoun in Greek (John 16:14). The Holy Spirit proceeds from both the Father and the Son (John 15:26; Rom. 8:9; Gal. 4:6), and is mentioned along with the Father and the Son in the baptismal formula (Matt. 28:19) and the apostolic benediction (2 Cor. 13:14). Even though in his ministry to the saints the Holy

Spirit does not speak of himself but points to Christ — thus almost hiding his own identity (John 14:26; 16:13f.) — the early church clearly had good reason to regard him as none other than God, as another one alongside the Father and the Son, who with them is to be obeyed, worshiped, and adored.

Undeniably, terms like "three persons and one essence," "Godhead," and "Trinity" are difficult. Given our contemporary understanding of the word "person," with its connotation of "independent individuality,"[5] trinitarian doctrine may sound like tritheism. Though unfamiliar to most people today the early church's term *hypostasis* is better — and even the relatively poor word "person" then carried a more wholesome meaning in this context than it does now. In the final analysis, however, any trinitarian discussion will use language that some will find objectionable and everyone will find difficult.

Calvin, who had his share of disagreements in this area, felt that in spite of difficulties in language and ideas, forthrightness is the best policy:

> Arius says that Christ is God, but mutters that he was made and had a beginning. He says that Christ is one with the Father, but secretly whispers in the ears of his own partisans that He is united to the Father like other believers, although by a singular privilege. Say "consubstantial" and you will tear off the mask of this turncoat, and yet you add nothing to Scripture. Sabellius says that Father, Son, and Spirit signify no distinctions in God. Say they are three, and he will scream that you are naming three Gods. Say that in the one essence of God there is a trinity of Persons; you will say in one word what Scripture states, and cut short empty talkativeness. ... We need not dally over words. But I have long since and repeatedly been experiencing that all who persistently quarrel over words nurse a secret poison. As a consequence, it is more expedient to challenge them deliberately than speak more obscurely to please them (*Inst.*, I, xiii, 5).

The Christian must simultaneously see the oneness and the distinctions in God, Calvin says. Admitting the mystery and counseling reverence and sobriety in handling the doctrine, he quotes a passage from Gregory of Nazianzus which he says "vastly delights" him: "I cannot think on the one without quickly being encircled by the splendor of the three; nor can I discern the three without being straightway carried back to the one" (*Inst.*, I, xiii, 17).

2. THE NAMES OF GOD

The enlarged conception of God which the early church received through Christ's coming and the gift of the Holy Spirit also brought some new names for God and a more profound understanding of those used for him in the Old Testament. This is significant because the names of the deity were important in Israel's religion. In Semitic thought a name was taken to express the nature of the person. It was no mere label pinned on, but synonymous with the individual himself. In Israel, with its sharp consciousness of the reality and the holiness of God, this was especially true. The name of God stood for his very being. To dishonor God's name was to dishonor him; to praise his name was to praise him. This explains the force of the third commandment: "You shall not take the name of the Lord your God in vain" (Exod. 20:7). Seeing that Israel was "called by the name of the Lord," which meant God's presence and help, the nations would be afraid (Deut. 28:10). "The name of the Lord is a strong tower" (Prov. 18:10). As is God's name, so is his praise (Ps. 48:10). Those who call on his name are saved (Joel 2:32; Acts 2:21). The Lord is jealous for his holy name (Ezek. 39:25).

In the first petition of the Lord's Prayer the believer utters "Hallowed be thy name" (Luke 11:2). Those who believed in Christ's name received him (John 1:12). Before his passion Jesus prayed, "Father, glorify thy name," and the response was, "I have glorified it and will glorify it again" (John 12:28). John's gospel was written so that believers may have life in Christ's name (20:31). To the Hebrew, to know someone's name was to share in the power or virtue residing in that name. To know God's name was to know *him*, and that means to share in his power, his purpose, his grace.[6]

Scripture claims that God's name is made known. Yet, here is the mystery; he is incomprehensible, unfathomable, the hidden God, as Isaiah, Luther, and Barth have described him. "The better we know God," says Brunner, "the more we know and feel that his mystery is unfathomable. The doctrine which lays the most stress upon the Mystery of God will be nearest to the truth."[7] Who can know or name God? The answer is: No one — on his own. In the biblical revelation, however, God has named himself.

After God had revealed himself to Abraham, Isaac, and Jacob, he came to Moses in the desert with a new name which he had not made known to the patriarchs. He had "appeared to Abraham, to Isaac, and to Jacob as God Almighty, but by my name the Lord," he declares, "I did not make myself known to them" (Exod. 6:3; 3:14). Thus God gave Israel a name for himself which was to be Israel's most precious possession. As God knew Moses by name (Exod. 33:17), he allowed Moses and Israel to know him by name. Strengthening the covenant relationship made with Abraham centuries earlier,

Yahweh gave himself to his people. As their leader, Moses became a channel of revelation to them: "Thus the Lord used to speak to Moses, face to face, as a man speaks to his friend" (Exod. 33:11; cf. 3:18–34:10).

The name Yahweh, or Lord, was the most important name by which God revealed himself to Israel. "Yahweh" signified his presence in Israel's midst in fulfilment of his covenant promise to be its God. It was a constant reminder that the sovereign God, having entered into fellowship with his people, would keep his covenant faithfulness towards them (Exod. 15:1-3; Isa. 42:6-8; Hos. 11; 12:2-9, 13; 13:4-6). When, in the fulness of time, he visited the covenant community personally, the name of Yahweh was ascribed to Christ because it was seen that God had indeed visited his people (Luke 1:68; 7:16).

Other names were also given to Christ, names which had been used in the Old Testament but now took on a new meaning. Jesus (the Greek form of Joshua), meaning Savior, was one of these. Used by God of himself in the Old Testament (Ps. 106:21; Isa. 43:3, 11; 45:21; 50:16; 63:8; Jer. 14:8; Hos. 13:4), it was given his Son in the New (Luke 1:21; 2:11; John 4:42; Acts 5:31; Titus 2:13). The Hebrew name Messiah, meaning anointed one, took on fresh significance when ascribed to Jesus in its Greek form "Christ" (John 1:41; 4:25).

The Old Testament expressions "Son of God" and "Son of Man" added rich associations in the New Testament. The former had been applied to angels, to the people of Israel, and to their officials, but when Jesus came he claimed it uniquely for himself. In some instances at least it seems to point to the eternal relationship of the Son to his Father (Rom. 1:3; 8:3; Gal. 4:4; Heb. 1:1). The expression "Son of Man," used by Ezekiel of himself some ninety times and by Daniel in the sense of Messiah (7:13), was applied by Jesus to himself more than sixty times. Denoting messiahship, it also kept the secret of his mission from those contemporaries who were not yet ready for an open declaration of it (John 12:34; Matt. 16:13) and expressed his identification with humanity. Christ, who had always been God, is now real man.

Thus God, who would otherwise be unknown, made himself known and gave his name. We may know who he is. A Hebrew once asked the angel of the Lord his name. The reply was: "Why do you ask my name, seeing it is wonderful?"—in other words, ineffable, beyond knowledge (Judges 13:18). The intent of the angel's warning was: Do not ask this so lightly; my glory I will not give to another; my name is holy ground. By grace Christians know that name and, reverently and joyfully, use it.

3. THE ATTRIBUTES OF GOD

The knowledge Israel acquired of God's manifold perfections was enhanced with the full revelation of God and the accomplishment of redemption in Christ. His abundantly attested love was given powerful new witness by Jesus Christ. "God shows his love for us in that while we were yet sinners Christ died for us" (Rom. 5:8). Language was inadequate to express what Paul thought of the gift of Christ, and his words spill out: In Christ God shows the "immeasurable riches of his grace in kindness towards us" (Eph. 2:7). The motivation for this is love: "God, who is rich in mercy," did it "out of the great love with which he loved us, even when we were dead through our trespasses" (Eph. 2:4). This love, known earlier, is now seen to be so great that nothing in all creation "will be able to separate us from the love of God which is in Christ Jesus our Lord" (Rom. 8:39).

The same was true of God's power. Often demonstrated in Israel's history, the power of God exhibited itself so strikingly in Christ's resurrection and subsequently in the lives of Christians that the Apostle is again hard pressed to express it in words. He prays that believers may know "what is the immeasurable greatness of his power in us who believe, according to the working of his great might which he accomplished in Christ when he raised him from the dead and made him sit at his right hand in the heavenly places, far above all rule and authority and power and dominion, and above every name that is named, not only in this age but also in that which is to come" (Eph. 1:19ff.; cf. Matt. 28:18 and the "signs" and "wonders" which Christ did).

So it is with God's wisdom. Though well known before, it is now fully seen in Christ, "in whom are hid all the treasures of wisdom and knowledge" (Col. 2:3; cf. 1 Cor. 1:24). Through Christ's church "the manifold wisdom of God [is] made known to the principalities and powers in the heavenly places" (Eph. 3:10) as well as to humankind. The same is shown in Christ of God's holiness (Heb. 9), justice (Rom. 3:21-26), will (Eph. 1:5-11), truth (2 Cor. 1:20), omniscience (Matt. 9:4; John 2:25), and eternity (John 8:58; 17:5). God's goodness and grace, mercy and patience — all are extolled, as a glance at a concordance indicates.

It is therefore nonsense to say that we cannot say what God *is* but only what he *does*. Eichrodt and Barth, among others, have shown the absurdity of this position. Introducing a chapter on "Affirmations About the Divine Being," Eichrodt writes:

By his own act of bestowing a name on himself, God chooses to be described as the definable, the distinctive, the individual. In this way the faith of Israel sets its face against both an abstract concept of deity and a nameless "ground of being." Both the intellectualist and the mystical misunderstanding of God are rejected.[8]

Barth claims that the nominalistic doctrine that God's attributes exist only in our minds and not in him makes God no longer "the living God" but instead "a lifeless shadowy abstraction."[9]

It is dangerous and ultimately fatal to faith in God if God is not the Lord of glory, if it is not guaranteed to us that in spite of the analogical nature of the language in which it all has to be expressed God is actually and unreservedly as we encounter Him in His revelation: the Almighty, the Holy, the Just, the Merciful, the Omnipresent, the Eternal, not less but infinitely more so than it is in our power to grasp, and not for us only, but in actuality therefore in Himself. Holy Scripture speaks to us of God in such a way as to give us this assurance.[10]

How much we say about God's attributes depends on many considerations. Barth wrote three hundred pages, partly because of his aversion to nominalism. The Puritan divine Charnock went on for eight hundred pages, some of the discussion good and some of it highly speculative.[11] But regardless of the length, there must be some discussion of God's perfections if we are to be true to the biblical revelation.[12] For although God is mystery and is one, so that his essence is identified with his attributes and the attributes are nothing other than various ways of looking at the biblical picture of the one incomposite God; and, although God is infinite, fathomless — think of the immensity of space, all of it contained within him — and we are finite with partial knowledge, we do know what God has revealed concerning himself. James Orr's comment is still relevant:

We may not know God in the depths of his absolute being. But we can at least know him in so far as he reveals himself in his relation to us. The question, therefore, is not as to the possibility of a knowledge of God in the unfathomableness of his being, but is: Can we know God *as he enters into relations* with the world and with ourselves? God has entered into relations with us in his revelations of himself, and supremely in Jesus Christ; and we Christians humbly claim that through this Self-revelation we do know God to be the true God, and have real acquaintance with his character and will. Neither is it correct to say that this knowledge which we have of God is only a *relative knowledge*. It is in part a knowledge of the *absolute* nature of God as well. The relations in which God stands to us — the revelations he makes to us — reveal something of what he is *truly*.[13]

Chapter 4

Jesus Christ: God and Man

In the long history of unusual and wonderful happenings in this world nothing is so unusual or wonderful as that event described by the simple statement: "And the Word became flesh and dwelt among us" (John 1:14). No other event has made a comparable impression on the world. The incarnation is in a class by itself. There will never be another event to compare with it, unless it is the day mentioned here and there in Scripture as "that day" or "the day of the Lord." Then the one who became flesh and dwelt among us will come again, this time "in his glory, and all the angels with him. Then he will sit on his glorious throne. Before him will be gathered all the nations, and he will separate them one from another as a shepherd separates the sheep from the goats" (Matt. 25:31ff.).

When Jesus came, however, the fact went virtually unnoticed. Except for the appearance of angels to a handful of simple shepherds, there seemed to be nothing earth-shaking about it. Babies were born every day. Prophetic insight was needed to grasp its real significance.

> Now there was a man in Jerusalem whose name was Simeon, and this man was righteous and devout, looking for the consolation of Israel, and the Holy Spirit was upon him. And it had been revealed to him by the Holy Spirit that he should not see death before he had seen the Lord's Christ. And inspired by the Spirit he came into the temple; and when the parents brought in the child Jesus, to do for him according to the custom of the law, he took him up in his arms and blessed God and said, "Lord, now lettest thou thy servant depart in peace, according to thy word; for mine eyes have seen thy salvation which thou hast prepared in the presence of all peoples, a light for revelation to the Gentiles, and for glory to thy people Israel" (Luke 2:25-32).

The phenomenon of prophetic insight, of which this is an instance, is an important aspect of the coming of Christ. Through it a people was prepared, and when Christ had come others became aware of it. All of prior sacred history was preparation. "Moses . . . and all the prophets who have spoken, from Samuel and those who came afterwards, also proclaimed these days" (Acts 3:22ff.). Not that they saw what would come in the same way as those who lived after the event, but the history and words of these forerunners found their true meaning and fulfilment in Christ.

The last of the prophets of the old covenant was John the Baptist. It was through prophetic insight that his father pronounced his mission: "And you, child, will be called the prophet of the Most High; for you will go before the Lord to prepare his way" (Luke 1:76). When the Baptist's ministry was near an end, Jesus eulogized him as "more than a prophet," inasmuch as John was the fulfilment of an important earlier prophecy: "Behold, I send my messenger before thy face, who shall prepare thy way before thee" (Mal. 3:1). Then Jesus made the startling statement that "among those born of women none is greater than John; yet he who is least in the kingdom of God is greater than he" (Luke 7:27f.). As great as he was, John was still a part of the old order. It was not to be his privilege to see redemption accomplished and the new covenant, with its outpouring of the Holy Spirit on God's people, instituted (Acts 2; John 7:37-39). John's vocation was to call people to repentance and point them to Jesus Christ (Matt. 3:1-12; Luke 3:1-18; John 1:15, 19-36).

The one to whom John pointed was an enigma to many (John 8:25), but Jesus' disciples and later the church believed him to be both man and God. His humanity could hardly be denied, for they could see he was a man among men. After being with him, hearing his teaching, and witnessing his works, after seeing him die and return from the dead in fulfilment, they believed, of prophecy, after receiving the promised gift of the Holy Spirit, they were convinced that Jesus was God. So the disciples enlarged their conception of deity to make room for Jesus Christ and his Spirit.

1. CHRISTOLOGICAL DEBATE

Not all accepted the apostolic witness, however. From the first, as the New Testament indicates, there were those who denied Jesus Christ. By the end of the first century some were denying his deity and others claiming that his humanity was unreal. In Palestine the Ebionites, a Judaizing sect on the fringe of the church, claimed that Jesus was the physical son of Mary and Joseph who was rewarded for his piety by God's Spirit at his baptism. Thus qualified for the messianic mission to which God had predestined him, he would return to reign on earth.[1] The Alogi ("deniers of the Logos") in Asia Minor believed in Christ's virgin birth and messiahship, but denied his eternity with the Father. They attacked John's gospel, claiming that its doctrine of the Logos was influenced by Gnosticism, and emphasized Christ's human life as set forth in the synoptic gospels.[2]

The Ebionites and Alogi were a prelude to a more serious challenge to the church voiced by Paul of Samosata in the middle of the third century. From his prestigious episcopal position at Antioch Paul taught that the Logos issued forth from God from eternity, so that it can truly be said that it was begotten. Personified, it can be called "Son," but the Logos is impersonal power. At work in the prophets, it was in Jesus in greater degree so that its presence in him can be termed an "indwelling." Here Paul appealed to John 14:10: "I am in the Father and the Father in me."

The Logos on this view is equivalent in Jesus to what the Apostle Paul called the "inner man" in a believer. The Logos did not dwell essentially in Jesus; nor did Mary give birth to the Logos but to a man, virgin born, but still a "mere man," as Paul's party put it, or as Paul said, "an ordinary man in nature." "Mary did not bear the Word, for Mary did not exist before the ages. Mary is not older than the Word; what she bore was a man equal to us, but superior in all things as a result of holy spirit." Anointed with the Holy Spirit at his baptism and preserved from sin, Jesus "advanced" to Godhead as the Father endowed him with divine attributes, gave him a name above every name, and made him the Savior of humankind. Paul said that Jesus was "made God" by interpenetration of divine power. "From man he became God," he affirmed; Christ was raised "dynamically" to divine rank.[3]

2. DOCETISM AND GNOSTICISM

Those groups who denied the humanity of Christ were known as Docetists (from Greek *dokein*, to seem). Motivated by Greek dualism, which believed that matter is evil as opposed to spirit which is good, Docetism was more "an attitude which infected a number of heresies" than "a simple heresy on its own."[4]

Docetists claimed that Christ's humanity was only an apparent humanity and his suffering was unreal. This latter idea came from the Greek notion that God cannot suffer, because suffering means the imposition from outside of something undesirable and that cannot happen to God. Already in New Testament days John's epistles refer to the spirit of antichrist, which denies "that Jesus Christ has come in the flesh" (1 John 4:1ff.; see also 2:22; 2 John 7; cf. John 1:14), but not until later was the full threat of Docetism experienced. It was a major concern of the church of the second century with church fathers from Ignatius to Irenaeus laboring to show the importance of maintaining the true humanity of the Savior.[5]

Many second-century Docetists were Gnostics (from Greek *gnostes*, knower). Gnosticism was a syncretistic, dualistic religious philosophy. Its significance, as Harnack says, "must not be sought chiefly in the particular doctrines, but rather in the whole way in which Christianity is here conceived and transformed."[6]

Gnostic Christology made a sharp distinction between the heavenly "aeon" Christ and the human appearance of that aeon on earth. Each acted distinctly in his (or its) own way. Some Gnostics, like Basilides and some Valentinians, saw no real union between Christ and the man Jesus; others among the Valentinians held that Jesus' body was a heavenly, psychical formation which only *seemed* to come from Mary; a third group, following Saturninus, taught that Christ's body was a phantom devoid of physical substance and consequently denied his birth altogether.[7]

Another group that had difficulty with Christ's humanity was the modalistic monarchians, those who held the doctrine of a succession of three persons in the Godhead (see above, p. 38), for they did not know what to do with Christ's humanity after the ascension when he was transformed into the Holy Spirit. According to one church father, Sabellius taught that at the ascension Christ's humanity was reabsorbed or lost in divinity.[8]

3. SUBORDINATIONISM AND ARIANISM

In struggling to relate Christ to God and the two natures of Christ to each other, the early church did not want to compromise either nature of Christ. Nor did it want to be monarchian or tritheistic in its thinking about God. A tendency which endangered both trinitarian theology and the two-nature thinking in Christology was the doctrine that the Son was subordinated to the Father in a way that prejudiced the Savior's Godhead and sometimes denied it altogether.

Although Origen contributed a great deal to trinitarian theology and Christology, there are emphases in his writings that are more representative of neo-Platonic philosophy than of Christianity. Thus in his heavy accent on gradation of being, in spite of the good teaching of the eternal generation of the Son, the Son is subordinate to the Father, a "second God," the "executive officer" of the Father, doing his will. Prayer should not be addressed to Jesus but to the Father, the "fountainhead of deity," to whom Christ himself prayed. Emphases like these in Origen helped make possible later subordinationism, which ended in the Arian crisis in the church.[9]

Another movement that contributed to subordinationism and the Arian heresy was the continuing emphasis in Antioch of the kind of christological thinking we saw in Paul of Samosata. Unlike the theological thought centered in Alexandria, which tended to be speculative and allegorical, the theological school which developed in Antioch was sober and rationalistic, with a stress on historical and grammatical exegesis. Arius himself was a leading presbyter in Alexandria, but in his theological method he was a devotee of the Antiochian school. Moreover, he was influenced by the atmosphere created in Alexandria by the more radical subordinationist teachings of Origen, which were mediated through men like Eusebius of Caesarea.[10]

Although Arius is known for his denial of the deity of Christ, the fundamental problem was his doctrine of God. Convinced that God is utterly transcendent, far removed from creation, Arius held that God could never come into direct contact with creation. He is "one God, who is alone ingenerate [self-existent], alone eternal, alone without beginning, alone true, alone possessing immutability, alone wise, alone good, alone sovereign, alone judge of all."[11] In Arius' thinking God is so aloof from all creation that sharing his substance with any other is inconceivable. To do that would make him divisible and subject to change, and that is impossible. God dwells alone.

Against this background Arius projected his view of Jesus Christ, bringing into bold relief details which had not been so clearly seen before. In spite of the many high-sounding titles he was willing to ascribe to Christ—Son of God, Son, Logos, the pre-existent one, only-begotten, the holy triad, Word, Mediator, even unchangeable and perfect God—he thought of the mediator as a creature, an exalted being far above all the rest of creation, but a creature nonetheless. When asked why he then ascribed such titles to him, he replied that they were given by way of courtesy. It is "by grace" that they are used.

The reason for the creation of the Logos, according to Arius, was that God is so remote that an intermediate being was required to effect the rest of creation. Arius made it clear that Christ was on this side of the wide gulf between God and creation. He did not share God's eternity: "there was a *then* when he did not exist." Nor could Christ comprehend the mind of the Father or share in his immutability.

The issue in Arianism was thus the distance between creation, including Christ, and God. Because of this distance it is not God who has come into our world for our salvation but another creature, like ourselves and yet unlike us, because Arius held that Christ's soul was unlike ours. Hence he is neither God nor man. God himself remains in the distance, uncondescending. This, however, was directly contrary to the earliest teaching of the church. In the New Testament and the earliest post-apostolic literature Christ was declared to be God. The deity of Christ is professed in the oldest surviving Christian sermon, in the oldest surviving report of the death of a Christian martyr, in the oldest pagan report of a church service, and in the oldest surviving liturgical prayer.[12]

Since the teaching of Arius was a clear departure from the apostolic faith, the orthodox party, led by Bishop Alexander of Alexandria and Athanasius, worked to demonstrate its consequences for faith. If Arius is right, they argued, the triune God we worship is not eternal; baptism is administered in the name of a creature; the Father was not always the Father for there was a time when he had no Son; Polytheism is introduced into Christianity, for we have the addition of gods; we worship a creature, Christ. If the Logos is mutable, how could he reveal the Father? In the end Arianism deprives us of the certainty of salvation, for we have no real savior. This was the primary concern of Athanasius in the long struggle against Arianism: our salvation depends on the fact that Jesus is God. Harnack's devastating critique shows what was at stake in the long contest:

> Only as cosmologists are the Arians monotheists, as theologians and in religion they are polytheists. Deep contradictions lie in the background: a Son who is no Son; a Logos who is no Logos; a monotheism which does not exclude polytheism; two or three *ousias*, who are to be worshipped, while still only one is really distinguished from the creation; an indefinable nature which first becomes God when it becomes man, and which still is neither God nor man. ... The opponents were right; this doctrine leads back to heathenism. The orthodox doctrine has, on the contrary, its abiding worth in the upholding of the faith that in Christ God Himself has redeemed men, and led them into His fellowship. This conviction of faith was saved by Athanasius against a doctrine which did not understand the inner nature of religion generally, which sought in religion only teaching, and ultimately found its satisfaction in an empty dialectic.[13]

4. THE NICENE CREED

In its statement of faith the Council of Nicea (A.D. 325) declared:

> We believe in one God, the Father almighty, maker of all things, visible and invisible;

And in one Lord Jesus Christ, the Son of God, begotten from the Father, only-begotten, that is, from the substance of the Father, God from God, light from light, true God from true God, begotten not made, of one substance with the Father, through Whom all things came into being, things in heaven and things on earth, Who because of us men and because of our salvation came down and became incarnate, becoming man, suffered and rose again on the third day, ascended to the heavens, and will come to judge the living and the dead;
And in the Holy Spirit.

But as for those who say, There was when He was not, and, Before being born He was not, and that He came into existence out of nothing, or who assert that the Son of God is from a different hypostasis or substance, or is created, or is subject to alteration or change — these the Catholic Church anathematizes.[14]

The intention of Nicea was to make clear that the faith of the church is that Jesus Christ is whatever God is, that he is of the same, identical substance as the Father. In contrast to the creaturely status the Arians gave him, he is fully God.

One would think that the language of the creed could not have been made more explicit. It had no more than been promulgated, however, than there was disagreement as to its meaning. The church historian Eusebius of Caesarea was among the first to challenge the orthodox interpretation, and soon a majority was opposing it. During the next decades the orthodox party was persecuted, and Athanasius was banned from the empire five times. From 350-361 the Emperor Constantius tried to crush the Nicene doctrine, and the success of the Arian party seemed assured.

Their very success, however, led its leaders to state their positions so boldly at a series of synods that the majority gradually saw the issues for what they were and declared its support of the orthodox faith. The Council of Constantinople in 381 reaffirmed Nicea. Because questions had arisen concerning the person and deity of the Holy Spirit, it stated the consubstantiality of both the Spirit and the Son to the Father. In addition to Athanasius, the three Cappadocian fathers — Gregory of Nyssa, Gregory of Nazianzus, and Basil the Great — were the principal champions in the development of the doctrine of the Holy Spirit. Against the Pneumatomachians ("Spirit-fighters") or Macedonians (as they were called after 380), it was declared that the Spirit, like Christ, is fully God.

5. APOLLINARIANISM, NESTORIANISM, EUTYCHIANISM

Another item of business at the Council of Constantinople was occasioned by the theorizing of Apollinaris of Laodicea. In the interests of preserving the strictest unity between the two natures of Christ, he fabricated a theory which denied full humanity to the Mediator. Apollinaris insisted that salvation depends on the union of God and man, and he greatly feared the dualism which he saw in areas of the church.

In order to have true and complete union Apollinaris argued that the divine Logos took the place of the animating spirit (*psyche*) and mind (*nous*) of the man Jesus, giving him his life and energy. Thus he spoke of one nature in Christ, or, as he put it, "one incarnate nature of the divine Word." Through the close union Christ's flesh was glorified, becoming "divine flesh" or "the flesh of God," and can be worshiped and received in communion, through which we become partakers of the divine nature.

The church responded to this by charging that there was a subtle docetism in Apollinaris' Christology, since Christ was not real man but only seemed to be. Apollinaris gratuitously assumed that two natures could not be one person. In his theory Christ lacked the most important parts of humanity and an injustice was done to the New Testament picture of Jesus. In Apollinarianism, the church asserted, the whole man is not saved. As Gregory of Nazianzus said: "What has not been assumed cannot be restored; it is what is united with God that is saved."[15]

Apollinaris' fears were not unfounded, however. Dualism was a genuine threat to sound doctrine in the church, particularly to a biblical Christology. The proof of this was a controversy which centered on Nestorius, Patriarch of Constantinople. The key term in this dispute was "Mother of God" (*theotokos*), an expression the fathers in Alexandria had used for over a century to express the real union of the two natures in the incarnation and the fact that it was the Logos which was born of Mary as the God-man. Antiochian theology, unable to envision a human nature without a human person, tended to separate the two natures, often using the expression "indwelling" for the union of the Logos with the man Jesus.

In asserting the distinction of the two natures, both Nestorius and his chief theologian, Theodore of Mopsuestia, denounced in strong language what they considered a denial of the full humanity of Christ. The point of contention was whether it was merely the man Jesus who was born of Mary or whether it was truly God whom she bore. The insistence of Theodore and Nestorius that Mary bore only the man Jesus and that God could not have been born of her raised a general alarm in the church, as the memory of the adoptionism of Paul of Samosata haunted many minds.

In the ensuing controversy the extreme language of Nestorius was matched by the arrogance and discourtesy of Cyril of Alexandria. All things considered, however, Cyril had a better position, and thanks to Antiochian influence, it was adopted in modified form at the Council of Ephesus (431). In the formula agreed upon, the Antiochians accepted the term *theotokos* and the Alexandrians the expression "unconfused union" of natures.

The peace in the church was short-lived, however. Extreme parties in both Antioch and Alexandria were unhappy with the settlement. Theodoret of Cyprus was one Antiochene who would never make peace with Alexandrian thinking. In Alexandria things came to a head with Eutyches, who held the old position that the incarnate Christ was of but one nature. Conceding under pressure that the Lord was "of two natures," he argued that that was true before the incarnation; "after the union I confess one nature," he said.

To compound the difficulty Eutyches refused to say that the incarnate Christ is consubstantial with mankind until he was forced to do so, and then he soon reverted to his former position. The eventual result was the important Council of Chalcedon in 451, in which the church, weary of exaggerated statements and heretical opinions, sought a balanced pronouncement that would be true to Scripture. While the formula adopted did not settle any of the mystery of christological doctrine, it stated the faith of the church clearly and settled once for all, it would seem, the issues that had been debated for generations.

> We, then, following the holy Fathers, all with one consent, teach men to confess one and the same Son, our Lord Jesus Christ, the same perfect in Godhead and also perfect in manhood; truly God and truly man, of a reasonable soul and body; consubstantial with the Father according to the Godhead, and consubstantial with us according to the Manhood; in all things like unto us, without sin; begotten before all ages of the Father according to the Godhead, and in these latter days, for us and for our salvation, born of the Virgin Mary, the Mother of God, according to the Manhood; one and the same Christ, Son, Lord, only-begotten, to be acknowledged in two natures, *inconfusedly, unchangeably, indivisibly, inseparably*; the distinction of natures being by no means taken away by the union, but rather the property of each nature being preserved, and concurring in one Person and one Subsistence, not parted or divided into two persons, but one and the same Son, and only begotten, God the Word, the Lord Jesus Christ himself has taught us, and the Creed of the holy Fathers has handed down to us.[16]

This statement was accepted along with the Nicene Creed. Setting itself against Eutychianism with the adverbs "inconfusedly" and "unchangeably," and against Nestorianism with "indivisibly" and "inseparably," the Creed of Chalcedon has directed christological doctrine away from these eddies and into the main channel of biblical teaching.

Negative in form, the four adverbs of Chalcedon were not intended to suggest a solution to the problem of the relation of the two natures in Christ to each other or to his single person. Rather, with the memory of bitter theological quarrels still fresh, they were meant to serve as warnings to help keep the church of the future from error.

Chapter 5

Scripture

We observed in the first chapter that the church takes as norm for its faith the Scriptures of the Old and New Testaments. Now we shall look further into the process which led the early church to that dogmatic position and ask what the church meant by it. The importance of that position requires no argument when we remember that in all matters of faith and conduct Christ exercises his kingship through the Word, his royal sceptre.

1. SCRIPTURE AND TRADITION

To exalt Scripture in this fashion does not imply that it functioned exclusive of other realities. In the early church the written Word was one part of a whole Christian tradition which had sprung up and was to be transmitted within the covenant community from generation to generation. Within the tradition, as understood in the early church, were not only the canon of the Old Testament and the emerging books of the New Testament, but also independent collections of the sayings of Jesus, creedal statements and baptismal formulas, customs and rites, and (as in Irenaeus, to give a concrete example) the structure of the church, the gift of love, and a body of precepts.[1]

"So palpable was this apostolic tradition," says Pelikan, "that even if the apostles had not left behind the Scriptures to serve as normative evidence of their doctrine, the church would still be in a position to follow 'the structure of the tradition which they handed on to those to whom they committed the churches.' "[2] A look at the rich literature of the ante-Nicene age attests this. The New Testament itself alludes to the ample store of tradition. John's gospel closes with the intriguing comment that if everything Jesus did were written down, "I suppose that the world itself could not contain the books that would be written" (John 21:25); and Paul exhorts the Thessalonians to hold to the traditions he taught them "by word of mouth or by letter" (2 Thess. 2:15). The early church had both.

As the distance between the apostles, who had been "eye-witnesses of [Christ's] majesty" (2 Pet. 1:16), and the believing community became greater, it became increasingly difficult to regulate the faith of the church by the oral traditions even though at first these, along with the Old Testament, had been most important to it and closest to the hearts of the faithful.[3] Moreover, traditions multiplied. Some Gnostic sects claimed to have received a secret apostolic tradition. Discerning true from false tradition therefore became complicated and, for some, impossible.

This was the immediate cause for the rise of the canon of the New Testament. The books had been written earlier, but there was no need to duplicate and distribute them in the church until after the death of the last of the apostles and the growing spread of rumor and fancy. Thus the church decided on the New Testament canon when it was able to make the decision intelligently and when the need for that decision lay before it. The process by which the canon was selected is not completely known, but we do know enough to appreciate the sense of responsibility and concern which was exercised. Although writings were being circulated before the end of the first century, it was in the first half of the second century, Hanson notes, that "the Church was in a position to know what were authentic and original records of Christianity and what were not; but as the years went on the Church inevitably found itself no longer in this position."[4]

It was no optional matter for the church to do what it did, therefore, or when it did it. The canon had to be determined and it had to be determined during that period. The Muratorian Canon, an important late second-century witness to canonicity, says that "one [letter] to the Laodiceans is in circulation, and another to the Alexandrians, forged in the name of Paul for the heresy of Marcion, and many others which cannot be received into the catholic church, because it is not fitting to mix gall with honey."[5] Others in this period spoke similarly. Irenaeus complained about "the multitude of apocryphal and spurious writings" and contrasted them with "the writings of truth." The Greek New Testament began to be translated into Latin not later than 150, for the Scillitan martyrs (executed in 180) and Tertullian had copies. By 150 Justin knew and used all four gospels and remarked that they were being used in church services.

About the same time Marcion drew up his own canon of the New Testament in Rome. Marcion's work was once assumed to be the first attempt to form a canon, which in turn stimulated the church to do the same in self-defense, but Hanson remarks that this assumption is "precarious, and it is more likely that Marcion picked and chose among an already existing collection."[6] The expression "New Testament" was first used for a collection of books by an anonymous person who wrote around A.D. 192 to Abercius Marcellus about "the list of the New Testament of the Gospel." Hanson comments that the expression "must have meant a written and determined testament, a collection of writings."[7]

Without marshalling further evidence for this phenomenon of the setting of the canon of the New Testament, we must note that this development distinguishes the apostolic tradition from the ecclesiastical tradition which came after it. This is a conclusion with far-reaching theological implications, for if the early church did establish the apostolic tradition by fixing the canon, distinguishing it from subsequent tradition, the church thereby indicated its subordination to the apostolic canon as normative for faith and life.[8] Later centuries were to see this thesis contested as the Roman Catholic Church declared at the Council of Trent that "both saving truth and moral discipline" are "contained in the written books and the unwritten traditions," and that it belongs to "holy mother church . . . to judge of the true sense and interpretation of the holy Scriptures."[9] The justification for this position was that the church had produced Scripture and tradition in the first place, and thus through its teaching office had the right and duty to determine the identity of Scripture and to draw from both it and tradition in setting forth the faith.

Calvin called this "a most pernicious error," which he sought to correct by reference to Ephesians 2:20: the church is "built upon the foundation of the apostles and prophets." The teaching of the prophets and apostles, he argued,

> must have had authority before the church began to exist. . . . While the church receives and gives its seal of approval to the Scriptures, it does not thereby render authentic what is otherwise doubtful or controversial. But because the church recognizes Scripture to be the truth of its own God, as a pious duty it unhesitatingly venerates Scripture (*Inst.*, I, vii, 1, 2).

Calvin was aware that the canon came from the bosom of the church: in one sense the church did make the canon. But in a deeper sense, what constituted the heart of the canon, the gospel, made the church.

In submitting to the judgment of Scripture to settle the many disputes that came before them, the fathers of the early church thus acknowledged it as the sole normative, apostolic witness beside which no other criterion might stand. For this reason the church may be considered apostolic today. Subordinating all other tradition and cultural influences to this one ancient norm, in which the voice of Christ and the apostles is still heard, the church of the ages remains just as truly apostolic as it was at the end of the first century. Indeed, in one sense the later church is in a more favorable position with respect to apostolicity than the church of the second century. For then the oral tradition was becoming uncertain and spurious writings and false prophets were plentiful. The process of sifting, at least in the early part of the second century, was not complete. The testing of writings for apostolicity would go on far beyond the second century, and when that process was finally concluded the church had the best authentication possible for the treasures it claimed to be the very Word of God.

2. THE OLD AND NEW TESTAMENTS

The first-century church had the same Scripture Jesus read in the synagogue (Luke 4:17), to which he often referred (Luke 4:4, 8, 12; 6:3; 24:27; John 3:14; 5:46; 6:32; 8:37; 10:35). The writers of the books that came to be the New Testament quoted from Scripture incessantly, for they wanted to lace their own writings with divine authority and show that the Old Testament received its true meaning in the light of Christ. He "fulfilled" it (Matt. 5:17). They saw the Old Testament as a book filled with hidden messianic prophecies which had not been clear until the appearance of Christ.[10]

In acquiring the Old Testament as its book, the Christian church took the position that Jews who did not accept Christ as Messiah failed to understand their Scriptures and had cut themselves off from their own spiritual inheritance. In rejecting Christ "their minds were hardened," says Paul; "for to this day, when they read the old covenant, that same veil remains unlifted because only through Christ is it taken away. Yes, to this day whenever Moses is read a veil lies over their minds; but when a man turns to the Lord the veil is removed" (2 Cor. 3:14ff.). Thus the early church looked on the Old Testament as a Christian book which had been instrumental in gathering a people and had prepared the way for the coming of Jesus Christ. To him all the prophets bore witness (Acts 3:24; John 5:39).

Not all professing Christians were of this mind, however. The Gnostics, whose religion borrowed from a number of sources, were not guided by Scripture, but used it as they pleased. To them the God of the Old Testament was the Demiurge, a lower, shadowy figure associated with creation, not the God and Father of Jesus Christ. They did not hold the Old Testament in high regard but preferred their own writings which included excerpts from the New Testament. To other persons, like Marcion, the Old Testament seemed incongruous with the New. He repudiated the Old Testament and everything in the New Testament that seemed to have been colored by the Old. Teachings like those of Marcion and the Gnostics, however, were repudiated by the Christian community at large as false. To it the Old Testament was the Word of God.

By the middle of the first century new Christian writings began to appear alongside the Old Testament. While some collections of them — for example, the sayings of Jesus or the epistles of Paul — appeared relatively early, they were probably not given the same standing as the Old Testament Scriptures at first. But they were associated with the Old Testament as similarly authoritative and as having similar religious merit. The Second Epistle of Peter (3:15f.) places Paul's writings on a level with "the other scriptures," meaning the Old Testament. Jesus had clearly set his own authority above that of the scribes and alongside the Old Testament (Matt. 5:27-44; Mark 1:22; John 5:24, 36; 7:16). It is not surprising then that to Ignatius the authority of the gospels is equivalent to that of the prophets; that 2 Clement introduces a quotation from Matthew with the words, "another Scripture says"; and that Barnabas and Justin preface New Testament selections with the well-known formula, "it is written."[11] From the time of Irenaeus and Tertullian (180) the association of the literature of the New Testament with the Old Testament was "universally acknowledged," as Kelly remarks.[12]

A problem existed with respect to the extent of the Old Testament canon. The Old Testament that had come into the church was the Greek translation known as the Septuagint, dating from some time before the middle of the third century B.C. Whereas the canon of the Hebrew Scriptures in Palestine was sharply delimited, the attitude of Greek-speaking Jews outside Palestine was more relaxed and allowed the inclusion of additional writings. The Apocrypha, as these books were called, was accepted as sacred literature and cited as such by the early church until near the end of the second century, when doubts began to arise as to its authenticity as revelation. These doubts increased when Palestinian Judaism repudiated the Apocrypha, and by the middle of the fourth century the eastern church had relegated these writings to a place outside the canon. In the west, however, the old attitude prevailed, and the Apocrypha continued to enjoy status as a part of the Old Testament. Augustine, for example, quoted often from the Apocrypha, particularly in his writings against the Pelagians.

Weighing heavily in the decision of the eastern church was the absence (with one exception) of quotations from the Apocrypha in the canonical New Testament writings, thus suggesting that it was not endorsed as Scripture by Christ and the apostles. In the east, therefore, and later in the judgment of the Reformers, these books were valued for their history and literature but not for purposes of doctrine. The settling of the Old Testament canon in the east was relatively simple once the decision had been made with respect to the Apocrypha. The collection of writings that Jesus and the apostles had recognized as Scripture remained such for the church.

The determination of the canon of the New Testament, as we saw in the previous section, was much more complicated. Some felt that John's gospel, for example, was influenced by Gnosticism and so they excluded it. But suspicions such as these led to searching inquiry, which served a good purpose in assuring the later church that what was given it was considered Holy Scripture by those in the best position to know.

The relation of the two Testaments to each other became a problem as soon as the words of Jesus and the letters of Paul were laid alongside the Old Testament. The place of honor given these new writings is a most remarkable historical phenomenon, for the new writings were in fact given preference over the Old Testament. Paul's terse statement, "the old has passed away, behold, the new has come" (2 Cor. 5:17), symbolized the attitude. As a result the tendency was to find things in the Old Testament which could be related to Christ and to read the rest of it in the light of him. Christ had taken up leading Old Testament motifs and applied them to himself: he was the expected Messiah, the Suffering Servant, the Son of Man, the Lord of Glory, the one in whom God's kingdom had come. All the New Testament writers give the impression that what happened in Christ was according to God's predestined plan foretold in the Old Testament. Little wonder, then, that the first Christians, steeped as they were in the Old Testament, found in Jesus the one for whom Israel had been waiting, the one whom the Old Testament was all about.[13]

What was true of the writers of the New Testament was equally true for the early church. With the exception of Marcion and the Gnostics, the church saw the same remarkable unity in the two covenants that is seen in the New Testament.[14] The reason given by some was that Christ is at the center of each; by others that the same Holy Spirit had inspired both. Leaders in the early church — like Justin in his dialogue with Trypho the Jew, and Irenaeus and Tertullian in their lucid debates with the Gnostics and others who threatened the purity and peace of the church — saw themselves as the people of God under the new dispensation, as Israel had been his covenant community under the old. The end of the ages had come upon them, and whatever had happened or been written before Christ's coming found its real interpretation in him. As Augustine put it: "In the Old is the New concealed; in the New is the Old revealed."

3. THE INSPIRATION OF SCRIPTURE

The church took over the idea of inspired Scriptures from Judaism. This is reflected in the attitude of Christ and his apostles towards the Old Testament. To them it was the Word of God. Jesus' direct references to the inviolable character of the Old Testament (Matt. 5:18; Luke 16:17; John 5:35), his quotations from it, and the way he used it show beyond doubt his high estimate of it as having divine and absolute authority. The apostolic view is similar. The Second Epistle to Timothy directly attests to the divine origin of Scripture: "All Scripture is inspired by God and profitable for teaching, for reproof, for correction, and for training in righteousness" (3:16). Peter's teaching is similar: "No prophecy of Scripture is a matter of one's own interpretation, because no prophecy ever came by the impulse of man, but men moved by the Holy Spirit spoke from God" (2 Pet. 1:20).

For the apostles no question is possible about the origin of the Word: it is from God. Human instruments in its writing added nothing to its content. This view corresponds with the general Jewish opinion of Scripture as coming from God. Moses and the prophets were reckoned to have divine authority because God was believed to have spoken through them; their word was the Word of God. Their writings were holy writings, the rule for faith and life, with a superhuman content. Nothing in them was superfluous; everything was there for a purpose.

This exalted view of Scripture was carried to excessive lengths in later Judaism, so that every word and every letter were said to be invested with divine meaning — and sometimes this meaning was considered in detachment from the body of Scripture. Prophetic ecstasy was said to deprive a person of his own consciousness. Along with the written word an oral tradition was given to help interpret it. Set down in writing in the Mishna and Gemara, this tradition, with the help of certain rules of interpretation known to the rabbis, could be shown to be in perfect harmony with the Old Testament.

Jesus and the apostles broke with this later Jewish teaching (Matt. 15:2ff.; 23:16ff.; Mark 7:11f.; 2:23ff.; John 5:10ff.), but held fast to the fundamental doctrine of the divine origin and authority of the Word of God. The common belief was that the author of Scripture was God's Spirit and that the human writer was a passive instrument used by the Spirit. The post-apostolic church shared this teaching. Origen, Basil, and Jerome, among others, say that Scripture was written by the Holy Spirit, and Psalm 45:1 — "my tongue is like the pen of a ready scribe" — was cited as proof of the human passivity and divine initiative in inspiration.[15]

However, some early Christian theologians had a more sophisticated view of inspiration and inscripturation. Theodore of Mopsuestia distinguished between various kinds of inspiration: the gift of prudence given Solomon, for example, differed from the insight given a prophet. Moreover, as the Spirit used the individual writers in accordance with the gifts he had given them, his action varied from person to person. Theodore sought to understand the phenomenon of prophetic ecstasy. What happened when the Spirit took possession of a person and used him as a channel of revelation? Theodore was interested in the conditioning of the prophet's sight, hearing, and mind, but behind it all he saw the living God, who used a person to give his people an inspired book. Augustine likewise speculated about these matters in attempting to probe the mystery of the revelation and inspiration which produced the Bible.

The chief reason the early church modified the earlier notion, shared with Judaism, that the sacred writers were utterly passive in the communication of the Word of God was the shock of Montanism. The Montanists claimed that the human author lost all consciousness when the Holy Spirit seized him, so that what he wrote was entirely a product of God. Convinced of the unreality of this position, Irenaeus, Origen, Eusebius, Jerome, Epiphanius, Chrysostom, Cyril of Alexandria, and Augustine strongly emphasized the human author's consciousness, his background before being called to special service, his training, use of sources, spiritual development, and memory, and the differences in language and style among the biblical authors. They noted the early life, gifts, and personal contributions of Moses, John, and Paul, and pointed out the memory of the evangelists in recalling the words and deeds of Jesus. Using the gifts he had given them and preparing them so that they could produce the desired effect for the church, the Spirit supervised the entire operation and kept it free from error.

This doctrine of Scripture, developed in the early church, went unchanged through the Middle Ages into the time of the Reformation, when it was modified only slightly. In post-Reformation orthodoxy a strict notion of inspiration prevailed, with the accent on the divine character of the Word. Since then, biblical studies have come to emphasize the human side of Scripture, so that it is possible to see more clearly what it means to say that the Word of God has come in and through the words of men. These men, while channels through whom the Holy Spirit has spoken, were children of their age in other respects, and Scripture reflects that fact.

Speaking to this subject at the turn of the twentieth century, Herman Bavinck wrote that the Bible is a "religious" book, which sets forth God's Word in the language and thought-patterns of the day in which the message was originally given. Because this is true, he says:

> Therefore it is no scientific book in the narrow sense. Wisdom, not learning, is its hallmark. It does not speak the exact language of science and the school but that of intuition and of daily life. It judges and describes things, not according to the conclusions of scientific inquiry, but according to intuition, according to the first, living impression which phenomena make on man. Therefore, it speaks of the approach of the land, of the rising and standing still of the sun, of the blood as the soul of the animal, of the kidneys as the seat of the emotions, of the heart as source of thoughts, etc., and does not at all concern itself with the precise scientific language of astronomy, physiology, psychology, etc. It speaks about the earth as the center of God's creation and does not take sides between the Ptolemaic and the Copernican world view. . . .
>
> The writers of Holy Scripture apparently knew nothing more than all their contemporaries in all these sciences: geology, zoology, physiology, medicine, etc. It was also not necessary. For Scripture uses the language of daily experience which always is and remains true. If, in place of this, Scripture had used the language of the schools and had spoken a scientifically exact language, it would have had to rely on its own authority. If it had decided for the Ptolemaic world-view, it would have been incredible in our age which recognizes the Copernican. Then it would not be able to be a book for life, for mankind. But, as it is, it speaks in a universal-human language, intelligible for the most simple, clear to both the learned and unlearned. It employs the language of observation which will always stand alongside that of science and of the school.[16]

We should note here Luther's and Calvin's accent on the organic nature of Scripture and on God's intention in giving it to the church. As an organism, these Reformers held, Scripture presents a unified message concerning God's grace made manifest in Jesus Christ and the Christian's call to live unto him. That is the Bible's single theme, and everything drawn from Scripture must be related to that theme.

God's intention in giving his Word is that it may function as the vehicle for Jesus Christ, the Word made flesh. Given for no other purpose, it should not be used for any other purpose. Idle speculations about the Bible were repugnant to the Reformers. Typical of this emphasis is Calvin's statement: "The Word of God is not intended to teach us how to chatter, or to make us eloquent and subtle, but to reform our lives."[17]

Used properly, with the help of the same Holy Spirit who inspired its authors, Scripture gives us just as truly the Word of God as if we were to hear it spoken by "his own most hallowed lips" (Calvin, *Inst.*, I, vii, 1). Though Luther and Calvin sometimes used the language of a severe biblicism, far from being slaves to the letter of Scripture, they meant to penetrate through the words to the mind of the sacred writers in order to reach the message God spoke and speaks through them. Then Scripture becomes the living word, which breaks down and builds up, kills and makes alive. As the sword of the Spirit it pierces the hardened heart so that Christ may enter and take control. As the message from God it is the channel through which the Holy Spirit conveys grace — which is Christ himself.

The fathers of the early church, in their struggles over heresy and canonization, tradition and false writing, gave the covenant community a doctrine of Scripture which has maintained its general features until today. As Irenaeus and Tertullian tested the spirits by the Word, so does the church today. As Chalcedon measured the imbalances of Antioch and Alexandria by Scripture, so the church today measures everything by that same rule of faith.[18] For the church today, as always, has been

> born anew, not of perishable seed but of imperishable,
> through the living and abiding word of God; for
>> "All flesh is like grass
>> and all its glory like the flower of grass.
>> The grass withers, and the flower falls,
>> but the word of the Lord abides forever" (1 Pet. 1:23ff.).

Chapter 6

Man, Sin, and Grace

The next major development in the faith of the church was in the area of human nature, sin, and grace. Augustine (354-430), one of the most gifted leaders in church history, was responsible for investigating and clarifying these doctrines, and he bequeathed to the Christian community a legacy of inestimable value. While the church had given occasional minor attention to nature, sin, and grace before Augustine, it was the challenge of the system known as Pelagianism which forced the church and its great theologian to lay bare the issues so that the biblical teachings could be understood and appreciated. Augustine had worked out the doctrines in question long before the Pelagian controversy but that struggle elicited from his opponents clear statements of their positions. In response he produced a long list of anti-Pelagian writings, which have served the church as guidelines in the disputed areas ever since.[1]

Augustine claimed that "the Pelagian heresy . . . is not an ancient one, but has only lately come into existence."[2] Athanasius and other Greek fathers in the east and Tertullian, Ambrose, and Ambrosiaster in the west had written about the effects of the Fall on humanity and the need for grace.[3] However, there was ambiguity in the teaching: uncertainty about the degree to which infants participate in the human situation after the Fall and disagreement about the effects of sin on the human race and the consequent need for grace.

Manicheism, with its pessimistic doctrine that matter, including the human body, is inherently evil, led to a determinism which forced the Greek fathers to lay heavy emphasis on free will. As a result, some statements in the writings of reputed leaders of the church made it appear that the human condition in sin is not so desperate and that people are able to take care of themselves if only they will to do so. Other statements, by contrast, led one to believe that, apart from a special act wrought by God, the human situation is hopeless. What was needed was a clear, authoritative statement of dogma, which would be received officially as the teaching of the church. This was to be provided by Augustine.

1. THE IMAGE OF GOD

We noted that the church's legacy from Israel included the conviction that the world had been created by God. As the crown of creation man and woman had been made in the likeness of God (Gen. 1:27; 2:7). But although Israel's doctrine of humanity had been taken over by the early church, foreign ideas were bound to threaten Christian belief. It was not long before speculation arose about the pre-existence of the soul and its fall in a pre-mundane state, as in Origen.[4] Christian thinkers asked whether the soul of a child is transmitted by the parents or is a special creation; they explored the nature of the soul; and they raised questions about the constitutional nature of humankind. The nature of matter was a particularly disputed issue because of the Greek and Oriental tendency to view matter, including the human body, as essentially evil.

Augustine's conception of the individual's relation to God is a good place to begin our examination. Having been made for fellowship with God, humanity was originally righteous and holy, living in perfect beatitude with all gifts undimmed. Nothing clouded the relationship men and women sustained to their maker, Augustine wrote; and had they maintained this happy condition they would conceive children "without the prurience of lust" and give birth "without excruciating pain."[5] The reason for this blessed state was twofold: God had created people that way, and they in turn constantly depended on God for grace and strength. "They [Adam and Eve] were pleasing to God, and God was pleasing to them."[6] Unlike some of his opponents, therefore, Augustine could not conceive of man and woman ever, even in their unfallen state, living independent of God. They were always to live in dependence on him, enjoy him, receive grace from him, and finally be confirmed in righteousness so that defection from him would be impossible.[7]

Condemning as "blasphemy" the heathen notions that the soul is a part of God, or that it is corporeal, or that it becomes polluted through the body,[8] Augustine saw it as a rational-spiritual substance, made "like God" and made by him, which sustains and directs the body. He never quite made up his mind concerning the origin of the soul — whether it is created or transmitted by parents but he was certain of its "proper abode" and "homeland," and that is God.[9] Orr characterizes Augustine's position well: "The soul is not a self-acting unit, but a receptive vessel; and its life consists in God continually imparting himself to it, sustaining it, and informing it with goodness."[10]

This, according to Augustine, is what freedom consists of: when men and women know and love and serve God, and no sin is lying at the door to rob them of their ability to do so. While people in sin have freedom to sin, so that they always have free will in the making of decisions, they do not have freedom in the positive sense of knowing and loving God such as they had before the Fall.[11] At this point Augustine's difference from his opponents is fundamental. Freedom for Julian of Eclanum meant that creation gave men and women the status of independence from God. By free will, he said, "man is set free from God."[12] That is, when God made Adam and Eve he gave them a certain independence; from this state they could make decisions for or against the good.

But we are getting ahead of ourselves. Our purpose here is only to show Augustine's doctrine of grace: that men and women even when unfallen still depended on God and lived on God's grace from day to day "for every moment and for every action."[13] Thus they were free. Harnack quotes Augustine's statement: "For me it is good to cling unto God." In the passage of which that statement is the theme, he says, "Augustine reveals his soul."[14]

2. PELAGIANISM

In order to see Augustine's doctrine of sin and grace as clearly as possible, we must set it against the background of a contrary system of thought begun by Pelagius, developed by Coelestius, and completed by Julian of Eclanum. Here we cannot probe the fascinating history of this movement in the church. But we must emphasize that this system was a pulsating organism within the church, not a dry and theoretical skeleton.

Pelagianism was motivated by a high moral sense and a passionate desire that people live responsibly. Convinced that God would not and could not make impossible demands of his creatures, it began with the premise that one cannot even think of God without thinking of him as just and good. Because God is just and good, the creature made in his image is also just and good. This, according to Augustine, explains the continual Pelagian emphases on "the praise of the creature, the praise of marriage, the praise of law, the praise of free will, the praise of saints."[15]

The optimistic Pelagian view of human nature is rooted in the conviction that the basic components of human nature cannot be changed. One of those basic components is the ability to will the good, and this capacity is given by God and can never be taken away without destroying human nature. "I am ... free not to have either a good volition or action; but I am by no means able not to have the capacity of good. This capacity is inherent in me, whether I will or no."[16] Men and women can always will good or evil. Free choice, that which makes them human, is ever theirs to exercise as they wish. The Manichean idea that they are necessarily sinners is demoralizing to humans and insulting to God.

Sin, according to Pelagian thought, is willing that which is contrary to the will of God. It can be avoided. It is not located in the body or in any necessity of nature, as the Manicheans held, for that would make God its author. Nor is it located in human nature. Sin is always an act of will, and the will is free. Nature remains unperverted and good. There is always the possibility of refraining from evil and there is always the possibility of sinless people. The sin of Adam and Eve affected only themselves, since human nature itself cannot be corrupted. Thus, the nature they transmitted to their offspring was as whole and uncorrupted as it was when it came from the hand of God. Adam and Eve did set a bad example for posterity to follow, but if those who came later wished, they could continue to live as Adam and Eve had been before the Fall, in natural holiness—that is, in free will with the right use of reason. Having been created mortal, men and women do not die as the result of sin. The notion that death came into the world through sin, like the idea of the transmission of guilt, was considered a blasphemous Manichean error. The spread of evil in the world was said to be due to imitation; infants and children are corrupted by their elders. The reign of sin might darken understanding, but through free will men and women are always able to do the good.

The elements in the Pelagian doctrine of grace were creation with the capacity to will the good, the law, the teachings and imitation of Christ, and the forgiveness of sins. Because of the reign of sin in the world, the incarnation had become a necessity. Now that Christ has come, grace is abundantly manifest in his teaching and works. Yet there is no internal work of the Holy Spirit in renewing corrupt nature. Augustine quotes Pelagius as speaking of our "deserving the grace of God, and by the help of the Holy Ghost, *more easily* resisting the evil spirit." Calling attention to the words "more easily," he charges Pelagius with teaching that there is no internal work of the Holy Spirit whatever. The fact is, says Augustine, that Pelagius treats Christ's grace "with great brevity, simply mentioning its name, so that his only aim seems to have been to avoid the scandal of ignoring it altogether."[17]

3. AUGUSTINE ON SIN AND GRACE

Like his opponents Augustine emphasized the element of human will in his doctrine of sin. Unlike the Manicheans, who lodged sin in nature, he stressed its personal and ethical dimensions and its character as the creature's decision to forsake its creator. In turning from God the soul brought death on itself and its posterity, so that human nature was infected with and altered by sin.[18] Men and women under the dominion of sin can no longer live in accordance with God's purpose in creating them. Their actions, rooted in their evil nature, are so tainted with sin that, unless God intervenes, they will perish.

Since the God from whom men and women have turned away is love, human love has become perverted. Self-love and hatred have replaced the original love of God. Inasmuch as God made everything good, that which is called evil is a privation of good; without the good, evil cannot exist.[19] When the good disappears, evil causes disturbance. One evidence of this is what Augustine called concupiscence, the inordinate power of sensuous desire, which works against the law of reason and righteousness. Concupiscence is present in procreation and is a means in the transmission of sin. Thus original or inherited sin is present from the time of conception.[20]

As men and women were the crown of creation, and as they were made with infinitely greater dignity than any other creatures on earth, so their fall has plunged them into abysmal depths which no other creature would have the capacity to experience. A "mass of perdition," humanity finds its only hope in God, who is rich in mercy and desires to save. Salvation, however, requires people to acknowledge that they cannot help themselves and to turn to God for grace. Unlike "those enemies of the cross of Christ who say that righteousness is by the law, to which it belongs to command, not to assist," Augustine appeals to the "grace of God through Jesus Christ the Lord [which] in the Holy Spirit helps our infirmity."[21] Augustine's strong opposition to Pelagian doctrine was based on a very clear perception, learned in his own personal experience as well as from Scripture, that men and women cannot extricate themselves from sin without God's help. That is why he could not lay down his pen; and when he died he was still writing against the proud claims of Julian, his last work incomplete.

As we have seen, Augustine claimed that grace was needed in Paradise. How much more is it needed today when humanity is a "condemned mass" with no resources of its own to help. Guilty before

God, humanity stands condemned. Separated from the fountain of all good, it lacks the grace it so desperately needs. Corrupt and under the dominion of Satan, it cannot even desire to will the good. What it needs is a transformation of nature as well as forgiveness and reconciliation to God. God gives that in Jesus Christ and the Holy Spirit, and this is what Augustine defines as grace. Christ, having become incarnate and suffered for humanity, now comes to sinners in the power of his Spirit and changes them, so that with their nature renewed the dispositions of their will may be changed also.

God is able to do this great work because as Creator he has more power over the wills of men and women than they have themselves. His is an "omnipotent power" with which he inclines hearts as it pleases him. Yet this irresistible grace does not coerce their wills but heals and renews them, along with their hearts, so that men and women desire what is good. Grace is not an imposition but a gift of freedom by which men and women can live for God and receive the blessing that is in Jesus Christ. Even sinners exercise free will, but only those to whom it is given enjoy "freedom," for this is free will put to proper use, a gift from the Spirit of God. Grace is the refrain running throughout Augustine's writings from beginning to end. For him grace is everything. With it there is salvation, without it only hell. Baptism, prayer, the Lord's Supper, Scripture, the church — all are means that convey grace and lead to that end which God has predestined for his children.[22]

Even a cursory reading of Augustine shows that he anchored his doctrines of sin and grace in Scripture. Much of what he wrote is citation and exposition of Scripture, designed to show that the message of the Bible is nothing other than a message of grace, of God coming to fallen humanity to seek and to save, to dwell among us in the person of his Son, and to give his Holy Spirit to undo the corrupting effects of sin. Augustine's doctrine of the effects of sin was (to use a later expression) one of total depravity, meaning that human nature is corrupt in the totality of its faculties, intellect, affections, and will. So, too, Augustine's doctrine of grace was a doctrine of sovereign grace — that God comes in the fulness of power in his work of re-creation. Election, regeneration, calling, faith, justification, adoption, sanctification, glorification — all are from him. Our good deeds, too, are from him, for we have nothing good from ourselves. "If, then, your good merits are God's gifts, God does not crown your merits as your merits, but as his own gifts."[23] Later he elaborates this thought:

As your good life is nothing else than God's grace, so also the eternal life which is the recompense of a good life is the grace of God; moreover it is given gratuitously, even as that is given gratuitously to which it is given. But that to which it is given is solely and simply grace; this therefore is also that which is given to it, because it is its reward; — grace is for grace, as if remuneration for righteousness; in order that it may be true, because it is true, that God "shall reward every man according to his works."[24]

"Grace for grace" is the best description of the Christian life, for all is of God. Little wonder that Augustine's prayer offended Pelagius: "Give what thou commandest, and command what thou wilt." And little wonder that Augustine was so offended when he heard, while in Carthage, that since infants have no inherited sin their baptism has nothing to do with sin or forgiveness; or when he heard that the petition "forgive us our debts" need not be offered by persons who by the exercise of their wills "lived above sin."

Such fallacious reasoning Augustine attributed to an unbiblical and unrealistic view of human nature, like that found in pagan culture, and to ingratitude for God's great kindness towards us in Jesus Christ. Only Scripture could dispel the ignorance of those who entertained such error. Pelagius, Coelestius, and Julian, who disseminated this teaching even after being shown that it contradicted the Word, were to be excluded from the fellowship of the church until they confessed the evil of their teaching and their constant need of grace.

4. SIN AND GRACE IN THE BIBLE

Our purpose in this book does not include a critique of such elements in Augustine's teaching as his neo-Platonic assessment of sin as privation of good or his doctrine of concupiscence. Rather we shall focus on his contribution to the development of the doctrines of sin and grace and their biblical roots. An obvious and persistent element here is the universality of sin.

Paul's statement on this point in Romans 3 is lucid and sufficient for those who accept the biblical revelation as normative:

All men, both Jews and Greeks, are under the power of sin. . . . None is righteous, no, not one; no one understands, no one seeks for God. All have turned aside, together they have gone wrong; no one does good, not even one. . . . No human being will be justified in [God's] sight by works of law. . . . All have sinned and fall short of the glory of God (vv. 9-12, 20, 23).

This position is evident elsewhere in Romans (5:12-21; 10:3ff.), in Paul's other writings (Gal. 3:22; Eph. 2:3), and in his addresses (Acts 17:30); in short, it is the presupposition of all his work. He saw himself as called to spread the good news of Christ, "who gave himself for our sins to deliver us from the present evil age" (Gal. 1:4). Those who believed and received forgiveness and grace would be saved, while those who did not believe would remain in darkness (2 Cor. 3:12–4:6).

The other New Testament writers either taught the same explicitly (e.g., 1 John 1:8-10) or assumed it (e.g., Heb. 9:22; 1 Pet. 4:17f.). That Jesus assumed the universality of sin is evident from his teaching of the necessity of a new birth if one is to be a part of the kingdom of God (John 3:3ff.). That which is born of the flesh only is a part of a fallen creation (vs. 6).

This New Testament revelation was built on the Old Testament, which had also explicitly taught the fallenness of the whole world in the first man and woman (1 Kings 8:46; Gen. 6:5ff.; Ps. 143:2; Jer. 13:23; Prov. 20:9; Eccl. 7:20). To elaborate this doctrine was unnecessary, since its truth was assumed within the covenant community. That community had been given as a "light to the nations that were dwelling in darkness" (Isa. 42:6); through the seed of Abraham all the families of the earth would be blessed (Gen. 12:3). That seed in its quintessence is Christ (Gal. 3:16). Scripture assumes that Israel and the nations are in need of him. Christians today take the same position, for humanity's solidarity in sin in so strong and pervasive that it finds solidarity in nothing else. In Christ alone there is reconciliation and peace.

A further element in Augustine's teaching which needs testing against Scripture is the doctrine of original, or inherited, sin. As unpalatable today as it was in the early church, original sin is nevertheless an important doctrine, because it determines whether the human condition in a universe governed by God is normal or abnormal. The answer of the church has been that humankind since the Fall has been in an abnormal condition. With a single exception, sin has deeply affected every member of the human race (John 8:46). How is it that "all have sinned?" The reason lies deeper than mere imitation. All have sinned because all have been infected as sons and daughters of the first parents whose transgression has been transmitted to us.

> Man after the Fall begat children in his own likeness. A corrupt stock produced a corrupt offspring. Hence all the posterity of Adam, Christ only excepted, have derived corruption from their original parent, not by imi-

tation, as the Pelagians of old asserted, but by the propagation of a vicious nature.[25]

These are hard words. The question is whether they are true. If they are judged to be true, it should not only be because it is easy to believe in human depravity these days with sin so evident everywhere, but because the thought expressed in them comes out of the Word of God. And Scripture, as we have seen, does indeed depict humanity as described in that statement. Men and women *do* beget children in their own likeness; children *are* partakers of the condemnation in Adam.

Scripture does not dwell on this teaching at greater length because it is "good news," whose purpose is not to spread gloom but to bring the message of salvation. Only incidentally does it speak extensively of the misery of the human situation, but the fact of sin and its inheritance is everywhere presupposed. Even in Romans 5:12-21 and 1 Corinthians 15:21ff., where the apostle refers to the representative character of Adam and of our having sinned in him, the purpose is not to teach sin but salvation in Christ. Paul's argument uses an analogy: the question is how salvation is possible through another, and the answer is that we can be saved through another (Christ) just as we fell through another (Adam). The fact of the Fall in Adam needed no argument; Paul's readers would have assumed it on the basis of their acquaintance with the Old Testament. Thus the case for the doctrine of original or inherited sin is even stronger from a biblical point of view. God "made from one every nation of men to live on all the face of the earth" (Acts 17:26). All are members of the same human family. Biologically and physiologically, psychologically and spiritually, the unity of the human race cannot be disputed, but our chief concern is our having received a vicious nature which needs redemption in God's Son.

A third element to be noted in Augustine's teaching is the nature of sin as guilt and depravity. Because sin originates in the creature's will, it is an ethical decision to revolt against God, and thus makes the sinner guilty. Guilt implies relation to a law which has been broken. It entails blameworthiness and deserved punishment. Sin brings guilt because it is rebellion against God, an emphasis which emerges in both Testaments. Guilt implies deserved punishment because God's world is a moral order in which sin and penalty are riveted together. From the first warning that the consequences of sin are death (Gen. 2:17) to the harsh words about the "second death" (Rev. 2:11; 20:6, 14) this is the testimony of Scripture throughout.

God wants guilt to be recognized and confessed. The law was given "to increase the trespass" (Rom. 5:20) or, as Paul puts it earlier, "that every mouth may be stopped and the whole world may be held accountable before God" (3:19). Jesus taught his disciples to pray "forgive us our debts" (Matt. 6:12). He made it clear that he assumed that they were "evil" and in need of forgiveness (Luke 11:13). Augustine's pervasive emphasis on sin as guilt is thus on target and, because it is scriptural, it is relevant today. Sin entails guilt before the Holy One of Israel, who will by no means clear the guilty (Exod. 34:7). "The wages of sin is death, but the free gift of God is eternal life in Jesus Christ our Lord" (Rom. 6:23).

As depravity, sin corrupts humanity's originally good nature. The splendid gifts of reason, will, and right affection have been spoiled and perverted. The "original righteousness" has been lost and, were it not for the restraining hand of God, depravity would be even more in evidence in the world than it is. Depravity is not merely localized in the material substance of the human body, as the Manicheans affirmed; nor is it a mere privation of good, as Augustine said in his struggle to avoid Manichean dualism. Rather, it is a positive disposition to sin, located in the very soul of men and women, causing them to "call evil good and good evil" and to "put darkness for light and light for darkness" (Isa. 5:20). Because sin is irrational it can never be understood. It is the "mystery of iniquity" that is at work (2 Thess. 2:7), to use the words of the apostle, that which supremely ought not to be.

In its teaching on the renewal of human nature the New Testament suggests aspects of the degradation to which humanity has been subjected through sin. We are bidden to "put on the new nature, created after the likeness of God in true righteousness and holiness"; to "put off the old nature with its practices . . . [and to] put on the new nature which is being renewed in knowledge after the image of the creator" (Eph. 4:24; Col. 3:10). Through the corrupting influences of sin the good nature God gave humanity has been so ruined that, apart from grace, it cannot dwell with God (Matt. 25:41-46; 23:33; Rev. 22:11, 15). That is the message of Scripture.

We have already seen the biblical character of Augustine's doctrine of grace as God's free gift in Christ and the Holy Spirit. His passionate rebuttal of the Pelagian teaching on sin was intended to drive his opponents to seek the grace of God, for as long as they felt well, he believed, they would not seek the physician. He tried to help them see themselves as he believed God saw them so that they would seek the help they needed. And if they would seek, they would find, for those who go to Christ will not be cast out. In its long pilgrimage of faith Israel had directly experienced the grace of God time and again. The first Christians saw that same grace personally manifested in Jesus. Pondering that history in the context of his personal struggles and the problems that confronted him in the church, Augustine became the chief champion of grace in the history of the church. Later theologians would see the nature of justification or the meaning of atonement more clearly than he could, but no one has had a firmer grasp of the basic scriptural doctrine of salvation by the grace of God than Augustine.

Later in the history of the church the positions on sin and grace worked out by Augustine were sometimes challenged or forgotten. "Semipelagianism" in the fifth and sixth centuries was the first such challenge, but it was condemned by the 25 canons of the Second Synod of Orange (529), which strongly affirmed Augustine's position on sin and the necessity and priority of grace.[26] In the late Middle Ages neo-Semipelagianism was a prevailing doctrine taught in the church, with Gabriel Biel its main proponent. Martin Luther, an Augustinian monk, had been trained in this school of thought and began to react against it in 1515. His early instruction had been so defective, he tells us, that when he became a doctor of theology he did not yet know that we cannot expiate our sins. When, through the study of Scripture and Augustine, he discovered the meaning of grace, he wrote *The Bondage of the Will*, directed against Erasmus and declaring that the question of sin and grace was "the real issue, the central concern." This conviction led Luther to attack the theology in which he had been trained, for it attributed the beginning of salvation to unfallen human free will instead of to the prevenient grace of God, which converts the will and enables it to assent to grace.

Although the Council of Trent improved Roman Catholic teaching on sin and grace, its positions left much to be desired. Subsequent official action, such as the condemnation of Jansenism, indicated that the stance of the church was still essentially the Semipelagian one.[27] Dutch Arminianism, which we shall discuss later, is one of several similar theological influences within Protestantism. But in official dogmatic pronouncements, most church bodies, Protestant and Roman Catholic alike, have sought to be faithful to the positions on sin and grace given in Scripture and worked out by Augustine early in the fifth century.

5. PREDESTINATION

An integral part of Augustine's doctrine of grace was his understanding of predestination, which he saw as salvation grounded in the eternal will of God. What God does in time was determined before time in his own counsel. Unable to save himself, the sinner must be saved by God. God does not merely react to man's initiatives to save himself, but has planned and is now carrying out a predetermined salvation.

Augustine's doctrine of grace was thus joined to a philosophy of history, which he delineated most fully in *The City of God*. He envisioned God's will as the ultimate cause for the creation, preservation, and salvation of the world. Everything, including the salvation of sinners, is taken up into this grand conception, in which the sovereign God is the chief actor and humanity, helpless in its sin, is the recipient of sheer grace. As we have seen, Augustine could not conceive of men and women being able to extricate themselves from their present fallen condition. In his earlier years, he tells us, he did not understand this, imagining "that faith whereby we believe on God is not God's gift, but that it is in us from ourselves, and that by it we obtain the gifts of God whereby we may live temperately and righteously and piously in this world."[28] A deeper understanding of Scripture convinced him, however, that faith is preceded by grace, which opens the heart, renews the will, and illumines the mind; and broader reflection on his own experience and that of others confirmed him in that conviction. The mature Augustine saw that faith is a gift, "given to some, while to some it is not given," and that "in the elect the will is prepared by the Lord." "Between grace and predestination," he avers, "there is only this difference, that predestination is the preparation for grace, while grace is the donation itself."[29] Grace carried back to the heart of God therefore means predestination; and predestination carried into time means the manifestation of grace in the lives of God's children.

Augustine quotes Cyprian: "We must boast in nothing, since nothing is our own." The verse which gave rise to Cyprian's statement is: "What have you that you did not receive? If then you received it, why do you boast as if it were not a gift" (1 Cor. 4:7)? Paul meant thereby to counter human pride, so that "no one should glory in man; and thus, no one should glory in himself."[30] In the strife-ridden church of Corinth Christians were boasting of being of Paul, or Apollos, or Cephas. But who is Paul? Or Apollos? Ministers by whom the Corinthians believe. Paul "planted and Apollos watered, but God gave the growth. So neither he who plants nor he who waters is anything, but only God who gives the growth" (1 Cor. 3:3ff.). Augustine asks: "Do you not see that the sole purpose of the apostle is that man may be humbled and God alone exalted?"[31]

To this Augustine adds what has since come to be the usual array of passages expressing God's sovereignty in salvation. Romans, especially chapters 9 and 11, is used heavily, as are other epistles, the Psalms, Proverbs, the prophets, and the gospels. He stresses God's initiative in salvation in the face of humanity's impotence, ignorance, and perversion of affections and will. All of this is intended to make luminous the doctrine of grace and to show that it stems from God's determination "before the foundation of the world" to gather a people to himself. Predestination is the term used to describe that fact, and Augustine's argument for it is elaborated in several of his writings.[32]

Always the meaning is that God is God in disposing grace to his creatures, and none of them would be saved apart from it. The manifestation of grace in time reflects a divine decision motivated by God's great love and made in his eternal counsel before the beginning of time. "This is the predestination of saints," he writes, "nothing else; to wit, the knowledge and the preparation of God's kindnesses, whereby they are most certainly delivered, whoever they are that are delivered."[33] The "most illustrious Light of predestination and grace is the Saviour himself." His assumption of our nature in its weakness, his humiliation, and his death on the cross constitute a predestination "so great, so lofty, and so sublime that there was no exalting it more highly. . . . As, therefore, that one man was predestinated to be our Head, so we being many are predestinated to be his members."[34]

We noted that Augustine sees predestination as "unto faith." From first to last faith is a gift of God. People are not "elected because they have believed, but are elected that they may believe."[35] Election is to life, so that God may have a people on whom he may bestow his grace. It is an election out of a race that is already lost, so that the elect may regain that life and fellowship with God which God intended for them from the beginning. In this alone they find their freedom, "because the human will does not attain grace by freedom, but rather attains freedom by grace."[36]

With rare insight Augustine saw man's true relationship to God in sin and grace, and he understood from his own experience and the teaching of Scripture that one can never have an adequate doctrine of salvation without understanding one's salvation as effected by the sovereign grace of God, which precedes all human effort. Knowing that salvation is anchored in God's "eternal purpose which he realized in Christ Jesus our Lord" (Eph. 3:11), believers, who once were dead through the trespasses and sins in which they lived, were made alive together with Christ and raised up with him. The one who did it all was God, "who is rich in mercy, out of the great love with which he loved us"; and his purpose is "that in coming ages he might show the immeasurable riches of his grace in kindness towards us in Christ Jesus" (Eph. 2:4-7). Twice in that passage the apostle injected the reminder "for by grace you have been saved," adding in the latter instance the comment: "this is not your own doing, it is the gift of God—not of works, lest any man should boast."

Augustine caught the Apostle Paul's spirit, and in more than a dozen writings on grace he quotes him constantly. Like Paul, he concentrates on the purpose of predestination rather than trying to look back into its reason in the heart of God. For both of these great Christian thinkers, predestination has a forward look: what engages the attention is God's purpose in creation and salvation—that we may serve him as his children and share his glory forever.

Augustine's teaching limits predestination to the elect, and the question of the relation of the non-elect to God's sovereign determination is left unanswered. They are left in the "mass of perdition" which they have wilfully brought on themselves by sin, and they are abandoned by God there. God foreknew that they would perish but is in no respect the cause of their condition. Here Augustine makes a distinction between foreknowledge and foreordination. Predestination "cannot exist without foreknowledge, although foreknowledge may exist without predestination. . . . He is able to foreknow even those things which he does not himself do, as all sins whatever."[37] Thus Augustine avoided deductions made by later theologians who came to teach a "double predestination" as they pondered the mystery of the eternal purpose of God.

6. LATER DEVELOPMENTS

Augustine's teaching on grace and predestination is one of the richest parts of the church's legacy. Later theologians fell far short of his understanding, even while they sought to benefit from his immense prestige. Few denied predestination entirely but the usual form of the doctrine was a watered-down version which bore little resemblance to Augustine's. Notable exceptions were the ninth-century monk Gottschalk, Thomas Aquinas (d. 1274) and others in the scholastic tradition, Thomas Bradwardine (d. 1349), John Wyclif (d. 1384), and the Reformers of the sixteenth century.

In Luther one encounters teaching reminiscent of Augustine, but with a necessitarian logic employed to counter Erasmus' notion of free will. Basing his thinking on the "all-working" character of God, Luther argues in the strongest terms for a rigid predestinarianism.[38] It is "fundamentally necessary and salutary for a Christian to know that God foreknows nothing contingently, but that he foresees and purposes and does all things according to his immutable, eternal, and infallible will. Here is a thunderbolt by which free choice is completely prostrated and shattered," he declares.[39] "God foreknows and wills all things, not contingently, but necessarily and immutably."[40] Luther assumes the fact of predestination and uses it in his argument as an incontestable fact to prove the bondage of the will.[41]

Zwingli and Calvin took similar positions on predestination. In part because of controversies in which he became involved, Calvin worked out the doctrine more theoretically than either Zwingli or Luther.[42] From Zwingli and Calvin the doctrine passed into the Reformed confessions and became an integral part of the faith of the Reformed churches. It is found in the confessions with varying emphases. The Heidelberg Catechism does not mention predestination at all, though election is presupposed in questions 1, 53, 54, 59-62, and 86. In the Scotch Confession, the Thirty-Nine Articles of the Church of England, and the Second Helvetic Confession there is a mild statement of predestination, while in other confessions it is given more detailed treatment.

The first "head of doctrine" of the Canons of Dordt, written after a long and bitter controversy, is devoted to predestination. In the first five articles of this head of doctrine, the cause or guilt of unbelief is "in no wise in God but in man himself, who refuses to repent and believe the gospel while salvation is the free gift of God." Article VI makes an abrupt change in method and introduces a new subject, "God's eternal decree." Sin and unbelief are no longer left with man while salvation is attributed to the grace of God; instead, the discrimination between elect and reprobate is said to rest in the eternal decree of God.

> That some receive the gift of faith from God, and others do not receive it, proceeds from God's eternal decree. ... According to which decree he graciously softens the hearts of the elect, however obstinate, and inclines them to believe; while he leaves the non-elect in his just judgment to their own wickedness and obduracy. And herein is especially displayed the profound, the merciful, and at the same time the righteous discrimination

between men, equally involved in ruin; or that decree of *election* and *reprobation*, revealed in the Word of God, which, though men of perverse, impure, and unstable minds wrest it to their own destruction, yet to holy and pious souls affords unspeakable consolation (Art. VI).

Election is the unchangeable purpose of God, whereby, before the foundation of the world, he hath, out of mere grace, according to the sovereign good pleasure of his own will, chosen, from the whole human race, which had fallen through their own fault, from their primitive state of rectitude, into sin and destruction, a certain number of persons to redemption in Christ, whom he from eternity appointed the Mediator and head of the elect, and the foundation of salvation . . . (Art. VII).

There are not various decrees of election, but one and the same decree respecting all those who shall be saved both under the Old and New Testament; since the Scripture declares the good pleasure, purpose, and counsel of the divine will to be one, according to which he hath chosen us from eternity, both to grace and to glory, to salvation and the way of salvation, which he hath ordained that we should walk therein (Art. VIII).

Mention of the eternal decree is found again in a later article:

What peculiarly tends to illustrate and recommend to us the eternal and unmerited grace of election is the express testimony of sacred Scripture, that not all, but some only, are elected, while others are passed by in the eternal decree; whom God, out of his sovereign, most just, irreprehensible and unchangeable good pleasure, hath decreed to leave in the common misery into which they have willfully plunged themselves, and not to bestow upon them saving faith and the grace of conversion; but permitting them in his just judgment to follow their own way; at last, for the declaration of his justice, to condemn and punish them forever, not only on account of their unbelief but also for all their other sins. And this is the decree of reprobation, which by no means makes God the author of sin (the very thought of which is blasphemy), but declares him to be an awful, irreprehensible, and righteous judge and avenger (Art. XV).

While the Synod of Dordt set forth a strong—some would say harsh—statement on predestination, it did not go beyond Calvin in its teaching. Nor does the position taken differ from that in other Reformed confessions. By comparison with statements found in Calvin, Luther, and Zwingli, Dordt was remarkably restrained in its language considering the history that preceded it and the position of certain delegates to the synod, who placed predestination at the head of their entire theological system.

Moreover, the third and fourth heads of doctrine of the Canons of Dordt offer one of the most perceptive and succinct biblical statements on sin and grace in the confessional literature of the church; and its articles on the efficacy of the atonement and the preservation of the

saints are faithful to Scripture and masterpieces of theological precision.[43] Where Dordt erred was in allowing the Remonstrant party to
establish the agenda for the treatment of topics. By responding point
by point to the Articles of the Remonstrants, it made predestination
the first matter of concern. Predestination, particularly that part of it
known as reprobation, was *the issue* for the Remonstrants, and that
is what they wanted to talk about. The more fundamental questions
were those of sin and grace, and the Synod might better have begun
there and treated predestination later in connection with the doctrines
of grace and the assurance of salvation.

This was Calvin's order of treatment in his *Institutes of the Christian Religion*. He did not discuss "God's secret predestination" in the
first book, saying that "it would be out of place" there (*Inst.*, I, xv,
8). Hence, he placed the discussion at the end of the third book.
Wendel claims that he placed it there "in order to show more clearly
that it is in Christ that election takes place."

> Just as the doctrine of providence, placed at the conclusion of the doctrine
> of God, might be said to complete the latter as the keystone finishes an
> arch, so also does the doctrine of predestination complete and illuminate
> the whole of the account of the Redemption.[44]

Calvin had made up his mind early about predestination and the
eternal counsel of God, but he sought to keep them associated with
the doctrine of salvation. He singled them out for special attention in
tracts only when he felt that he had to do so in order to defend the
truth of God.[45] Had Dordt followed Calvin's lead here and been more
consistent in its method in the first head of doctrine, there would have
been less room for criticism of the Canons over the years. Nevertheless, if there is room for criticism of Dordt, the fact is that the synod
did and said what had to be said and done in the circumstances in
which it found itself.[46] What was at stake was nothing less than the
preservation of the doctrines of sin and grace for which Augustine,
Luther, and Calvin had struggled. Both were being compromised by
those who wanted to change the confession of the church. The struggle
was a recurrence of Semipelagianism, with a very real threat of Socinianism[47] and of the domination of the church by the state.[48] The
issues were complicated further by the extreme predestinarianism of
some in the Reformed party and a bad political situation during the
Eighty Years' War of the Netherlands with Spain.

To assume that the Synod of Dordt was merely a controversy over
the doctrine of predestination is therefore a gross oversimplification.
Even on that disputed doctrine, however, Dordt followed Calvin, and

Calvin simply elaborated the general teaching of the church. Attempts to make Calvin or Dordt look original betray an ignorance or misunderstanding of church history. "One need only recall," Wendel reminds us, "the parallel passages in Luther and in Bucer to find out here again, the *Institutes* move along lines that had been traditional since St. Augustine."[49] And Augustine sought nothing more than faithfulness to the message that he heard from God through prophet and apostle.

Chapter 7

Hope and History

Our discussion of the faith of the early church began by noting that Christ came into the world as the one for whom Israel had been waiting. He was the fulfilment of the Old Testament (Matt. 5:17), the long-expected Messiah (John 1:41; 4:26), the hope of Israel (Acts 28:20).

Throughout the long years of its life with God, Israel had been taught to look ahead. The "day of the Lord" *would* come (Isa. 2:12; 13:6; Joel 1:15; 2:1f.; Zeph. 1:7; Zech. 14:1; Mal. 3:2); someday God would bare his mighty arm and redeem his people. Future expectation was built into their religious life.

> The entire redemptive history of the Old Testament tends towards the goal of the incarnation. . . . [The Old Testament] meaning for redemptive history is recognized only when this entire section of time is placed in relation with the unique, once-for-all event of the mid-point, and this relation may be understood only as a relationship, conceived in a strict time sense, between *preparation* and *fulfillment*.[1]

With those words Cullmann describes the significance of the period that preceded the coming of Christ.

When that coming had occurred and the Old Testament was fulfilled, Jesus, having accomplished the work the Father had given him to do (John 17:4), redirected the disciples' attention towards the future. Redemption had been achieved when Christ "appeared once for all at the end of the age to put away sin by the sacrifice of himself" (Heb. 9:26; ch. 12). Now, "Christ, having been offered once to bear the sins of many, will appear a second time, not to deal with sin but to save those who are eagerly waiting for him" (Heb. 9:28). The kingdom has already come in Christ (Matt. 3:2; 12:28), and it will come in all its fulness when he comes again. In the meantime his disciples are to wait expectantly for that coming (Matt. 24:30, 36 – 25:13; 1 Cor. 15:24; 1 Pet. 1:4f.; 2 Pet. 3:10-13).

The church is living in the "last days" (Acts 2:17) foretold by the prophets. The new day has dawned when the dayspring from on high will give light to those who sit in darkness and in the shadow of death (Luke 1:78). The principalities and powers have been vanquished by the Saviour's death and resurrection (Col. 2:14f.; Heb. 2:14f.), and the Holy Spirit has been poured out on all flesh as the sign of the end (Acts 2:17). Promised by the prophet (Joel 2:28) and by Jesus before his passion (John 14:15-18; 16:7-14), the Spirit could not be given until Jesus was glorified (John 7:39). Now he has become the "guarantee of our inheritance until we acquire possession of it" (Eph. 1:13f.; cf. 4:30 and 2 Cor. 1:22).

The disciples were taught to look ahead to the completion of their own redemption and that of all creation (Rom. 8:19-25). Thus eschatology, the doctrine of the last things, was a major theme of the early church from the outset. Christ ushered in the last age and his people await his appearance.[2] The New Testament and post-apostolic literature hold together salvation "as already achieved and salvation as something to be attained hereafter, whether after the death of the individual believer or at the end of the age. The process of salvation is a unity."[3] So acutely did the early Christian community feel this sense of the end as an integral part of the Christian experience of salvation that Christian worship was organized with this in mind, as Cullmann has shown.[4]

The church of the first centuries retained the New Testament vision of the ascended and reigning Christ who would come again, and his tarrying required certain adjustments in its thinking. Not until Augustine, however, was there any significant development in this area. Retaining the Christian hope, his massive *City of God* introduced a new sense of history into Christian thought, and this has become an important part of the Christian understanding of time and historical development. Writing at a time of unprecedented calamity in the ancient world, when Rome had fallen, he sought the meaning of events around him in the light of God's Word. After 1100 years of "the eternal city" many believed that Rome would indeed last forever. Its downfall would mean the destruction of all civilization.

Surveying the scene, Augustine was aware of the inner corruption which had eaten away Rome's former strength. He saw the pride of its citizens, their profligate manners, their love of ease, and their lack of discipline. Its humiliation, when Augustine contemplated it, was not a complete surprise, and he saw in it a symbol of how fragile all worldly ambition and power are. But through faith Augustine was able to look beyond the ruins of Rome to another city which would not be subject to destruction and decay. It was "the holy city, new Jerusalem, coming down out of heaven from God, prepared as a bride adorned for her husband" (Rev. 21:2). The destiny of God's people is not bound up with the city that has fallen, whose corruption is evident to all as a sign of the universal sinfulness of the race; rather, it is bound together with this "city which has foundations, whose builder and maker is God" (Heb. 11:10).

Augustine laboriously sought to show his contemporaries that they should take a longer and deeper look at history, so that they would be able to discern God's hand in what had happened in recent Roman history and in the more distant history of Christ and the people of God. Then they would see that alongside and within the history of Rome that other history, which was gaining in strength while the other was diminishing. Compared with the cities of this age, the "city of God" is so incomparably superior in morality and virtue, in its blessings and example, in doctrine and origin in the heart of God that its success is assured.

Augustine traces the histories of the two cities back to their origins in the Fall and in God's elective love, and ahead to the perfection of the redeemed community and the judgment of the wicked. Saints and martyrs, the devil and the lost, all will be judged by Christ when the meaning of human history as a whole and individual destinies is made clear. He ridicules the pagan cyclical view of history, contrasting it with the Christian apprehension of time as a line running between creation and the second advent. Cochrane describes how Augustine scorns

> "those argumentations whereby the infidel seeks to undermine our simple faith, dragging us from the straight road and compelling us to walk with him on the wheel; argumentations which, if reason could not refute, faith could afford to laugh at" (*The City of God*, XII, 18). According to him the real basis of this theory may be traced to the inability of the scientific intelligence to grasp the notion of "infinity" and to its consequent insistence upon "closing the circle." But this, he goes on to point out, is a demand of the human reason which, not unlike the human stomach, is disposed to reject what it cannot assimilate. It is therefore to be deprecated as an attempt to measure "by the narrow standards of a mutable human mentality the divine mind, wholly immutable, capable of apprehending whatever degree of infinity and of numbering the innumerable without alteration of thought (Ibid.)."[5]

In this great work of Augustine, written intermittently over thirteen years, there is the " 'first real effort to produce a philosophy of history,' to exhibit historical events in connection with their true causes, and in their real sequence."[6] The *City of God* was a beacon to many during the dark days of the millennium when the empire had been swept from history and the modern age had not yet appeared. For it demonstrated that history, like the heart of the king, is in the hands of God, who turns it wherever he wills (Prov. 21:1). That conception alone, fortified by biblical argument and public example, was adequate to sustain the church and give it hope when darkness deepened and no star appeared.

Chapter 8

Atonement

1. THE EARLY CHURCH

One might assume that the central position of the doctrine of atonement in the Christian faith would have meant that it would be worked out early in the history of the church. But even though a number of treatises were written on the incarnation, death, and resurrection of Christ (those of Athanasius and Gregory of Nyssa being especially worthy of notice), the doctrine of atonement developed relatively late, perhaps because other, more fundamental teachings had to be worked out first. Not until the doctrines of the Trinity, of the person of Christ, and of human nature and sin had been carefully thought through was the church ready for advanced thinking about the work of the Saviour in his death.[1]

A quick reading of these earlier treatises on the atonement might make it appear as though they are adequate statements of faith. But only in Anselm (d. 1109) do we finally meet a statement which, from the point of view of Reformation theology, handles the problems associated with atonement with some degree of adequacy. Subsequent understanding would make some improvements on Anselm, but every history of dogma acknowledges Anselm's epoch-making work in redirecting thought in this area. Hence it is proper to consider the doctrine of atonement here.

Not that the church for the first thousand years of its history was ignorant about salvation through the death of Christ. The writings of the ancient fathers of the church are filled with warm-hearted evangelical statements about our being saved through the blood of Christ or by his death on the cross.[2] The cross was indeed central to faith from the first, but there is nothing of great consequence beyond the recitation of Scripture and a relatively few elaborated statements of theory, and the latter do not really do justice to biblical teaching.

The earliest *theory* of atonement is that of Irenaeus (d. 200), who saw Christ as recapitulating the experience of the human race. Christ's whole life was said to be one continuous redemptive purpose culminating in his death for ours. Thus he restored us and led us back in the way that we should go. Restoration, summing up, recapitulation —

all these ideas are included in the term· *anakephalaiosis*. Irenaeus grasped the truth of the corporate wholeness of humanity and the need for Christ to enter into our experience if we are to be saved, but he missed the biblical motifs that are necessary for an adequate statement of doctrine.[3]

Origen (d. 254) likewise developed a doctrine of the death of Christ which is worth noting. In attempting the first systematic statement of Christian doctrine, he organized Christ's work under five heads: teacher, lawgiver, example, redeemer, and priest. Under the fourth head, he saw the significance of Jesus' death as a triumph over the demonic, as a ransom paid to Satan for human souls, and as a sacrifice to God. Although Origen struggled to remain faithful to Scripture, he was influenced by his age; and he too failed to see or respect certain biblical priorities. So, for example, while he held that sin made propitiation necessary, he grounded that necessity in the mysterious cleansing power of the blood of sacrifice rather than in the nature of God. While he spoke of substitution, he left the idea undeveloped. When he mentioned justice, it was remedial and equitable, rather than absolute and retributive justice which he had in mind. Origen tended to see the whole race deified in Christ, with universal salvation (including that of the devil) as the final condition.[4]

In Athanasius one finds biblical emphases and consistency of statement on the death of Christ not seen before. The first single work on the subject, *The Incarnation of the Word,* was written shortly after the last great persecution when he was barely twenty. In it Athanasius describes man as having been made in the divine image for a life of blessedness with God. This blessedness was contingent on obedience to God in Paradise, after which man would have become immortal and enjoyed God in heaven forever. If he should sin, the sentence of death would rest on him. Since man did indeed fall, he now finds himself in bondage to corruption and death. It is

> unthinkable that God would go back upon his word and that man, having transgressed, should not die; but it was equally monstrous that beings which once had shared the nature of the Word should perish and turn back again into non-existence through corruption. ... What, then, was God to do?[5]

This was the divine dilemma. The way God solved it was that the eternal, immortal Word, who had made the world, entered it with "a body capable of death" that he, "in solidarity with mankind," might receive the penalty and give the creature that immortality that he lost.

This he did out of sheer love for us, so that in his death all might die, and the law of death thereby be abolished because, having fulfilled in his body that for which it was appointed, it was thereafter voided of its power for men. This he did that he might turn again to incorruption men who had turned back to corruption, and make them alive through death by the appropriation of his body and by the grace of his resurrection. Thus he would make death to disappear from them as utterly as straw from fire.[6]

Since the Word was who he was, when he offered himself as a "substitute for the life of all, he fulfilled in death all that was required."[7]

Athanasius spelled out his solution to the divine dilemma believing that "it is better to put the same thing in several ways than to run the risk of leaving something out."[8] He affirmed that the ascended Lord had shown his great power in the conversion of multitudes from sin to holiness of life, in the destruction of idolatry, and in giving steadfastness to his disciples in the face of persecution and death.[9]

One reads in Athanasius a clear statement of a theory of atonement: God has guarded his own "consistency of character"[10] while saving his creation. There is a satisfaction (though the word "satisfaction" is not used) of the sentence of death against sin while God's veracity is maintained. The incarnation and resurrection give immortality and life to humanity. The entire argument is closely knit and put in a systematic form. Aspects of teaching on the atonement appear in Athanasius which made a permanent impression on the church; and we shall meet them again in later thinking.

A theologian whose treatment of atonement is inferior to Athanasius—while more typical of Greek thinking in general—is Gregory of Nyssa (d. 394). In his *Great Catechism* Gregory sought to show the reasonableness of faith, arguing that salvation in Christ demonstrates God's goodness, wisdom, justice, and power. Because he is good, God wills to save men; and because he is wise, he knows how to do it justly. Since man freely gave himself to the devil, God cannot justly use force to deliver him but must pay a price. Taking a cue from 1 Corinthians 2:8, Gregory said that Christ's deity was hidden beneath the veil of flesh. Satan, always jealous, wanted Christ's power but failed to recognize him as God. So God demonstrates his goodness towards men and his justice towards Satan in offering Christ as a ransom for the souls of men. His wisdom is evident in duping Satan, and his power is attested by his doing something contrary to his nature in becoming man. To the objection that God used deception in this transaction, Gregory replies that Satan deserved it.[11]

For Gregory of Nyssa, therefore, the reason for the incarnation is to deliver humanity from sin, death, and the devil and to convey

Christ's benefits through the sacraments. He understood the Saviour's work as both a remedial process within humanity and a victory over the devil, a view common to that day. A new emphasis, which would be retained in later thinking, was Gregory's belief that Christ's work of salvation destroyed sin as well as death.

The unworthy notion of God trafficking with the devil was rejected by some church fathers and softened by others. Gregory of Nazianzus, a contemporary and compatriot of Nyssa, called the idea of payment to the devil an "outrage" while retaining most other aspects of Greek thought.[12] Augustine substituted the idea that Satan's claim over the race was annulled in the sacrifice and victory of Christ for that of payment to Satan.[13] Augustine also placed the mystery of atonement deep in God's nature and emphasized his love and grace as the motivating factors. This helped turn the direction of later thought toward God; nevertheless, the devil remained prominent in atonement theory until Anselm entered the discussion and changed the thinking of the western church.

2. ANSELM

Anselm is important in the development of the doctrine of atonement for two reasons: (1) he focused attention on the nature of God as that which makes the atonement of the God-man necessary for the salvation of humanity; and (2) his treatment was a comprehensive one, picking up many strands of thought related to the subject and organizing them under a single theme: the nature of God and the gravity of human sin necessitate the satisfaction for sin which only Jesus Christ can give. Without satisfaction there can be no salvation.

Prior to Anselm, much had been written about Christ's death as a victory over sin, death, and the devil. But little had been said about its real necessity in relation to God. Augustine had explored the depths of sin and grace, but even he had not asked the ultimate question framed by Anselm. Only Athanasius had made the point that Christ assumed the *necessary* penalty of the sentence of death against sin, thus grounding the need for atonement in the very nature of God, relating it to God's veracity. For Athanasius it was "unthinkable" that God, having warned against sin, should lie; therefore punishment was necessary. Apart from Athanasius, however, the church failed to appreciate the scriptural emphasis on the nature of God as that which makes atonement necessary if sinful humanity is to have fellowship with its Maker.

Anselm's starting point is to ask "for what cause or necessity God became man, and by his own death, as we believe and affirm, restored life to the world."[14] Rejecting earlier theories as unsatisfactory, Anselm argues that "the world could not otherwise be saved . . . but by his death."[15] The argument begins with the assumption that "man was made for happiness, which cannot be attained in this life" because of sin.[16] Then he goes on: "Every wish of a rational creature should be subject to the will of God." He who lives subject to God does not sin; he who does not, sins, for sin robs God of honor due him. "Every one who sins ought to pay back the honor of which he has robbed God; and this is the satisfaction which every sinner owes to God."[17]

Nothing is more intolerable than the thought that one sin should go unpunished. If that were to happen, God would not discharge his duty; and it would mean that for him there is no difference between the guilty and the innocent. This would be "unbecoming" to God.[18] Moreover, "satisfaction should be proportionate to guilt. Otherwise sin would remain in a manner exempt from control (inordinatum), which cannot be, for God leaves nothing uncontrolled in his kingdom. . . . Even the smallest unfitness is impossible with God."[19]

Protesting "repentance, a broken and contrite heart, self-denial, various bodily sufferings, pity in giving and forgiving, and obedience," Boso, a party to the dialogue, hopes for divine acceptance on the basis of these. Anselm responds that man always owes these to God, so that future obedience of this type does not pay for past debt. When Boso continues his plea, Anselm replies: "You have not as yet estimated the great burden of sin."[20] This is the center of the debate. Boso errs in thinking that sin can be set aside lightly. He has not considered the nature of God and his moral rule over the world, with its necessary opposition to sin. God cannot forgive without satisfaction, because he is God and God cannot deny himself.

Earlier Anselm has argued that "if God wishes to lie, we must not conclude that it is right to lie, but rather that he is not God."[21] Any honor taken away from God "must be repaid, or punishment must follow; otherwise, either God will not be just to himself, or he will be weak in respect to both parties; and this it is impious even to think."[22] Thus Anselm argues that God's will is not free to do as he pleases, but that he must act in accordance with his nature, which cannot condone sin, even the most trifling.[23]

With that foundation laid, Anselm goes on to show that no mere creature is able to satisfy for human sin. Yet he argues (as we also saw in Athanasius) that "God as it were bound himself to complete the good which he had begun" in creating humankind.[24] But satisfaction can only be effected if "the price paid to God for the sin of man be something greater than all the universe besides God" and this can only be the God-man, Jesus Christ.[25] It must be offered by man, inasmuch as mankind has sinned, but so great is mankind's debt that one greater than man is needed to pay it. God could not justly require the death of Christ as sinless man,[26] but voluntarily assuming humankind's debt he "freely offered to the Father what there was no need of his ever losing, and paid for sinners what he owed not for himself."[27] Because of who he is, "his death outweighs the number and greatness of all sins."[28]

Thus Anselm, digging deeper than his predecessors, saw the meaning of the atonement for God himself as a satisfaction rendered to the divine nature. Influenced by his medieval milieu, he related sin to the category of honor (rather than of God's justice, as the Reformers were to do later), but he succeeded in showing the exceeding sinfulness of sin and the absolute necessity of atonement for salvation.

3. LATER DEVELOPMENTS

Our consideration of the strengths and weaknesses of Anselm's doctrine is limited to those elements that bear on the church's later development of the doctrine of atonement. We should see Anselm's treatment against the background of the medieval doctrine of penance. By Anselm's time this had become an elaborate system, and one of its key notions was that of merit — the right to claim a reward for acts beyond the call of duty. The penitential system included an assessment of the value in the sight of God and men of particular deeds, and a shrewd believer took a keen interest in how he stood in the books of heaven. Anselm applied this thinking to the work of Christ, which gave his argument much of its outward trappings. But his inner ideas are fundamental to the Christian revelation, and this is why Anselm has made a lasting contribution to the faith of the church.[29] Later thinkers would correct his weaknesses. Thus as early as Bernard (d. 1153) emphasis came to be placed on the union of the believer with Christ,[30] and the Reformation was to relate Christ's death to the penal dimensions of God's law, which Anselm had failed to do, and to see his death as a satisfaction made to the justice of God.

The Reformation, of course, was not primarily concerned with the doctrine of the atonement. Its immediate doctrinal concerns were the Semipelagian doctrine of sin current in Luther's time and the question of how one is justified before God. But the latter issue immediately leads to the question of the foundation of justification: on what basis does God forgive sin and reckon one righteous? And so the atonement is the foundation on which justification becomes operative, as Luther pointed out:

> Justification is the disburdening of the personality from guilt at the tribunal of God's primitive justice, and therefore from punishment; but this in such a way that the believer has the consciousness that divine justice itself has been satisfied by Christ; that no exception has been made at the cost of justice; that his is not simply the experience of divine long-suffering, including neither definitive forgiveness, nor satisfaction made to justice. . . . Since it is only faith in Christ which knows itself justified, Christ's acts and sufferings enter into direct relation with the penal law, and without guilt which has to be blotted out, Christ being thus the Atoner, to whom the consciousness of justification attaches itself.[31]

In harmony with this position, all the Reformation creeds define justification as being grounded in the work of Christ. The Heidelberg Catechism (Q. & A. 60–61) is an example:

> *How are you righteous before God?*
> Only by true faith in Jesus Christ. In spite of the fact that my conscience accuses me that I have grievously sinned against all the commandments of God, and have not kept any one of them, and that I am still ever prone to all that is evil, nevertheless, God, without any merit of my own, out of pure grace, grants me the benefits of the perfect expiation of Christ, imputing to me his righteousness and holiness as if I had never committed a single sin or had ever been sinful, having fulfilled myself all the obedience which Christ has carried out for me, if only I accept such favor with a trusting heart.
> *Why do you say that you are righteous by faith only?*
> Not because I please God by virtue of the worthiness of my faith, but because the satisfaction, righteousness, and holiness of Christ alone are my righteousness before God, and because I can accept it and make it mine in no other way than by faith alone.

The Reformers were also impelled to develop an adequate doctrine of atonement by the scholastic speculation after Anselm about the possibility that God could forgive sin by an act of will alone. While Aquinas had stated this as possible, Duns Scotus (d. 1308) and later nominalism went far beyond him in arguing for the arbitrary will of God. On this view something is right because God wills it, not because it is right in itself. Everything depends on the sovereign and arbitrary will of God. In formulating the doctrine of the atonement Duns Scotus argued that Christ's death had merit because of the divine decree and acceptance. However, God could have decreed to save humanity in some other way, through an angel or a righteous man. The fact is, said Duns Scotus, Christ has saved us, not in his divine nature, but in his humanity, through human merit which is finite, for as the eternal Word he cannot offer anything to God. As sin is finite, so Christ in his finite nature offered a finite satisfaction. A finite person could have offered this same merit, for all depends on the divine decree and estimation of merit by God.[32]

Taking their cue from Duns Scotus, certain sixteenth-century theologians reasoned that not only could God have effected salvation without an incarnation of a divine Savior, but that he has in fact done so. Salvation comes to us through a man only. Prominent among these was Faustus Socinus (d. 1604). Belief in the incarnation of God was too much for these men, and they found comfort in Duns Scotus' doctrine of God as one in whom there is no inner necessity to deal with sin.[33]

With an appreciation for the main thrust of Anselm's position, the Reformers — with some hesitation, as we shall see — insisted that the just and holy nature of God is the ground for the necessity of atonement. They saw sin as "a violation of the order of public law that is upheld by God's authority, a violation of the law that is correlate with the eternal being of God himself."[34] While they emphasized the mercy and love of God behind the program of salvation, and spoke clearly about the subjective effects of Christ's saving work in the repentant sinner's heart, they did not highlight mercy and love at the expense of other perfections in God. Grace reigns, but it reigns "through righteousness to eternal life through Jesus Christ our Lord" (Rom. 5:21).

Calvin speaks the mind of Reformation theology, and he is worth quoting at length:

> God, who is the highest righteousness, cannot love the unrighteousness that he sees in us all. All of us, therefore, have in ourselves something deserving of God's hatred. With regard to our corrupt nature and the wicked life that follows it, all of us surely displease God, are guilty in his sight, and are born to the damnation of hell.
>
> But because the Lord wills not to lose what is his in us, out of his own kindness he still finds something to love. However much we may be sinners by our own fault, we nevertheless remain his creatures. However much we have brought death upon ourselves, yet he has created us unto life. Thus he is moved by pure and freely given love of us to receive us into grace.
>
> Since there is a perpetual and irreconcilable disagreement between righteousness and unrighteousness, so long as we remain sinners he cannot receive us completely. Therefore, to take away all cause for enmity and to

reconcile us utterly to himself, he wipes out all evil in us by the expiation set forth in the death of Christ; that we, who were previously unclean and impure, may show ourselves righteous and holy in his sight. Therefore, by his love God the Father goes before and anticipates our reconcilation in Christ. Indeed, "because he first loved us" (1 John 4:19), he afterward reconciles us to himself.

But until Christ succors us by his death, the unrighteousness that deserves God's indignation remains in us, and is accursed and condemned before him. Hence, we can be fully and firmly joined with God only when Christ joins us with him. If, then, we would be assured that God is pleased with and kindly disposed toward us, we must fix our eyes and minds on Christ alone. For actually, through him alone we escape the imputation of our sins to us — an imputation bringing with it the wrath of God (*Inst.*, II, xvi, 3).

In this passage Calvin mentions most of the elements of the doctrine of atonement: the reality of sin and our helplessness; the nature of God which makes him react against sin; the tension between God's love for us and his hatred of sin in us; satisfaction through Christ's vicarious sacrifice seen as penal suffering; the necessity of union with Christ so that our sin may be imputed to him and that we may receive his righteousness; and God's initiative in reconciling himself and us through Christ. God, who is both the subject and the object of atonement, is seen as the one who has done it all from beginning to end, and he has made sinful humanity the recipients of this incredible grace.

A measurement of this doctrine by Scripture shows that it comes from a searching scrutiny of the Word of God. Into his teaching on the atonement Calvin incorporates a variety of biblical truths: the necessity for atonement (Rom. 3:25f.; Gal. 3:21; Heb. 2:10; 9:23); God's necessary wrath against sin (Exod. 34:7; Num. 14:18; Nah. 1:2f.; Deut. 27:26; Ezek. 18:4); substitution (Lev. 1:4; 16:20ff.; 17:11; Isa. 53:6, 12; John 1:29; 2 Cor. 5:21; Gal. 3:13; Heb. 9:12-14, 28; 10; 12; 1 Pet. 2:24; 3:18; cf. the passages which speak about Christ dying "for" or "in behalf of" his people — e.g., Rom. 5:6-8; Gal. 2:20; 2 Cor. 5:15); our union with Christ (John 15:1ff.; Rom. 6:3ff.); the many protestations of God's love for us; the emphasis that Christ bore punishment in being condemned and put to death; that God has conciliated himself, appeased his own wrath; and the fact that all this has been done for believers freely, that they do not have to suffer the cost since Christ has paid it (1 Pet. 1:18f.). Thus Calvin's succinct statement is set firmly on the scriptural foundation required for acceptance as a part of the faith of the church.

In the introduction to the christological section of the *Institutes* Calvin cites as the reason for redemption in Christ the decree of God rather than any "absolute necessity."

> Now it was of the greatest importance for us that he who was to be our Mediator be both true God and true man. If someone asks why this is necessary, there has been no simple (to use the common expression) or absolute necessity. Rather, it has stemmed from a heavenly decree, on which men's salvation depended. Our most merciful Father decreed what was best for us (*Inst.*, II, xii, 1).

Later in the same paragraph Calvin writes as though redemption through the incarnation and death of Christ is absolutely necessary. So "hopeless" is the condition of humanity that we could never get to heaven by our own strength.

> Hence, it was necessary for the Son of God to become for us "Immanuel, that is, God with us" [Isa. 7:14; Matt. 1:23], and in such a way that his divinity and our human nature might by mutual connection grow together. Otherwise the nearness would not have been near enough, nor the affinity sufficiently firm, for us to hope that God might dwell with us. So great was the disagreement between our uncleanness and God's perfect purity! Even if man had remained free from all stain, his condition would have been too lowly for him to reach God without a Mediator (*Inst.*, II, xii, 1).

There is equivocation here. One cannot be sure just what Calvin believed concerning the absolute or relative necessity of redemption through Christ and his atonement. Perhaps Hunter is correct:

> Whether redemption could have been effected without it [atonement] or some equivalent, Calvin would have refused to consider, in consistency with his whole attitude to ultimate mysteries. Certainly as God could suspend even moral law according to His pleasure, He was not bound by some high necessity to justify the dictates of His will. Whatever He commanded or determined was right by virtue of His mere command or decree. It was enough for Calvin that God chose the "way of salvation" through Christ. It might not be intrinsically necessary, but that there was in it some inherent reasonableness might be taken for granted.[35]

Whether or not Hunter is correct, Calvin does seem to have been influenced in his doctrine of God, and of the absolute will of God, by the tradition of Duns Scotus.[36] Nevertheless, as we have seen, the Reformer's conception of the just and holy nature of God and God's necessary abhorrence of sin is likewise fundamental.

From the ancient fathers of the church, from Anselm, and from the Reformers, a doctrine of the atonement developed which brings out various strands of New Testament teaching. This doctrine has stood as the heart of the faith. In it Christ is seen as Irenaeus saw him, as the second Adam who entered fully into human experience and thereby restored humanity. He is seen as having overcome the powers of darkness in his death and resurrection, thereby ransoming his people;[37] as having made satisfaction through the blood of his cross when he bore in himself God's necessary wrath against sin; as having bound himself to us so that what is ours became his and what is his became ours;[38] and as having kindled in believers by his sacrifice a depth of gratitude and love which would be impossible and incomprehensible apart from his suffering and death. So rich is this teaching that no single motif does justice to it; rather, all must be seen as attempts to express the "inexpressible gift" of God (2 Cor. 9:15).

Chapter 9

The Recovery of the Gospel

The time preceding the outbreak of the Protestant Reformation has sometimes been compared to the first century.[1] Spiritual stagnation, widespread corruption, a decline in morality, and an attitude of frustration and despair characterized both periods. Likewise both boast great personalities and stirring events that changed the history of the world. In order to understand the contribution of Martin Luther to the faith of the church, we must turn our attention to the circumstances in the church in the pre-Reformation period.

During the century before the Reformation three great councils — Pisa, Constance, and Basel — had been called to deal with the lamentable situation in the church. Although there was great "need for reform in head and in members," as the Council of Constance had stated,[2] the church found itself unable to make the necessary corrections in doctrine and practice. Those in power sold church offices (simony) or gave them to their children or other relatives (nepotism). One person might hold several church offices while residing in only one — or even none — of them, nevertheless receiving income from each. Priests promised and professed celibacy but lived in open concubinage or even promiscuity. Many who held spiritual offices lacked proper qualification; gross ignorance and moral debauchery were tolerated among clergy and laity alike. The breakdown of monasticism had a demoralizing effect on society. Popes such as Alexander VI, Julius II, and Leo X were notoriously corrupt.

Doctrinal error was more serious, though less obvious than the immorality within the church. This included an unbiblical doctrine of merit for salvation; Semipelagian teaching on sin and grace; the view of the mass as a propitiatory sacrifice; the teaching and selling of indulgences; the doctrine of purgatory with papal claims of control over it; an unbiblical view of the papacy, priesthood, authority, and teaching office of the church; nominalism and mysticism in theological method, both of which were destructive of the faith.

There was also a brighter side to the picture when Luther appeared on the scene. Besides revealing certain errors, the new learning encouraged by the Renaissance had created a thirst for understanding, learning, and reform. The invention of printing had greatly increased the availability of written materials, and made possible the wider distribution of Erasmus' translation of the Greek New Testament. Invention and discovery had given rise to a desire for more of the same and to a spirit of optimism. Growing ethnic and national consciousness fostered a desire for independence and freedom, thus threatening central control. Peasant unrest and dissatisfaction promised support when change would finally come.

In the light of the New Testament Martin Luther's work was not so much a change for something new as a return to the teachings of the Bible. One of the doctrinal errors prevalent when Luther began his career — though the church had condemned it centuries earlier — was Semipelagianism. It had too weak a view of sin and too high a view of human ability, thus playing down the biblical teaching on the need for grace. In the late Middle Ages William of Occam (d. 1349) and Gabriel Biel (d. 1495) revived this teaching and made it the popular theology of the day. Luther had been trained in it:

> I was a good monk and kept my order so strictly that I could say that if ever a monk could get to heaven through monastic discipline, I should have entered in. All my companions in the monastery who knew me would bear me out in this. For if it had gone on much longer I would have martyred myself to death with vigils, prayers, readings and other works. . . .
>
> I tried to live according to the Rule with all diligence, and I used to be contrite, to confess and number off my sins, and often repeated my confession, and sedulously performed my allotted penance. And yet my conscience could never give me certainty, but I always doubted and said, "You did not perform that correctly. You were not contrite enough. You left that out of your confession." The more I tried to remedy an uncertain, weak, and afflicted conscience with the traditions of men, the more each day found it more uncertain, weaker, more troubled.[3]

Luther's effort to expiate his own sins grew out of a faulty understanding of sin and grace. He imagined that his will was free to do good and to merit the grace of God. He had learned from Biel that while the formula *facere quod in se est* [doing what is in oneself] "means different things for different people, everyone is by nature in a position to discharge this first duty. For God, however, the *facere quod in se est* means only one thing: He is obliged, because he has placed the obligation on himself, to infuse his grace in everyone who has done his very best."[4] Moreover, as Oberman shows, Biel felt that the absolute love which the creature ought to give the creator "is within the reach of natural man *without the assistance of grace.*"[5]

Not until after Luther had lectured on the *Sentences* of Peter Lombard (1509-10) and had begun lecturing on the Psalms (1513-15) and Romans (1515-16) did he show a change in his thinking. Luther's work in Scripture showed him the error of his earlier positions, and his reading of Augustine's anti-Pelagian writings confirmed him in his new stance. From 1515 on he began to react against the semi-Pelagianism of his day, "struggling against those who so exalt the free will that the necessity of the grace of God is ignored."[6]

This struggle reached a peak in Luther's controversy with Erasmus over free will. Encouraged by the great humanist's demonstration of the need for church reform, Luther had hoped that Erasmus would join his movement and lend it his tremendous prestige. But Erasmus was more interested in his "good letters" and feared that an alliance with Luther would hurt his own cause, already under attack by the papal party in the church; so he declined. Luther's friends pressed Erasmus, who then wrote *The Sponge,* wiping out Ulrich von Hutten for printing a piece challenging Erasmus to come out boldly for reform by joining Luther's movement.

Luther wrote Erasmus a conciliatory letter suggesting that, in order not to hinder reform, each party should refrain from attacking the other, but it was too late. Stung by the insinuation that he was lacking in courage, Erasmus wrote a book on the point of doctrine at which he disagreed with Luther, free will. Responding to a 1520 publication in which Luther had denied human freedom, Erasmus argued the other side of the question.

In this repetition of the Semipelagian doctrine of the will and human ability, Erasmus had found an excuse for abstaining from the rough and tumble of real reform. As he put it, man must be free to be accountable to God. Obligation to do the good implies the ability to do it. Luther's doctrine, Erasmus argued, dishonors man, discourages striving, encourages apathy and irresponsibility, and insults God, who is said to punish those who sin by necessity. Luther would have preferred to disregard the attack, but because of its wide circulation — there were six printings in two months — and consequent public pressure, he could not. Thus Erasmus' *De Libero Arbitrio* (*Of Free Will*) was answered a year later, in 1525, by Luther's *De Servo Arbitrio* (*The Bondage of the Will*); and all hope of cooperation was shattered.

Luther stated repeatedly that Erasmus had hit upon the real difference between them. Satisfied that he had grappled with a worthy problem precipitated by a worthy opponent, Luther wrote:

> I praise and commend you highly for this also, that unlike all the rest you alone have attacked the real issue, the essence of the matter in dispute, and have not wearied me with irrelevancies about the papacy, purgatory, indulgences, and such like trifles (for trifles they are rather than basic issues),

with which almost everyone hitherto has gone hunting for me without success. You and you alone have seen the question on which everything hinges, and have aimed at the vital spot.[7]

The real issue between Luther and Erasmus was salvation by the grace of God. The question was how one becomes a Christian: is salvation in part a matter of human achievement, or is it wholly a gift of God? What is the condition of persons in sin? Can they extricate themselves? Can they give themselves faith? Or are they utterly dependent on God? "Bondage of the will" did not mean for Luther that humanity has no freedom of choice, but rather that it is unable to put itself into a right relationship with God. Men and women must understand the hopelessness of their condition before they will look to Christ for the help that only he can give. They must see that they are slaves of Satan unless they are slaves of God, and when by grace they become slaves of God they gain true freedom.

A main contention of Luther is that people in their depravity must be told not only about the objective redemption in Christ, or that they must now get themselves in shape to receive it through works of merit, but even more that God, having predestinated his creatures to eternal life, comes to them in their helplessness and gives them faith and repentance. Whereas Erasmus had agreed with the scholastics in seeing salvation as effected in part by God in Christ and in part by humankind in free will which is able to perform meritorious acts (synergism), Luther like Augustine ascribed all to God's grace. This, Luther reasoned, is an absolute necessity inasmuch as humankind can do nothing on its own for salvation. Both the objective work of God in Christ and the subjective appropriation of that work by faith are gifts of God which must not be separated. God is not a half-Savior; the gospel is the good news that all of our salvation is from him.

To prove that this was no new doctrine, Luther quoted copiously from Scripture and from Augustine. He was maintaining the earlier church dogma of salvation by grace. In Harnack's judgment, although Erasmus' tract is "the crown of his literary work . . . it is an entirely worldly, at bottom an irreligious treatise," for it compromises God's grace.[8]

What was new in Luther's teaching was the comprehensive treatment he gave to the subject of the gift of God's grace in salvation. He saw it as including, besides all else, God's gratuitous justification of the sinner by the righteousness of Christ reckoned to him without human merit or "free choice." This is received by simply trusting the promise of God given in the gospel.[9] No one before Luther had seen the sovereignty of grace so clearly and comprehensively. God has taken our salvation out of our hands into his; from start to finish it is a work of God.

> Even if I lived and worked to eternity, my conscience could never be assured and certain how much it ought to do to satisfy God. For whatever work might be accomplished, there would always remain an anxious doubt whether it pleased God or whether he required something more, as the experience of all self-justifiers proves, and as I myself learned to my bitter cost through so many years. But now, since God has taken my salvation out of my hands into his, making it depend on his choice and not mine, and has promised to save me, not by my own work or exertion but by his grace and mercy, I am assured and certain both that he is faithful and will not lie to me, and also that he is too great and powerful for any demons or any adversities to be able to break him or to snatch me from him.[10]

Chapter 10

Justification by Faith

In his response to Erasmus, as we have seen, Luther stated the Augustinian doctrine of salvation by the grace of God. Consistent with the doctrine, he affirmed God's free justification of the sinner received through faith alone apart from human merit.

Augustine had not seen all the dimensions of the doctrine of justification as clearly as Luther. To be sure, he had attributed everything to the grace of God, and the general tenor of his teaching was consistent with Luther's thinking on sin and grace. But Augustine dealt with the doctrine of grace in his many anti-Pelagian writings at the point of the controversy over whether or not we have in ourselves the inner strength and ability to keep God's law and gain heaven on our own. His response was clear and unequivocal: sinners need grace. To be more specific, they need the righteousness of Jesus Christ.

However, Augustine did not address himself to whether the righteousness of Christ by which one is justified is strictly speaking one's own — in the sense of having been worked into him by the Holy Spirit — or whether it is not one's own but reckoned to him by virtue of his faith in Christ. In other words, Augustine did not ask whether justifying faith gives one an *infused* or an *imputed* righteousness from Christ. It would seem that, had he been asked the question which later confronted Luther, he would have answered very much as the Reformer did. As it is, he tended to blend the doctrines of justification and sanctification into each other as one work of the Holy Spirit in renovating fallen humanity.

After Augustine the doctrine of grace became enveloped in the sacramental system of the church, which saw God's grace as conveyed through certain ecclesiastical rites. The biblical doctrine of justification as a free gift of God given on the basis of faith was left to the side. The sacramental scheme of the impartation of grace allowed no room for seeing justification as God's *declaration* giving the sinner a *standing* of complete acceptance by God and setting him free from the guilt of sin. Although set forth in the Pauline epistles, this insight had been lost in the intervening ages. Justification came to be understood as *making* a sinner righteous by the gradual infusion into him of the grace of God. Through baptism, penance, and the eucharist one is made right with God.

Woven throughout the sacramental system was an involved doctrine of merit — the property of a good work which entitles the doer to a reward from God because of God's promise. Different kinds of merit were distinguished: *condign* merit was motivated by the Holy Spirit, *congruous* merit proceeded from one's own free will. Christ merited salvation for us. Having been placed in a state of grace, we must merit it by our good deeds. All merit depends absolutely on God's ordination and promise. Having ordained the system of merit and the sacraments through which grace is conveyed, God has made it possible for humanity to cooperate in its own salvation.

Thus while the sinner is told that he must merit salvation, the scheme of merit is seen within the context of the grace of God who has thus enabled him to work out his salvation. Christ was declared to be the *meritorious cause* of justification, but its *formal cause* is the righteousness of Christ infused in us.[1] Moreover, the Council of Trent said, there is an "increase of justification" when believers "through the observance of the commandments of God and of the church, faith cooperating with good works, increase in that justice which they have received through the grace of Christ, and are still further justified."[2] Prior to Trent (1545-63), theologians opposing the Reformers had insisted that before they are justified persons must merit grace, not through condign merit but through the merit of congruity which proceeds from their own free will. Cautious because of the Reformers' polemics, Trent still spoke about "preparation for justification" in "the prevenient grace of God" whereby "without any merits existing on their parts" sinners are called through grace "to convert themselves to their own justification, by freely assenting to and cooperating with that said grace."[3]

Statements about "preparation for" and "increase of justification" sound strange to Protestants, for Scripture does not describe justification as a *process* fitting one more and more for the kingdom of God but as a judicial *act* of God who declares the sinner forgiven and reckons him righteous for Jesus' sake. To Luther and the other Reformers Rome before Trent was obscuring and compromising God's grace and endangering human souls by teaching a false ground and process for the bestowal of the blessings of Jesus Christ on humankind.

Even after Trent, when the Roman Catholic Church for the first time defined and sought to improve its dogma of justification, Rome's position was confused and unscriptural. Cunningham somewhat harshly describes it as "characterized by vagueness and verbiage, confusion, obscurity, and unfairness. . . , [contrasting] strikingly with the clearness and simplicity that obtain in the writings of the Reformers and the confessions of the Reformed churches regarding it."[4] To test that judgment one must compare the teaching of Rome with that of the Reformation and, as a final court of appeal, with Scripture itself.

1. LUTHER'S DOCTRINE

Reformation teaching spoke with one voice on justification. On nothing were all the Reformers more agreed, and to no other name is the doctrine of justification more attached than that of Luther. He described justification as "the summary of Christian doctrine," "the sun which illuminates God's holy church," "the article on which the church stands or falls," that which "distinguishes our religion from all others," "master chief, lord, ruler, and judge above every kind of doctrine, which preserves and directs every doctrine of the church."

> Nothing in this article can be given up or compromised, even if heaven and earth and things temporal should be destroyed. . . . On this article rests all that we teach and practice against the pope, the devil, and the world. Therefore we must be quite certain and have no doubts about it. Otherwise all is lost, and the pope, the devil, and all our adversaries will gain the victory.[5]

Noting that Luther says similar things about the doctrine of Christ, Althaus remarks: "The fact that Luther could say the same things about both doctrines shows that they belong very close together and are interdependent in his theology."[6] Justification through faith in Christ means simply relying on Christ, trusting in him alone for salvation. Justification means Jesus Christ, and an appropriation of him through simple faith means justification.

Since justification is Luther's message compressed into a single word, there is a wide variety of sources in his writings where one can find an exposition of this doctrine. A year before his death he wrote a preface for the complete edition of his Latin writings, in which he related the story of his Reformation struggle and told how he wrestled with the question of his standing before God. After mentioning his university lectures on various books of the Bible, he continues:

> I had indeed been captivated with an extraordinary ardor for understanding Paul in the Epistle to the Romans. But up till then it was not the cold blood about the heart, but a single word in Chapter 1[:17], "In it the

righteousness of God is revealed," that had stood in my way. For I hated
that word "righteousness of God," which, according to the use and custom
of all the teachers, I had been taught to understand philosophically regarding the formal or active righteousness, as they called it, with which
God is righteous and punishes the unrighteous sinner.

Though I lived as a monk without reproach, I felt that I was a sinner
before God with an extremely disturbed conscience. I could not believe
that he was placated by my satisfaction. I did not love, yes, I hated the
righteous God who punishes sinners, and secretly, if not blasphemously,
certainly murmuring greatly, I was angry with God, and said, "As if,
indeed, it is not enough, that miserable sinners, eternally lost through
original sin, are crushed by every kind of calamity by the law of the
decalogue, without having God add pain to pain by the gospel and also
by the gospel threatening us with his righteousness and wrath!" Thus I
raged with a fierce and troubled conscience. Nevertheless, I beat impor-
tunately upon Paul at that place, most ardently desiring to know what St.
Paul wanted.

At last, by the mercy of God, meditating day and night, I gave heed to
the context of the words, namely, "In it the righteousness of God is revealed, as it is written, 'He who through faith is righteous shall live.' "
There I began to understand that the righteousness of God is that by which
the righteous lives by a gift of God, namely by faith. And this is the
meaning: the righteousness of God is revealed by the gospel, namely the
passive righteousness with which merciful God justifies us by faith, as it
is written, "He who through faith is righteous shall live." Here I felt that
I was altogether born again and had entered paradise itself through open
gates. There a totally other face of the entire Scripture showed itself to me.
Thereupon I ran through the Scriptures from memory. I also found in
other terms an analogy, as, the work of God, that is, what God does in
us, the power of God, with which he makes us strong, the wisdom of God,
with which he makes us wise, the strength of God, the salvation of God,
the glory of God.

And I extolled my sweetest word with a love as great as the hatred with
which I had before hated the word "righteousness of God." Thus that
place in Paul was for me truly the gate to paradise. Later I read Augustine's
The Spirit and the Letter, where contrary to hope I found that he, too,
interpreted God's righteousness in a similar way, as the righteousness with
which God clothes us when he justifies us. Although this was heretofore
said imperfectly and he did not explain all things concerning imputation
clearly, it nevertheless was pleasing that God's righteousness with which
we are justified was taught.[7]

For Luther then justification is God's imputing or reckoning his
own righteousness in Jesus Christ to sinners. On that basis they have
acceptance and the forgiveness of sins. It is incorporation into Christ,
so that the sinner and Christ are seen as one before God. Thus Luther

defines a Christian "not as someone who has no sin or feels no sin; he is someone to whom, because of his faith in Christ, God does not impute his sin."[8] The righteousness which justifies us is an "alien" righteousness, one outside of us. When a Christian becomes one with Christ by grace through faith, this alien righteousness becomes the Christian's so that he can stand before God.

Luther's doctrine of justification is therefore called a *forensic* doctrine, defining justification as a divine judicial act by which a sinner is declared righteous even though he is yet a sinner. Hence Luther's famous formula: *simul justus ac peccator* (at one and the same time righteous and a sinner).

We who, by the grace of God, accept the doctrine of justification know for certain that we are justified solely by faith in Christ. Therefore we do not confuse the Law and grace, or faith and works; but we separate them as far as possible. . . .

To live to God is to be justified through grace or through faith for the sake of Christ, without the Law and works. Therefore if you want to live to God, you must die to the Law. But if you live to the Law, then you are dead to God. . . .

This is our theology; and when it is said that I am not only blind and deaf to the Law and free from it but completely dead to it, these are paradoxes strange to reason and absurd. And this statement of Paul's, "I through the Law died to the Law," is full of comfort. If it could come to a person's mind at the opportune time and cling firmly to his mind with genuine understanding, he would stand bravely against all the dangers of death and the terrors of conscience and of sin, no matter how much they attacked him, accused him, and wanted to drive him to despair. Of course, everyone is tempted, if not during his life, then at his death. Then, when the Law accuses and manifests his sin, his conscience immediately says: "You have sinned." If now you hold to what Paul, the apostle of Christ, teaches here, you will reply: "It is true. I have sinned." "Then God will punish and damn you." "No." "But that is what the Law of God says." "I have nothing to do with this Law." "Why is that?" "Because I have another Law, one that strikes this Law dumb. I am referring to liberty." "What liberty?" "That of Christ, for through Christ I am liberated from the Law." . . .

Christ and I must be so closely attached that He lives in me and I in Him. What a marvelous way of speaking! Because He lives in me, whatever grace, righteousness, life, peace, and salvation there is in me is all Christ's; nevertheless, it is mine as well, by the cementing and attachment that are through faith, by which we become as one body in the Spirit. . . .

Faith must be taught correctly, namely, that by it you are so cemented to Christ that He and you are as one person, which cannot be separated but remains attached to Him forever and declares: "I am as Christ." And

Christ, in turn, says: "I am as that sinner who is attached to Me, and I to him. For by faith we are joined together into one flesh and one bone." Thus Eph. 5:30 says: "We are members of the body of Christ, of His flesh and of His bones."[9]

In the development of this doctrine of justification by faith, Luther knew that he was breaking with the official teaching of the church, but he also knew that he was expounding the message of salvation found in the New Testament. The thunderous pages of his Commentary on Galatians, from which the lines above are taken, make it clear that Luther had captured the mind of Paul. Nothing matters to him but Christ. Luther also stood in the line of the best of the fathers, particularly Augustine and the medieval mystics, even though they had not defined the doctrine of justification as precisely. They had *felt* the truth that he was articulating, and in their sermons and writings they like Luther found refuge in Christ alone. Among those whose spirit Luther shared, Orr lists not only Augustine, but also Bernard, Thomas à Kempis, Tauler, and the *Theologica Germanica*. Quoting Ritschl, Orr remarks that the whole strain of Bernard's sermons is to lead his hearers

> to disregard their own contribution to their merits, and to take into account only the operation of God's grace in them; or, generally, to direct their attention from these particular works to God as the Founder of every hope of salvation. Paradoxically, he says that the humility which renounces all claim to merit, and trusts in God alone, is the only true merit.[10]

Luther was aware that such piety had always existed in the church, and he affirmed repeatedly that it was the pope, the sophists, and the monks who led people away from a simple trust in the righteousness and mercy of God. Thus he praises those who "walked in simplicity and humility," who "found in themselves no good works or merits to pit against the wrath and judgment of God, [hence] they took refuge in the suffering and death of Christ, and in that simplicity they were saved."[11] Orr is correct then in his thesis that the Reformers, "in their proclamation of the doctrine of justification by faith, could uniformly claim to stand in unbroken connection with the Church of God in the past," and in repudiating the idea that this doctrine was wholly new.[12]

We may close this brief exposition of Luther's thought concerning *the* question that troubled him — how a sinner can stand before God — by quoting his dramatic words:

> I, Dr. Martin Luther, the unworthy evangelist of the Lord Jesus Christ, thus think and thus affirm: — that this article, viz., that faith alone, without works, justifies before God, can never be overthrown, for . . . Christ alone,

the Son of God, died for our sins, but if He alone takes away our sins, then men, with all their works, are to be excluded from all concurrence in procuring the pardon of sin and justification. Nor can I embrace Christ otherwise than by faith alone; He cannot be apprehended by works. But if faith, before works follow, apprehends the Redeemer, it is undoubtedly true that faith alone, before works, and without works, appropriates the benefit of redemption, which is no other than justification, or deliverance from sin. This is our doctrine; so the Holy Spirit teaches and the whole Christian Church. In this, by the grace of God, will we stand fast. Amen.[13]

2. SCRIPTURAL FOUNDATION

A good place to begin measuring Luther's doctrine of justification against Scripture is Genesis 15:6: Abraham "believed the Lord; and he reckoned it to him as righteousness." Paul used that statement to help clinch his own argument concerning justification in Romans (4:3) and Galatians (3:6). His argument turns on the verb "reckons," which he uses eleven times in Romans 4. The idea is that God counts sinners *as though* they are actually righteous in themselves. They are not, but he looks upon them as though they are because they trust in him and look to him for grace. So sharply does Paul make his point in these two epistles that he appears to discourage doing anything at all — and some have taken him to mean just that. If one tries to earn salvation, he says in Romans 4:4, he gets what he has coming to him — which, because of the universality of sin, is punishment. But if he does not try to earn salvation but simply believes "on him who justifies the ungodly," his simple faith will be counted as righteousness.

The teaching is that God does not sit around waiting to see how high we score in trying to achieve salvation ourselves and then reward us accordingly. According to Scripture, God is not impressed with human effort motivated by the "mind of the flesh," nor does he reward us on the basis of human merit or our self-styled "righteousness." Christ came not to call the righteous but sinners to repentance (Matt. 9:13; cf. Luke 5:31). It was the publican, smiting his breast and saying, "God, be merciful to me a sinner," who was justified, not the self-righteous Pharisee (Luke 18:14).

Sinners are justified freely, says the Apostle, as a gift, through redemption in Christ Jesus. The fact that salvation is not by works but through faith (Rom. 3:24ff.) rules out boasting. "The wages of sin is death, but the free gift of God is eternal life in Christ Jesus our Lord" (Rom. 6:23). Though the Apostle Paul had everything desirable, he counted it all as refuse compared to what he received in Christ. Paul wanted to be "found in him, not having a righteousness of [his] own, based on law, but that which is through faith in Christ, the righteousness from God that depends on faith" (Phil. 3:8ff.).

That is the mind of the writers of the New Testament and of Christ himself. Christian faith does not look at itself or at what it can do but only at Jesus Christ. Faith is the attitude of openness, of trust in God, that lays hold on Christ. It is a humble recognition of inability and unworthiness which looks to God for help and, clinging to his promise, gets new strength and joy from him. Thus Scripture sees faith as the one work which is acceptable to God, the single ground on which one is justified. Like the prophet, who saw all his "righteous deeds" and those of his people as a "polluted garment" in the light of God (Isa. 64:6), like Paul, who saw his pedigree and achievements as *skubala* — dung, refuse — in the light of Christ, the only recourse we have is the mercy of God. Those who come with this conviction and in this spirit are assured acceptance (Isa. 45:22; 55:1ff.; John 6:37).

Chapter 11

The Church

1. EARLY DEVELOPMENTS

The storm which broke in Western Europe over Luther's activity caused the church to take a long look at itself. As a result, intensive and extensive attention was given to definitions of the church during this period in history. Although the church had always been conscious of its identity and had been characterized in one way or another from time to time, there had been no comprehensive treatment of it, probably because there had been no great need: for the most part the church was simply assumed.

There had been a few early developments in a doctrine of the church. Ignatius, Bishop of Antioch (*ca.* 115), held that each congregation should have a bishop at the head of its presbyters and deacons, and he emphasized the church's unity, the sign of which is the eucharist.[1] Cyprian (d. 258) accented the unity of the church and its episcopate in his treatise *On the Unity of the Church*. The bishops are successors to the apostles and the church is founded on them, he said, citing Matthew 16:18. There is parity within the episcopate but every Christian is subject to his bishop and is thereby a member of the church, outside of which there is no salvation. To this line of thinking Augustine added the emphasis on predestination. His doctrine of the church therefore had both an external and an internal side: it was the visible community receiving the Word and sacraments from the apostles' successors and it was the fellowship of the elect — a feature which his opponents the Donatists criticized. The main thrust of Augustine's teaching was in the direction of the church as the community within which God's grace is received by faith through the means instituted by Christ, with the accent on the grace and faith that unites one to the Savior.

The tension in Augustine's teaching continued unresolved, and there was little significant development in theory until the Reformation. In practice, however, the development was considerable. The external structure of the church developed in a hierarchical fashion with the papacy at the top. The kingdom of God was identified with the Roman Catholic Church. The church and its head, the pope, claimed infallibility. In effect Cyprian's ancient formula "outside the church there is no salvation" came to be understood as "outside the *Roman* church there is no salvation."

On the basis of Matthew 16:18f. and John 21:15ff., the Apostle Peter was declared to have been the first pope; and on that basis medieval pontiffs claimed the power to set themselves above kings and emperors as well as other bishops. Here we need not catalog the errors and abuses within the church against which the Reformers protested: suffice it to say that Roman Catholic and Protestant scholars agree that the situation was deplorable and the reasons for the Reformation lay within the church itself.[2] Where agreement is lacking, however, is on important elements of the doctrine of the church, to which we must now direct our attention.

Citing Luther's great love for the church, of which he gratefully and humbly confessed himself to be a member, Althaus points out the Reformer's belief in the importance of the church. He quotes Luther as saying:

> Whoever seeks Christ must first find the church. Now the church is not wood and stone but the group of people who believe in Christ. Whoever seeks the church should join himself to them and observe what they teach, pray, and believe. For they certainly have Christ among them.

For Luther, "the reality of the church is thus an essential part of man's relationship to Christ. A man's relationship to the church obviously precedes even his relationship to Christ."[3]

2. THE COMMUNION OF SAINTS

Luther understood the church to be the people of God. He interpreted the phrase in the creed " the communion of saints" as a description of what precedes it: "I believe in one holy Christian church." "Here the creed clearly indicates what the church is, namely, a communion of saints, that is, a crowd or assembly of people who are Christians and holy, which is called a Christian holy assembly, or church."[4] Luther clearly did not like the word "church," which confuses the issue; he would have preferred the creed to say: "I believe that there is a holy Christian people."

> The words "Christian holy people" would have brought with them, clearly and powerfully, the proper understanding and judgment of what is, and what is not, church. Whoever would have heard the words "Christian holy people" could have promptly concluded that the pope is no people, much

less a holy Christian people. So too the bishops, priests, and monks are not holy Christian people, for they do not believe in Christ, nor do they lead a holy life, but are rather the wicked and shameful people of the devil. He who does not have the Holy Spirit against sin is not holy. Consequently, they cannot be "a Christian holy people." . . .

But since we use this meaningless word "church" . . . the common man thinks of the stone house called a church, as painted by the artists; or, at best, they paint the apostles, disciples, and the mother of God, as on Pentecost, with the Holy Spirit hovering over them. This is still bearable; but they are the holy Christian people of a specific time, in this case, the beginning. *Ecclesia*, however, should mean the holy Christian people, not only of the days of the apostles, who are long since dead, but to the end of the world, so that there is always a holy Christian people on earth.[5]

Luther's new interpretation of the "communion of saints" and his attempt to implement it in the life of the church was one of the fascinating aspects of his Reformation activity. In the words of Paul Althaus, who made a special study of this emphasis in Luther, he "brought down the community of the saints . . . out of heaven and down to earth."[6] Before Luther the saints were believed to be a select group in heaven, who were still a part of the church, just as the souls in purgatory. The three parts of the church — in heaven, on earth, and in purgatory — were related to each other in prayer and veneration, and in the application of the merits of the saints to those not yet in heaven. In contrast to this communion,

sharing within the earthly church is not particularly important, especially since the biblical meaning of "saint" was pushed into the background by the ordinary medieval meaning of that term. Second, the sharing with the saints was materialized and egocentrically distorted through moralism; Luther calls it "workism." Both of these characteristics are closely connected. We look up to the heavenly church because it possesses the treasury of merits. And the ordinary medieval concept of the "saints" is in itself moralistic.[7]

Luther had parted with the medieval conception of saints long before he posted his theses on the church door at Wittenberg. The "saints" are not a select few in heaven but God's people on earth:

The living saints are your neighbors, the naked, the hungry, the thirsty, the poor people who have wives and children and suffer shame. Direct your help toward them, begin your work here, use your tongue in order to protect them, your coat in order to cover them and to give them honor.[8]

The emphasis on ministering to the needs of the other in Christ's name is prominent in Luther's teaching. In the church as a community of saints, each works for the other and receives from others what they can give. This is what Paul meant by saying that believers are members of one another (1 Cor. 12:12ff.; Rom. 12:4ff.). Luther summarizes the meaning of this mutual sharing: "All the goods of Christ and the saints are my goods; my burden, trouble, and sin belong to Christ and all the saints."[9] Because of this community of true love and fellowship Luther believed that in life or in death he was never alone; Christ and the church were ever with him. Whatever concerned the one concerned the whole body; and this belief greatly encouraged him in his spiritual struggles and labors in reform. As Althaus says, "the fact that Luther spoke of the church only with great joy and overflowing thankfulness is to no small extent based on his certainty of this community of the saints."[10]

Christian love means no less than sharing one's self and one's possessions with others. Althaus finds three states in Christian community for Luther: the sacrifice of "temporal possessions and physical service"; doctrine, consolation, and intercession; and "bearing the weakness of the brother" wherever and whenever he is in need. He often cites Christ's example and the admonitions of the apostles in excoriating selfish Christians and Pharisaism in the midst of the church. His strong emphasis on love as the lifeblood of community bound him to the church in all its weakness and sin; thus he would not separate himself from the church but struggled for its purification and unity all his life.[11]

Althaus highlights two significant differences between the Lutheran and medieval doctrines of community:

> According to the medieval position, self-denial is meaningful as an ascetic achievement which a man brings about by himself apart from any relationship to the actual life of the brother. It thus becomes a merit which can be credited to the brother. For Luther, as for Paul, self-denial is substitutionary participation in the brother's situation and is meaningful only as identification with his particular burden and a means to his freedom from it. . . .
>
> Therewith, we touch the second point at which Luther restored the purity of the idea of *communio*. The medieval church simply could not understand the church as a real community because it was dominated by the moralistic principle that everyone must first of all take care of himself. "Love begins at home." And even where love acts for and in the life of another, its final goal is to secure one's own salvation. Luther relentlessly exposed this connection. Moralism is selfish in its very essence, because it does not allow the community of saints to come into existence. Instead of establishing this community, moralism destroys it. The drive to produce outstanding ascetic achievements creates religious classes. The equality of

all believers in their membership in the body of Christ is broken — most obviously by the haughty claim of some to serve as mediators for the ordinary Christians which resulted in work righteousness. The gospel destroys the foundation of this whole world of pious selfishness and leaves it in ruins.[12]

3. COUNCILS

Not until the Leipzig Disputation with John Eck in 1519 did Luther come to clarity in his understanding of what the church is. Before that time he had definite ideas about many articles of the faith, but his conception of the nature of the church was colored by his belief that church councils had a unique authority. Luther's thirteenth thesis in this debate read:

> The very feeble decrees of the Roman pontiffs which have appeared in all the last four hundred years prove that the Roman Church is superior to all others. Against them [the decrees of the pontiffs] stand the history of eleven hundred years, the text of divine Scripture, and the decree of the Council of Nicea, the most sacred of all councils.[13]

During the debate Luther contended that the papacy was a human institution. He was pressed into admitting that the Bohemian reformer John Huss may have been right and that the pope and Council of Constance may have been wrong in condemning him to death in 1415. This represented a shift in Luther's thinking, and the consequences of admitting that a general council may err drove him back to Scripture as his sole authority for articles of faith. Schaff writes:

> The importance of this theological tournament lies in this: that it marks a progress in Luther's emancipation from the papal system. Here for the first time he denied the divine right and origin of the papacy, and the infallibility of a general council. Henceforward he had nothing left but the divine Scriptures, his private judgment, and his faith in God who guides the course of history by his own Spirit, through all obstructions by human errors, to a glorious end. The ship of the Reformation was cut from its moorings, and had to fight with the winds and waves of the open sea.[14]

Both Eck and Luther claimed victory in the lengthy debate. The following spring, the Franciscan monk Augustine Alveld baited Luther with a pair of treatises seeking to prove the divine institution of the papacy. Luther disregarded the first one, but he feared that the second, written in German for simple laymen, would lead many astray. Within two weeks he wrote a reply, *On the Papacy in Rome Against the*

Most Celebrated Romanist in Leipzig — his first literary attack on the papacy. In it he was forced to define the church, a subject with which he was to be preoccupied throughout the rest of his life.

Against the Roman Catholic position that the church "must have a single physical head under Christ," Luther argued that "Christ's kingdom is spiritual and internal," a "spiritual community" which "exists in the Spirit." The church is "an assembly of all the people on earth who believe in Christ . . . a communion of saints." The "natural, real, true, and essential Christendom exists in the Spirit and not in any external thing." " 'Physical, external Christendom' is ruled by canon law and by prelates within Christendom. Included in it are all popes, cardinals, bishops, prelates, priests, monks, nuns, and all those who are regarded as Christians according to externals, no matter whether they are true and real Christians or not." Scripture teaches that "only Christ in heaven is the head [of the church] and he rules alone." As the head of the church Christ infuses into his people through the Holy Spirit dispositions of "faith, hope, and love."

> No one is able to instill either into another man or into his own soul the faith, mind, will, and activity of Christ except Christ alone. Neither pope nor bishop can cause faith and whatever else a Christian member should have to spring up in a human heart. What a Christian must have is the mind, sense, and will that Christ in heaven has.[15]

At this early stage Luther believed that the Roman pontiff held his position by the providence of God — not so much a gracious as an angry providence — and therefore, he claimed, he does "not want anyone to oppose the pope [but] endure it with all patience, just as though the Turks ruled over us." Luther insists on only two things:

> First, I will not tolerate it that men establish new articles of faith and scold, slander, and judge as heretics, schismatics, and unbelievers all other Christians in the whole world only because they are not under the pope. It suffices that we let the pope be pope. It is not necessary for his sake to slander God and his saints on earth. Second, I shall accept whatever the pope establishes and does, on condition that I judge it first on the basis of Holy Scripture. For my part he must remain under Christ and let himself be judged by Holy Scripture.[16]

Later, as the tempo of battle increased, Luther tossed this caution to the wind and attacked the papacy with every weapon at his command.

4. THE MARKS OF THE CHURCH AND THE KEYS OF THE KINGDOM

The definition of the church given thus far is incomplete. The stress on community, on the sole headship of Christ, and on the sole authority of Scripture in evaluating the church are indeed fundamental to Luther and to the entire Reformation. When it became evident after 1536 that if a general council would meet, its purpose would be to condemn the Reformers, Luther wrote the Smalcald Articles, whose definition of the church concludes: "Thank God, a seven-year old child knows what the church is, namely, holy believers, and the sheep who hear the voice of their Shepherd."[17]

But more important than Luther's early writings for understanding the Protestant view of the church is his tract *On the Council and the Church*. Written in 1539 when Luther's thought had matured, it not only enlarges on his previous emphasis but introduces new considerations. The Word remains fundamental, the first mark by which "the holy Christian people are recognized."[18] The other signs by which the church is recognized are all derived from Scripture, which is held to be so fruitful that wherever it is God's people must exist; conversely, wherever God's people are the Word must be present, for they cannot live without it. Baptism and the holy sacrament of the altar are second and third ways in which God's people are recognized, followed by the public exercise of the keys and the office of the ministry of the Word.[19]

Next Luther lists public worship and cross-bearing, followed by a discussion of "other outward signs that identify the Christian church, namely, those signs whereby the Holy Spirit sanctifies us according to the second table of Moses." Then comes a listing of Christian graces and fruits of the Spirit, followed by the assurance that Christians see the wisdom in the Pauline injunction to do all things "decently and in order" (1 Cor. 14:40).[20]

Similar teaching is found in a later tract *Against Hanswurst* (1541). Two different churches are said always to have existed in the world, as both Christ and Augustine inform us; and to the marks for recognizing the true church listed earlier he adds the creed, the Lord's Prayer, honor given the temporal power, refusal to kiss the pope's foot, honor given marriage, willingness to suffer, refraining from the shedding of blood or vengeance, and prayer. Responding to his opponents, Luther accuses them of fearing a council because the condition of their church would be exposed. His own church by contrast would welcome a council, so that its doctrine and practice could come to greater light.[21]

A major charge in this tract is novelty in the Church of Rome. The Reformation had been protesting this in returning to the "ancient" faith.

We have proved that we are the true, ancient church, one body and one communion of saints with the holy, universal Christian church. Now, you too, papists, prove that you are the true church or are like it. You cannot do it. But I will prove that you are the new, false church, which is in everything apostate, separated from the true, ancient church, thus becoming Satan's whore and synagogue [Rev. 2:9].[22]

His opponents, says Luther, "do not hold to the original, ancient baptism," having perverted it through "satisfactions" and their accompanying "indulgences, pilgrimages, brotherhoods, masses, purgatory, monasteries, convents, and [other] abominations."[23] Concerning indulgences he asks sarcastically: "Where do you find in the ancient church that you may institute such a new baptism and washing away of sins?" The new "head" of the church, the new saints, the new relics, the new idea of forgiveness through merit, the new denigration of marriage, the new decrees and decretals of which neither the "ancient church nor the apostles knew anything" — all come in for scathing review. He reminds readers that he is trying to restore original Christianity while "the papal asses are such stupid asses that they cannot and will not distinguish between God's Word and human doctrine but hold them both as one." His purpose is "to show that the church must teach God's Word alone, and must be sure of it," inasmuch as the church is the pillar and bulwark of the truth. Indulgences may have been the immediate occasion for his protest but the call for the preaching and teaching of God's Word alone was his fundamental concern.[24]

A topic to which Luther returned frequently in discussing the church was the keys of the kingdom of heaven and the power which Christ attached to them. The perversion of this biblical teaching into a papal instrument of terror irritated the Reformer constantly. Whereas the popes, with their "new key," bound the consciences of people with a multitude of rules and decrees based on whim or will rather than Scripture, Luther interpreted Christ's words as a reference to the powers given the whole church to console "poor sinful consciences" through Christ's promise of binding and loosing. Bound to the Word, the keys open and close the kingdom of heaven as persons respond to that Word.

5. MINISTERS OF THE WORD AND THE UNIVERSAL PRIESTHOOD OF BELIEVERS

In order for the keys to function in the church the preaching office is necessary. Christ has provided for that by giving his church pastors or ministers of his Word. This is how God, who is a God of order, uses the means of Word and sacrament in building his church.

All the members of the church are called to its ministry, but a special teaching and preaching office is necessary. The "keys" belong to the whole congregation, but unlike the Anabaptists Luther held that their public exercise is to be restricted to officials duly called to this function. In his letter *Infiltrating and Clandestine Preachers* Luther complains that Anabaptist preachers subvert order because they are not properly called and their work is not done openly and publicly.[25] A tract written to Bohemian Christians in difficulty with Rome assumes the importance of a duly appointed ministry and argues that the Bohemian congregations have the right to forget foreign (Italian) bishops and elect their own pastors.[26]

For Luther Paul's admonition to teach others (2 Tim. 2:2), his "glorying" not having been sent to baptize (1 Cor. 1:17) "as to a secondary office, but to the primary office of preaching the gospel," and Christ's example in proclamation indicate the necessity of the provision of office.

> Since the church owes its birth to the Word, is nourished, aided and strengthened by it, it is obvious that it cannot be without the Word. If it is without the Word it ceases to be a church. A Christian, thus, is born to the ministry of the Word in baptism, and if papal bishops are unwilling to bestow the ministry of the Word except on such as destroy the Word of God and ruin the church, then it but remains either to let the church perish without the Word or let those who come together cast their ballots and elect one or as many as are needed of those who are capable. By prayer and the laying on of hands let them commend and certify these to the whole assembly, and recognize and honor them as lawful bishops and ministers of the Word, believing beyond a shadow of doubt that this has been done and accomplished by God.[27]

Although Luther urges the Bohemians to elect "bishops and ministers of the Word" for their churches, there is no superiority of one office over the other. "Inasmuch as the office of preaching the gospel is the greatest of all and certainly is apostolic," there is no room for hierarchy in the church.[28] Luther's conception of the office of the ministry of the Word emerges most clearly in the *Instructions for the Visitors of Parish Pastors in Electoral Saxony,* which he and Melanchthon wrote. These instructions emphasized the importance of the office of local pastors in the evangelical church and sought to maintain and restore order in congregational life. Here again one observes Luther's conviction that special ministers are necessary to the well-being of the church.[29]

But the special office of the ministry of the Word did not invalidate Luther's fundamental conviction of the universal priesthood of all believers. "All Christians are spiritual and are priests,"[30] needing no hierarchy to authenticate their ministry. "Papist priests . . . regardless of their contention . . . have no other priesthood than that which the laity possesses, or they have a priesthood of Satan."[31] Christ teaches us to judge all trees by their fruits (Matt. 7:17f.). The fruits of the evangelical congregations were evident. Let the papist priests

> either show us other fruits than these or admit that they are not priests. For a difference in public or in private use of the kind of fruits does not prove that it is a different function or priesthood, but means only another function and another use of the same priesthood.[32]

Shaving, anointing, and wearing a long robe as signs of a peculiar priesthood are meaningless trifles arising out of human superstition, which could be done to a pig as well. To have a special order of priests in the church is either a vestige of Judaism or an imitation of heathen customs. In either case it is "greatly injurious to the church." The name "priest" should not be used in the church but rather the New Testament terms ministers, deacons, stewards, and presbyters. Since all God's people constitute a holy priesthood to him, each having his calling, with the special ministry of the Word entrusted to those called and set aside for that purpose, the notion of "indelible character vanishes and the perpetuity of the [peculiar priestly] office is shown to be fictitious."[33]

6. THE APPEAL TO SCRIPTURE

Since Luther's doctrine of the church called for a return to the biblical conception and practice, appeals to Scripture are naturally prominent in his writing. The papacy, the infallibility of church councils, sacerdotal priesthood, the medieval doctrine of the keys of the kingdom, the veneration of the saints, and the treasury of merit, Rome's understanding of the marks of the church — all are subjected to scriptural scrutiny and found wanting. What he approves is an understanding of the church as a caring fellowship, a new understanding of the keys of the kingdom as the proclamation of the Word of God, pastors chosen by the people to be ministers of that Word, and the priesthood of all believers.

Luther cites the example of Jesus, who came "not to be served but to serve, and to give his life as a ransom for many" (Mark 10:45).

When Jesus washed his disciples' feet (John 13:4ff.), he showed what their attitude towards each other should be. "The rulers of the gentiles lord it over [people], and their great men exercise authority over them," Jesus said. "It shall not be so among you; but whoever would be great among you must be your servant, and whoever would be first among you must be your slave" (Matt. 20:25ff.). His parable of the sheep and the goats condemns the absence of compassion and makes it clear that serving the needy *is* serving the Lord (Matt. 25:31ff.). It is evident from the book of Acts (2:43ff.; 4:32; 11:28f.; 16:15; 28:14ff.) and the epistles (Phil. 4:14; Rom. 12:3-21; 1 Cor. 12; 13; 16:1f.; 2 Cor. 9:1ff.; Gal. 6:1ff., 9f.; Eph. 5:21; 1 Thess. 4:9f.; 1 Tim. 6:17ff.; 1 Pet. 2:21; 3:8f., 16f.; 1 John 3:17f.; 4:20f.) that this spirit was caught by the first disciples.

Luther saw rightly that the keys were given to Peter not alone, but as representative of the entire apostolic band (Matt. 16:19). John 21:22f. makes it clear that the power of binding and loosing was given to all the disciples present. Moreover, Luther was correct in insisting that the keys did not represent selfish autocratic power, lest God become a servant of the pope; rather, they are the power given in the Word which binds and looses all who hear it proclaimed.

Luther was also right in accepting office in the church and the priesthood of all believers. He noted the appointment of leaders in the apostolic church (Acts 14:23; 20:17, 28; Eph. 4:11; 1 Tim. 3; 5:17; Titus 1:5ff.; Heb. 13:7, 17; 1 Pet. 5:1ff.) but pointed out that they are given their gifts for the sake of service, "for the common good," as Paul put it (1 Cor. 12:7). Leaders are to serve, "not as domineering over those in [their] charge but being examples to the flock," all of whose members are "a chosen race, a royal priesthood, a holy nation, God's own people" (1 Pet. 5:3; 2:9). Sacerdotal priesthood ended in the covenant community when Christ offered the perfect sacrifice once for all (Heb. 9:12, 32ff.; 10:12), and the leadership now consists of those who minister the Word in the name of the one head of the church, Jesus Christ.

7. LATER DEVELOPMENTS

There were few significant developments in the doctrine of the church after Luther's time. During the sixteenth century the churches influenced by Calvin distinguished between the temporary offices in the apostolic church and the permanent offices. The former were apostles, prophets, and evangelists; the latter elders, some of whom preached and taught (1 Tim. 5:17), and deacons. In his *Ecclesiastical Ordinances* for Geneva, written when he returned to that city in 1541, Calvin distinguished four offices: ministers, doctors or teachers, elders, and deacons. The tendency in Reformed churches since then has been to drop the separate office of teacher, seeing it as one function of the ministry of the Word.

The key office was seen to be that of elder. It is mentioned a hundred times in the Old Testament, and was carried over into the New Testament church, which entrusted the care of the flock to the elders (Acts 14:23; 15:6, 22; 16:4; 20:17, 28). Those "elders who rule well [are to] be considered worthy of double honor, especially those who labor in preaching and teaching" (1 Tim. 5:17). Agreeing with Luther's rejection of hierarchy, Calvin held that Titus 1:5, 7 and Acts 20:17, 28 refer to one *office,* that of elder (*presbyteros*), whose *function* is that of an overseer (*episcopos*). Calvin did not object to episcopacy as an expedient system of church government provided it relinquished all pretensions to divine right and served the people after the biblical model. What he did oppose was sacerdotal priesthood and the abuses of episcopacy, as outlined in the *Institutes* (IV, iv-xi).[34]

Calvin understood the office of deacon in the early church as twofold: "to receive, dispense and hold goods for the poor, not only daily alms, but also possessions, rents, and pensions"; and "to tend and care for the sick and administer allowances to the poor."[35] The *Ecclesiastical Ordinances* offer detailed instructions on behalf of the sick and the poor. Basing this office on Scripture passages like Acts 6:1-6 and 1 Timothy 3:8, 10, 12, Calvin and the Reformed church after him believed that it was an important function of the church, for which everyone was responsible even if its administration was entrusted to a few.

A further post-Reformation development in the doctrine of the church was the establishment of graded judicatories. In most of the church there came to be a series of church courts, from local consistories or church councils to regional synods, and then to the major assemblies of the church. Certain prerogatives were delegated to each judicatory, along with certain responsibilities, and these powers were to be zealously guarded. Like the New Testament examples of believers acting in concert (cf. in particular Acts 15), the reforming church continued the ancient practice of conciliar action and refined its policy in accordance with its understanding of Scripture and its own needs.

For Calvin, "there is nothing [in the church] in which order should be more diligently observed than in establishing government, for nowhere is there greater peril if anything is done irregularly" (*Inst.,* IV, iii, 10). His heavy emphasis on the oneness and catholicity of the church and on responsible local church government, in which everything would be done in accordance with the apostolic admonition (1 Cor. 14:40), made it certain that the Reformed churches would have a well-developed system of government, including graded courts, where the work of the kingdom would receive consideration and action.

A final development we should note in the doctrine of the church is the shift from territorial churches, which included virtually the entire population of an area on account of birth, to a church conceived as a voluntary association of believers with their children. During the days of the Reformation this was the Anabaptist position, but gradually it has become the most familiar form of the church.[36] While the entire population of a nation or territory *ought* to believe, the facts are otherwise; and the New Testament makes belief and confession of faith prerequisites for participation in Christ and fellowship with his people. Coercion is not the way to bring people into the kingdom. To be sure, the idea of a free church can easily degenerate from the biblical ideal into a stratified social club or a clique of like-minded people. There is something to be said for a "people's church" which feels a responsibility for the masses of the people of the land. Nevertheless, the principle of voluntary church membership and the assumption of the responsibilities that go with it is clearly the pattern set forth in the New Testament.

Chapter 12

The Sacraments

1. THE DEVELOPMENT BEFORE THE REFORMATION

The sacraments had been the occasion for discussion and controversy before the Reformation, of course. But it was in the sixteenth-century exchanges — those between the Reformers and the theologians of the Roman church on the one hand, and the disagreements among the Reformers themselves on the other — that the doctrine of the sacraments received its most sustained attention in the history of the church.

In the ninth century Radbertus, influenced by the hankering for the supernatural which characterized his time, taught that a miracle takes place at the words of institution in the eucharist. The elements of bread and wine are changed into the actual body and blood of Christ. Ratramnus opposed this view with the Augustinian teaching that the presence of Christ in the Supper was spiritual. But the practice of the church nevertheless moved in Radbertus' direction — a doctrine of transubstantiation. In the eleventh century Berengar's spiritual sense led him to reject the idea that pieces of Christ's flesh are received during Communion. In the interest of faith he claimed that the whole Christ (*totus Christus*) is given the believer. The elements remain unchanged but are invested with new meaning as they symbolize the body and blood of Christ with whom the believer is united inwardly. Berengar's view could not withstand the currents of the time. Transubstantiation became the official dogma of the church in 1059, though the term itself does not appear until the Fourth Lateran Council of 1215.[1]

The word "sacrament" itself, around which the controversies swirled, had a long history in civil and ecclesiastical life. Originally it had referred to the money deposited by a party in a lawsuit; if forfeited it was devoted to some sacred purpose. *Sacramentum* also came to signify the oath of loyalty taken by a soldier. The church applied it to religious rites, and it came to be synonymous with the familiar New Testament Greek word *mysterion*. (The Latin Vulgate's translation of *mysterion* by *sacramentum* in Eph. 5:32 was significant in the development of the theology of marriage as a sacrament.) Eventually, *sacramentum* came to be understood as a religious sign or rite with a hidden or mysterious meaning.

Augustine mentions sacraments frequently, saying that they are called such "when they pertain to divine things."[2] Later Hugo of St. Victor (d. 1141) made important contributions to sacramental theology. Medieval theologians wove these ideas into what became known as the sacramental system of the thought and practice of the church. Emphasizing mysticism and the supra-rational character of the Christian faith, Hugo elaborated a system of thirty sacramental rites, organized into three groups, with baptism and the eucharist having primacy.[3]

The common definition of a sacrament as "the sign of a sacred thing" was too broad, and the church found it necessary to make the meaning of the term more precise. Although theologians and church councils had difficulty here, the thirteenth century did see some progress in definition; and the number of the sacraments was set at seven, which the Council of Trent later confirmed.[4] Starting with Augustine's familiar definition of a sacrament as a visible sign of an invisible grace, medieval theologians argued that the sacraments are necessary for salvation; that they contain and confer grace; that they in fact work as the efficient cause of grace by a virtue inherent in themselves when the act is performed (*ex opere operato*); that baptism, confirmation, and ordination imprint an indelible mark on the soul; and that the sacraments must be administered by priests. All of these positions were confirmed and made a part of the church's dogma by the Council of Trent during the heat of controversy.[5]

Earlier challenges to church teaching on the sacraments were mild compared to the tempest unleashed during the Reformation. Luther's 1520 tract *The Babylonian Captivity of the Church* is a case in point. Written in Latin for those equipped to handle its radical ideas, it was translated into German by one of Luther's bitterest foes, who hoped that its dissemination among the masses would expose Luther's revolutionary thinking and discredit him. Its effect was indeed earth-shaking. Erasmus, who had been hoping for reconciliation, declared that the break with Rome was now "irreparable." Theologians and princes read it with shocked horror. Even King Henry VIII of England wrote a book condemning Luther and defending the seven sacraments—for which Leo X honored him with the title "Defender of the Faith," which the British crown has carried ever since. But others were provoked to thought or galvanized in their new-found conviction.

Beginning sarcastically by thanking his opponents for showing him that his earlier mildness with respect to indulgences and the pope was a mistake, Luther calls his present volume only "a prelude on the captivity of the Roman Church." He then launches into his argument:

> To begin with, I must deny that there are seven sacraments, and for the present maintain that there are but three: baptism, penance, and the bread. All three have been subjected to a miserable captivity by the Roman curia, and the church has been robbed of all her liberty. Yet, if I were to speak according to the usage of the Scriptures, I should have only one single sacrament, but with three sacramental signs, of which I shall treat more fully at the proper time.[6]

2. THE LORD'S SUPPER

In the church's theory and practice concerning the Lord's Supper Luther finds a threefold bondage: withholding the cup from the people, transubstantiation, and the sacrament of the mass. The whole sacrament belongs to the people, he argues from Scripture, and to restrict the wine to priests is unwarranted human tyranny.

The "second captivity of this sacrament," transubstantiation, Luther had learned to question from Pierre d'Ailly, one of his theological mentors. The theory of Thomas Aquinas, that the *substance* of bread and wine are changed into the body and blood of Christ during Communion while the *accidents* (appearance, taste, smell) remain the same, had bothered d'Ailly. So he had argued for real bread and real wine on the altar, "and not merely their accidents." This view "would be much more probable and require fewer superfluous miracles — if only the church had not decreed otherwise." Luther goes on:

> When I learned later what church it was that had decreed this, namely the Thomistic — that is, the Aristotelian church — I grew bolder, and after floating in a sea of doubt, I at last found rest for my conscience in the above view, namely, that it is real bread and real wine, in which Christ's real flesh and real blood are present in no other way and to no less a degree than the others assert them to be under their accidents. . . . Aristotle speaks of subject and accidents so very differently from St. Thomas that it seems to me this great man is to be pitied not only for attempting to draw his opinions in matters of faith from Aristotle, but also for attempting to base them upon a man whom he did not understand, thus building an unfortunate superstructure upon an unfortunate foundation.[7]

Luther would permit either opinion here, but he does not want a person called a heretic for believing that there are real bread and real wine on the altar. He challenged the Thomistic view that substance can be changed while accidents remain inasmuch as Aristotle, from whom this terminology is derived, allowed no such separation. But why get bogged down with philosophy when the Holy Spirit is greater than Aristotle!

The third captivity is for Luther "by far the most wicked of all": the doctrine of the sacrifice of the mass, the notion that the priest offers to God the very body and blood of Christ as a repetition of the atoning sacrifice of the cross, only in an unbloody manner. Fearing that this error may be so "firmly entrenched" that it is "perhaps impossible to uproot," Luther nevertheless takes heart because his Christ lives. So he launches into page after page of powerful polemic. The true mass, or the sacrament of the altar, he defines as "a promise of the forgiveness of sins made to us by God, and such a promise as has been confirmed by the death of the Son of God." Since it is a "promise," access to God is not gained by works or merits by which we seek to please God but by faith alone. "For where there is the Word of the promising God, there must necessarily be the faith of the accepting man."[8]

> Who in the world is so foolish as to regard a promise received by him, or a testament given to him, as a good work, which he renders to the testator by his acceptance of it? What heir will imagine that he is doing his departed father a kindness by accepting the terms of the will and the inheritance it bequeaths to him? What godless audacity is it, therefore, when we who are to receive the testament of God come as those who would perform a good work for him! This ignorance of the testament, this captivity of so great a sacrament — are they not too sad for tears? When we ought to be grateful for benefits received, we come arrogantly to give that which we ought to take. With unheard-of perversity we mock the mercy of the giver by giving as a work the thing we receive as a gift, so that the testator, instead of being a dispenser of his own goods, becomes the recipient of ours. Woe to such sacrilege![9]

Although he finds himself in general agreement with Rome on baptism, Luther declares the other five sacraments invalid. "There are, strictly speaking, but two sacraments in the church of God — baptism and the bread. For only in these two do we find both the divinely instituted sign and the promise of forgiveness of sins."[10]

The sacramental system lay at the heart of the church. In attacking it Luther was threatening the very life of Rome. He had made clear to his sympathizers that the church lay in bondage. As Israel had been taken captive from Jerusalem to Babylon and had languished there, the church, the Israel of the new covenant, had been carried away from Scripture and had been bound by ignorance and papal tyranny. But neither God nor his Word could be bound, and Luther was not bound either. He was determined to do his utmost to break the bonds that were holding the church captive, dispel the ignorance, and show what Christ intended when he gave his flock baptism and the Supper.

Luther continued his sacramental theology in a continuing series of essays. *The Misuse of the Mass* appeared the next year, followed a year later by *Receiving Both Kinds in the Sacrament*. The year after that he published *The Adoration of the Sacrament*, and two years later *The Abomination of the Secret Mass*. While attacking the Roman teaching, Luther also had to fight developments on his other flank. Hearing that the extreme positions taken by Carlstadt and other fanatics were hindering a proper appreciation for the sacraments, Luther felt it necessary in 1524 to write a letter to Christians at Strassburg "in Opposition to the Fanatic Spirit." This was followed the next year by *Against the Heavenly Prophets in the Matter of Images and Sacraments* and three years later by *Concerning Rebaptism*. In the meantime, in 1526, he wrote *The Sacrament of the Body and Blood of Christ — Against the Fanatics; That These Words of Christ, "This Is My Body," etc., Still Stand Firm Against the Fanatics* (1527); and a *Confession Concerning Christ's Supper* a year later.

Whereas Luther rejected transubstantiation and the sacrament of the mass, he still believed that Christ is bodily present in the Lord's Supper and that his body is received by all who partake of the elements. "On this we take our stand, and we also believe and teach that in the Supper we eat and take to ourselves Christ's body truly and physically."[11] How this takes place is a mystery but there is no question of the fact inasmuch as Christ declared: "This is my body." If Scripture cannot be taken literally here, he wrote, it cannot be believed anywhere and the way is prepared "for the virtual denial of Christ, God and everything."[12] Luther was more shaken emotionally by Reformers who denied the physical presence of Christ in the Supper than he was by the doctrine of transubstantiation, and he aimed the heaviest salvos of his sacramental battles against his fellow-Protestants.

3. ZWINGLI

Luther's main antagonist in the new battle was the German Swiss Reformer Ulrich Zwingli. He had independently come to evangelical convictions in Zurich about the time Luther's reform started. Though both were committed to the fundamentals of Christianity and the Reformation, Zwingli was of a different spirit from Luther and was far from him in the way in which he conceived the faith. Zwingli was a humanist who felt no deep commitment to the medieval faith. He appreciated reason, held a questionable doctrine of the noetic effects of sin, and disliked the very word "sacrament." It was not difficult for Zwingli to break with the Roman Church. Luther by contrast felt an attachment to the whole tradition of the church, was conservative by nature, and had a deep mystical strain and suspicion of the free use of human reason.

> Luther never escaped from the feelings of the monk and associations of the cloister; but Zwingli studied his New Testament with a fine sense of the sanity of its thought, the combined purity and practicability of its ideals, and the majesty of its spirit; and his ambition was to realize a religion after its model, free from the traditions and superstitions of men. It was this that made him so tolerant of Luther, and Luther so intolerant of him. The differences of character were insuperable.[13]

Theologically Luther and Zwingli were at variance because of dualism in Zwingli's thinking and Luther's inability to free himself from the medieval notion that the presence of Christ in the Supper could be real only if it were physical. Zwingli's dualism is reflected in a heavy emphasis on God's sovereignty, grace, and predestination over against any schemes of human merit or sacramental triumphalism, his doctrine of the Word of God as both outward and inward, his doctrine of the church as both visible and invisible, and his conception of the means of grace as having both an external human form and an inward content which is given by the Holy Spirit. The Spirit makes the external form of the Word and sacrament and their inward content one, but the two must always be distinguished, for not all who receive the external Word or sacrament believe.

No physical element can affect the soul, Zwingli argued. Inner grace is needed, and this depends on God's sovereignty. Thus we may not identify the sign in the sacraments with that which it signifies. Moreover, Zwingli believed that one approaches the spiritual reality as by faith he concentrates on it and rises above the world of sense. Luther by contrast taught that God comes to us precisely in physical realities discerned by sense. In an introduction to Zwingli's thought Bromiley writes:

> In his own expositions Zwingli concentrated almost exclusively upon the sign, that is to say, the sacrament in its purely external sense. Naturally, he had no great difficulty in showing that the presence of the sign is no guarantee of the presence of the thing signified. . . . In his reaction against the identification of sign and thing signified, he failed to give any very coherent account of the relationship between the two. He did not deny

that God can and does use the sacrament as a means of grace, but he so isolated the sovereign operation of God that for all practical purposes there was no connection between the internal and the external work. ... A possible link was true faith in the recipient, but even this was ultimately the gift of God and independent of the external sacrament. The fact remains that while Zwingli had a strong sense of the two "natures" of the sacrament, he did not show any clear sense of its unity.[14]

Zwingli held that the Lord's Supper is a visible reminder of salvation in Christ. The words of institution — "This is my body," "This is my blood" — must be interpreted in accordance with John 6, where Jesus spoke of eating and drinking his body and blood, especially verse 63: "It is the spirit that gives life; the flesh is of no avail." Therefore, said Zwingli, there is no physical presence of Christ in the Supper, and the doctrine of a physical eating is absurd and repugnant to reason and common sense. God does not require us to believe that which is contrary to sense experience. The word "is" in the words of institution means "represents" or "signifies"; it must be interpreted figuratively, as is commonly done in other "I am" passages in the New Testament. Christ's ascension means that he took his body from earth to heaven.[15]

Though one-sided and unsatisfying, Zwingli's argument is powerful. What it lacks is a sufficient emphasis on the real presence of Christ in the Supper in his Holy Spirit and a real feeding of the believer on the risen Lord. Although he uses the expressions, eating Christ spiritually means to him "trusting with the heart and soul upon the mercy and goodness of God through Christ" and thanking him for the pledge of salvation.[16]

Luther emphasized the reality of a communion with Christ and reception of him in the sacrament. Again and again he protests that reason cannot and must not be the arbiter of the mysteries of God. While a crude understanding of feeding on Christ is not to be tolerated, "it is contrary neither to Scripture nor to the articles of faith for Christ's body to be at the same time in heaven and in the Supper." The ascension means that Christ went to God's right hand; and since God's right hand is everywhere, Christ can be in various places at one time. This became possible through the communication of the attributes of Christ's divine nature to his human nature.[17]

There are various modes of Christ's presence, Luther argued. We do not have to think that Christ's body is in the Supper in the way that a bird is in a nest, wine in a cask, bread in a box, or money in a pocket. An object may be in a place *locally*, when it takes up all the space there is for it — as wine in a cask. Or an object may be in a place *definitively*, that is, when it is not in one place but can occupy more or less room, like a devil or an angel. Or an object may occupy space *repletively*, that is, supernaturally, "if it is simultaneously present in all places whole and entire, and fills all places, yet without being measured or circumscribed by any place."[18] This last mode of existence belongs to God alone.

Luther had learned these scholastic distinctions from William Occam and Gabriel Biel. With them he answered Zwingli's objections. He sought to show that in one of the last two modes of presence Christ's body can be present everywhere, so that it can truly be received in the sacrament. But finally the "sacramental union" of Christ with the elements was a mystery, a matter of faith. And the primary concern behind Luther's reaction to Zwingli was the same belief he maintained against Rome: "The sacrament is really to be understood as God's gift. . . . Human activity adds nothing to it."[19]

4. CALVIN

Calvin's position on the sacraments may seem to be mediate between the views of Luther and Zwingli, but it is in fact an independent position. Calvin rejected both Zwingli's memorialism and Luther's "monstrous notion of ubiquity" (*Inst.*, IV, xvii, 30). With Luther he held that there is a real reception of the body and blood of Christ in the sacrament, but in a spiritual manner. The sacrament is a means by which Christ communicates himself to us. Calvin held with Zwingli that after the ascension Christ retained a real body of flesh and blood which was located in heaven. Nothing should be taken from Christ's "heavenly glory — as happens when he is brought under the corruptible elements of this world, or bound to any earthly creatures." Moreover, "nothing inappropriate to human nature [should] be ascribed to his body, as happens when it is said either to be infinite or to be put in a number of places at once" (*Inst.*, IV, xvii, 19). Like Luther Calvin believed that the elements in the Supper are signs which exhibit the presence of Jesus Christ; he repudiated Zwingli's idea that they are signs which represent what is absent.

Inasmuch as the real presence of Christ in the sacrament was the key issue in the eucharistic controversies, the agreement between Luther and Calvin was greater than that between Calvin and Zwingli. When pressed, Zwingli would admit a presence of Christ in the Supper, but it was a presence "by the contemplation of faith," not "in essence and reality."[20] For Luther and Calvin communion with a present Christ who actually feeds believers with his body and blood is what makes the sacrament. The question between them was *how* Christ's body exists and is given to believers.[21]

Calvin repudiated the Eutychian doctrine that Christ's humanity was absorbed by his divinity, an idea he found in the sacramental theology of some of his Lutheran opponents (*Inst.*, IV, xvii, 30). Not only in the *Institutes* (IV, xvii, 26), but also in the *Geneva Catechism*, the *Mutual Consent of the Churches of Zurich and Geneva*, and the tracts of the Westphal controversy,[22] Calvin stressed that, while Christ is bodily in heaven, this distance is overcome by the Holy Spirit, who vivifies believers with Christ's flesh. Calvin readily uses the word "substance" in this context. "Without any change of place, [Christ's] virtue penetrates to us by the secret operation of his Spirit, so that our souls obtain spiritual life from his substance."[23] Thus the Supper is a true "communion of the body."[24] In order for Christians to believe in the reality of the body, the notion of "the immensity of the body" must be removed.[25]

> It is not necessary that the essence of the flesh should descend from heaven in order to our being fed upon it, the virtue of the Spirit being sufficient to break through all impediments and surmount any distance of place. . . . This mode is incomprehensible to the human mind; because neither can flesh naturally be the life of the soul, nor exert its power upon us from heaven, nor without reason is the communion which makes us flesh of the flesh of Christ, and bone of his bones, called by Paul, "A great mystery" (Eph. 5:30). . . . But we must have done with all inventions inconsistent with the explanation lately given, such as the ubiquity of the body, the secret inclosing under the symbol of bread, and the substantial presence on earth.[26]

In the *Geneva Catechism* Calvin put the matter as simply as he could phrase it, and his explanation is worth quoting at length:

> *Do we therefore eat the body and blood of the Lord?*
> I understand so. For as our whole reliance for salvation depends on him, in order that the obedience which he yielded to the Father may be imputed to us just as if it were ours, it is necessary that he be possessed by us; for the only way in which he communicates his blessings to us is by making himself ours.

> *But did he not give himself when he exposed himself to death, that he might redeem us from the sentence of death, and reconcile us to God?*
> That is indeed true; but it is not enough for us unless we now receive him, that thus the efficacy and fruit of his death may reach us.

Does not the manner of receiving consist in faith?
I admit it does. But I at the same time add, that this is done when we not only believe that he died in order to free us from death, and was raised up that he might purchase life for us, but recognize that he dwells in us, and that we are united to him by a union the same in kind as that which unites the members to the head, that by virtue of this union we may become partakers of all his blessings.

Do we obtain this communion by the Supper alone?
No, indeed. For by the gospel also, as Paul declares, Christ is communicated to us. And Paul justly declares this, seeing we are there told that we are flesh of his flesh and bones of his bones — that he is the living bread which came down from heaven to nourish our souls — that we are one with him as he is one with the Father, etc. (1 Cor. 1:6; Eph. 5:30; John 6:51; John 17:21).

What more do we obtain from the sacrament, or what other benefit does it confer upon us?
The communion of which I spoke is thereby confirmed and increased; for although Christ is exhibited to us both in baptism and in the gospel, we do not however receive him entire, but in part only.

What then have we in the symbol of bread?
As the body of Christ was once sacrificed for us to reconcile us to God, so now also is it given to us, that we may certainly know that reconciliation belongs to us.

What in the symbol of wine?
That as Christ once shed his blood for the satisfaction of our sins, and as the price of our redemption, so he now gives it to us to drink, that we may feel the benefit which should thence accrue to us.

According to these two answers, the holy Supper of the Lord refers us to his death, that we may communicate in its virtue?
Wholly so; for then the one perpetual sacrifice, sufficient for our salvation, was performed. Hence nothing more remains for us but to enjoy it.

The Supper then was not instituted in order to offer up to God the body of his Son?
By no means. He himself alone, as priest forever, has this privilege; and so his words express when he says, "Take, eat." He there commands us not to offer his body, but only to eat it (Heb. 5:10; Matt. 26:26).

Why do we use two signs?
Therein the Lord consulted our weakness, teaching us in a more familiar

manner that he is not only food to our souls, but drink also, so that we are not to seek any part of spiritual life anywhere else than in him alone.

Ought all without exception to use both alike?
So the commandment of Christ bears: and to derogate from it in any way, by attempting anything contrary to it, is wicked.

Have we in the Supper only a figure of the benefits which you have mentioned, or are they there exhibited to us in reality?
Seeing that our Lord Jesus Christ is truth itself, there cannot be a doubt that he at the same time fulfills the promises which he there gives us, and adds the reality to the figures. Wherefore I doubt not that as he testifies by words and signs, so he also makes us partakers of his substance, that thus we may have one life with him.

But how can this be, when the body of Christ is in heaven, and we are still pilgrims on the earth?
This he accomplishes by the secret and miraculous agency of his Spirit, to whom it is not difficult to unite things otherwise disjoined by a distant space.

You do not imagine then, either that the body is inclosed in the bread or the blood in the wine?
Neither is inclosed. My understanding rather is, that in order to obtain the reality of the signs, our minds must be raised to heaven, where Christ is, and from whence we expect him as Judge and Redeemer, and that it is improper and vain to seek him in these earthly elements.[27]

Joachim Westphal claimed that Calvin taught only a "spiritual eating" which took no account of Christ's body. Calvin sought to counter this by answering Westphal directly, and by writing to the Swiss churches:

He does not think that we discern a real body; as if, forsooth, like him, and fellows of his sort, we conjure up a phantom instead of a body. We on the contrary, when we know that there was but one sole body of Christ, which was offered up as a victim to reconcile us to God, assent at the same time that that very body is offered to us in the Lord's Supper, because, in order that Christ may communicate to us the grace of the salvation which he has procured, it behooves that body first to be appropriated by us and the flesh of Christ to be made vivifying in us, since from it we derive spiritual life.[28]

In expounding the difference between Calvin and Luther on the manner of the present existence of Christ's body, Hunter argues that the essence of Christ's body for the Genevan Reformer was its power.[29]

In itself the flesh is of no value, since it "had its origin from earth, and underwent death" (*Inst.*, IV, xvii, 24), but the Holy Spirit communicates its power to us so that we do receive the whole Christ. The difference from Luther's teaching is not great. Luther held that "the right hand of God" to which Christ ascended meant God's power; and that power is everywhere. "Luther's conception of Christ's body is that of the qualities and properties which go to make up the humanity divested of its materiality, and it is of these that the communicant partakes, which corresponds in all essentials with Calvin's teaching as to what is received in the sacrament."[30]

The difference in interpretation is in the present existence of Christ's body. Calvin said that it is in a place, heaven, while Luther said that it has the same omnipresence as Christ's divine nature. Both agreed that there is deep mystery here, which one cannot understand but yet accepts: "If anyone should ask me how this [partaking of the whole Christ] takes place, I shall not be ashamed to confess that it is a secret too lofty for either my mind to comprehend or my words to declare. . . . I rather experience than understand it" (*Inst.*, IV, xvii, 32).

The Lord's Supper then may be defined briefly as a rite instituted by Jesus Christ in which bread is broken and the fruit of the vine is poured out in thankful remembrance of Christ's atoning sacrifice, having become, through their reception and the sacramental blessing given by the Holy Spirit, the communion (that is, a partaking) of the body and blood of Christ and an anticipation of full future salvation.

In his introduction to the sacraments in the *Institutes of the Christian Religion* Calvin delineated their meaning and importance to faith. A sacrament is "an outward sign by which the Lord seals on our consciences the promise of his good will toward us in order to sustain the weakness of our faith; and we in turn attest our piety toward him" (*Inst.*, IV, xiv). With the meaning of the sign explained by the Word, the sacraments are helpful seals of God's promises, pointing to the trustworthiness of his Word, as they confirm and nourish faith, through the power of the Holy Spirit. While the sign is distinguished from that which it signifies, the sign points to and offers Christ, who is its true substance. Prefigured by sacrifices and circumcision in the Old Testament and set forth in the New Testament, the sacraments have the same office as the Word — to proclaim Christ — and they must be received in faith in order to effect their purpose.

The Supper, which unlike baptism is to be repeated, demonstrates the rich meaning of these sacred rites Christ has given the church. No empty sign, it gives what it promises as a means of grace used to build the church. As Christ exercises his sovereignty when the Word is proclaimed, so that the Word is indeed the sword of the Spirit, he is also the minister at his table, offering believers his flesh and blood.

5. SCRIPTURAL FOUNDATION

The doctrine of the Lord's Supper worked out during the sixteenth century and given classical expression by Calvin and the Reformed confessional statements attempts faithfully to express the teaching of the Word of God. "The Lord Jesus on the night when he was betrayed," we read, "took bread, and when he had given thanks, he broke it, and said, 'This is my body which is broken for you. Do this in remembrance of me.' In the same way also the cup, after supper, saying, 'This cup is the new covenant in my blood. Do this, as often as you drink it, in remembrance of me.' " The Apostle Paul, who related the institution of the Supper, then adds, "For as often as you eat this bread and drink the cup, you proclaim the Lord's death until he comes" (1 Cor. 11:23ff.; cf. Matt 26:26ff.; Luke 22:14ff.; Mark 14:22).

In a discourse with his disciples after feeding the five thousand, John tells us, Jesus spoke about the need for them to eat his flesh and drink his blood if they were to have life in themselves. Knowing that the multitudes sought him because he satisfied their temporal needs, Jesus warned them not to labor for sustenance that would perish but for that which lasts forever. That he would give them when they would believe on him. When they asked for a sign that they might believe, Jesus reminded them of the sign of manna their fathers had received in the wilderness:

> "Truly, truly, I say to you, he who believes has eternal life. I am the bread of life. Your fathers ate the manna in the wilderness, and they died. This is the bread which comes down from heaven, that a man may eat of it and not die. I am the living bread which came down from heaven; if any one eats of this bread, he will live for ever; and the bread which I shall give for the life of the world is my flesh."
>
> The Jews then disputed among themselves, saying, "How can this man give us his flesh to eat?" So Jesus said to them, "Truly, truly, I say to you, unless you eat the flesh of the Son of man and drink his blood, you have no life in you; he who eats my flesh and drinks my blood has eternal life, and I will raise him up at the last day. For my flesh is food indeed, and my blood is drink indeed. He who eats my flesh and drinks my blood abides in me, and I in him. As the living Father sent me, and I live because of the Father, so he who eats me will live because of me" (John 6:47-57).

The New Testament thus sets before us the necessity of partaking of Christ, of feeding on him, if we are to have eternal life. His word is to dwell in us, his Spirit is to renew us. Union with him means salvation. These and similar expressions are spread over the pages of the New Testament. The teaching about the Lord's Supper reinforces this emphasis on union with Christ. We are told that we must eat his flesh and drink his blood — not literally, to be sure, but symbolically and sacramentally in the sacred rite he gave the church.

To those who would play down the significance of the sacraments the church replies: when these rites are used as Christ gave them, they are as truly means of grace as the proclamation of the Word. Indeed, they *are* a proclamation of the Word, a dramatic proclamation God is pleased to use in edifying his people. To those who insist on a literal interpretation of receiving Christ's flesh and blood, the church repeats the words of Jesus: "It is the Spirit that gives life, the flesh is of no avail" (John 6:63). It is *totus Christus*, the whole Christ, not only his flesh and blood, which is received in the sacrament and *that* in a sacramental, spiritual manner. Through the power of the Holy Spirit he who is both God and man is communicated to believers. This was the faith of the church from the beginning, and it is the faith of the church today.

6. BAPTISM IN THE EARLY CHURCH

Compared to the eucharistic controversies of the Reformation, the differences of opinion over baptism seem less heart- and church-rending. Yet baptism has also helped divide the church. Moreover, baptism became an issue in the early church, long before there were serious differences of opinion over the Lord's Supper.

From the first, baptism was a rite of the church. Even when the number of sacraments had been greatly multiplied, baptism shared a position of honor with the Lord's Supper. As the rite of initiation into the fellowship of the people of God, it had a solid foundation in the New Testament (Matt. 28:19; Acts 2:38ff.; 8:12f., 16, 38; 9:18; 10:47f.; 16:15, 33; 18:8; 19:5; Rom. 6:3ff.; 1 Cor. 1:13ff.; 12:13; Gal. 3:27; Eph. 4:5; 5:26; Col. 2:12; Titus 3:5; 1 Pet. 3:21).

Baptism was meant particularly to symbolize the cleansing of the believer from sin through the blood of Jesus Christ. Paul relates that at his conversion he was told to "rise and be baptized" to wash away his sins (Acts 22:16). Later he refers to baptism as "the washing of regeneration and renewal in the Holy Spirit" (Titus 3:5).

This last text suggests another meaning of baptism: it points to a new birth through the agency of the Holy Spirit, symbolized by the laying on of hands after baptism (see Acts 8:17; 9:17; 19:6). John the Baptist had baptized with water but, as he declared, Jesus would baptize with the Holy Spirit and with fire (Luke 3:16; John 1:33). One must be born of water and the Spirit in order to enter the kingdom of God (John 3:5).

A third meaning of baptism is that the recipient has standing within the fellowship of God's covenant people. In this, baptism replaced circumcision, which had made that designation under the old covenant (Gen. 17:7, 10ff.; Rom. 4:11; Col. 2:11f.). It was a sign that the believer had identified himself with Jesus Christ.

This suggests a fourth meaning of baptism, which is in some respects the central one. Baptism is union with Christ in his death and resurrection. Thus the sinner has died to sin and been raised with Christ to newness of life (Rom. 6:3ff.).

The fathers of the post-apostolic and later church offer a variety of emphases on baptism and do not always present the fulness of New Testament teaching on the subject. Yet they agree on two points: that baptism means entrance into the kingdom of God and therefore salvation; and that it must not be repeated. Father after father of the church commented on the great importance of baptism as both an article of faith and a sacred practice.

The importance of baptism to the early church is seen in Augustine. Scrupulous about apostolic teaching, Augustine had a massive influence on successive generations of Christians, which gives him a unique place in pre-Reformation Christianity. Augustine's theology of Word and sacrament as means of grace was well developed. While the term *sacramentum* is applied to sacred rites besides baptism and the Lord's Supper, these two are in a class by themselves. With the Word they are the chief means by which God imparts grace to his people. Men preach and administer the sacraments; God gives the grace. Men work outwardly while God works within. Although we must not identify the sign and that which it signifies — for the sign may be an outward observance without an accompanying inner work of grace — the signs are not empty, because it pleases God to use them in building his church. Water, bread, and wine are symbols of an invisible grace which ordinarily accompanies them and are to be revered as such. Just as one who receives the elements of the Lord's Supper is really refreshed in Christ, so, too, in baptism God bestows the blessing which he promises. The sacraments retain their symbolic character but they also impart grace.

While Augustine always held that baptism works the forgiveness of sins, he increasingly emphasized original or inherited sin. As his controversy with Pelagianism led him to concentrate on the fallen condition of the race, it was the consequence of the Fall, that is, human solidarity in sin and guilt, which engaged his attention. His opponents, Augustine believed, saw no need for infant baptism, since they denied that infants needed forgiveness. He charged them with undermining the doctrine of infant baptism (which they denied doing). So serious in Augustine's eyes was their rejection of the doctrine of inherited sin, that he was led to explore the ramifications of the doctrines of sin and grace, which contributed to his appreciation of the sacrament of baptism, particularly infant baptism. In baptism sins are blotted out, and we stand forgiven before God. Daily sins after baptism are forgiven as we pray the Lord's Prayer, but this forgiveness depends on the forgiveness given once for all in baptism. With baptism, we are admitted to the church, the ark of salvation, and we become children of God. Without baptism, prayer and good works bring no forgiveness.[31]

Medieval theologians elaborated and systematized Augustine's ideas. The guilt of sin is forgiven, they taught, while concupiscence — not itself sin but the possibility of sin in a weakened human nature — remains. In the sixteenth century the Council of Trent confirmed the development of the doctrine of baptism in the medieval church when it declared that baptism removes all sin and renews the sinner. If anyone, Trent says,

> asserts that the whole of that which has the true and proper nature of sin is not taken away, but says that it is only erased, or not imputed, *let him be anathema*. For in those who are born again there is nothing that God hates. . . . [They] are made innocent, immaculate, pure, harmless, and beloved of God. . . . In the baptized there remains concupiscence, or an incentive to sin. . . . The Catholic Church has never understood [this concupiscence] to be called sin, as being truly and properly sin in those *born again*, but . . . it is of sin and inclines to sin.[32]

The catechism published in 1563, three years after the Council of Trent finished its work, lauded the Council for having "pronounced anathema against those who . . . should not hesitate to assert that sins, although forgiven in baptism, are not however entirely removed or utterly eradicated but are erased in such a manner, as to leave their roots still fixed in the soul." It repeats the judgment of the Council that those baptized "are made innocent, immaculate, pure, harmless, and beloved of God."[33]

7. THE REFORMERS AND BAPTISM

The Reformers, of course, had to differ with that teaching. They held to the sacramental character of baptism and its reality as a means of grace, but they denied that it eradicates all sin, even though they taught the removal of the *guilt* of sin (e.g., Calvin, *Inst.*, IV, xv, 10-12). Moreover, they rejected baptismal regeneration as taught by Trent, for the sign in baptism and that which it signifies must be distinguished or grace would be converted into magic.

Among the Reformers, Martin Luther came closest to Trent's doctrine of baptismal regeneration; but he too distinguished sharply between the sign and the grace which it signifies.[34] Baptism to Luther signified two great truths. First was regeneration through the power of the Holy Spirit, who cleanses from sin and imparts a new nature. The once-for-all character of baptism signifies God's constant readiness to renew the sinner, which obliges the sinner ever to seek to renew himself.[35] Second, baptism assures us that God is always ready to forgive us our sins. God has "bound" himself to forgive the sin of those baptized. Since it is he who baptizes, he embraces and assures us of his eternal kindness towards us in Christ. This greatest consolation which anyone can have is signified in baptism.[36]

Zwingli's teaching on baptism emphasized its symbolical, external character. Like his conception of the Lord's Supper, his understanding of baptism reflected his dualistic outlook and depreciated it as a means of grace. Baptism is an outward symbol, not intended to mediate grace: grace comes inwardly from God the Holy Spirit. "We dare not attribute to the symbols," writes Seeberg quoting the Reformer of Zurich, " 'things which belong to the divine power alone.' "[37] Baptism is a sign, a badge, worn by the Christian to set him apart as a servant of Christ. It is "nothing else than an initiatory ceremony or a pledging." Zwingli strongly doubted the propriety of infant baptism, but he advocated it largely out of antipathy for his Anabaptist opponents, who rejected the practice.

Calvin rejects the notion that baptism "is nothing but a token or mark by which we confess our religion before men, as soldiers bear the insignia of their commander as a mark of their profession" (*Inst.*, IV, xv, 1). Rather, he sees it much as Luther saw it, as a means of grace instituted and used by Christ to bestow rich blessing on believers. Distinguishing the sign from that which it signified, he sees baptism as the channel through which faith is strengthened and the certainty of salvation is given. It is not the water that cleanses and saves, but in the sacrament "the knowledge and certainty of such gifts" is received. This is the proper understanding of texts which speak of cleansing "by the washing of water with the Word" (Eph. 5:26), of our being saved "by the washing of regeneration and of renewal in the Holy Spirit" (Titus 3:5), or which say that "baptism . . . saves [us]" (1 Pet. 3:21).

> Paul joins together the Word of life and the baptism of water, as if he had said: "Through the gospel a message of our cleansing and sanctification is brought to us; through such baptism the message is sealed." And Peter immediately adds that this baptism is not a removal of filth from the flesh but a good conscience before God [1 Pet. 3:21], which is from faith. Indeed, baptism promises us no other purification than through the sprinkling of Christ's blood, which is represented by means of water from the resemblance to cleansing and washing. Who, therefore, may say that we are cleansed by this water which attests with certainty that Christ's blood is our true and only laver? Thus, the surest argument to refute the self-deception of those who attribute everything to the power of the water can be sought in the meaning of baptism itself, which draws us away, not only from the visible element which meets our eyes, but from all other means, that it may fasten our minds upon Christ alone (*Inst.*, IV, xv, 2).

A token of repentance and faith, baptism also signifies the forgiveness of sin, renewal, and union with Christ. These blessings come to God's people within the covenant of grace, first made with Abraham, which includes all the faithful (*Inst.*, IV, xv, 22; IV, xvi, 3 ff.). While baptism signifies salvation, salvation does not depend on it, for the blessing of the covenant does not depend "upon any additions" (*Inst.*, IV, xv, 22, cf. 20). Since God has given us this holy rite, however, neither "sloth, nor contempt nor negligence" may keep us from using it and receiving its rich blessing.

8. INFANT BAPTISM

Today as always, adults who desire baptism must repent and believe the gospel. No one is formally received into the church by baptism until he or she has declared acceptance of the Christian faith and an intention to lead a Christian life. With such a candidate for baptism the formula is as it has always been: believe and be baptized.

But what about little children? The question of whether or not they should be baptized has given rise to considerable dispute within the church, although it is estimated that as many as 95% of the world's Christians practice it. Nowhere does the New Testament explicitly state that children should receive this rite of the church, although there is also no statement that they should not receive it. The case for the baptism of infants can be set forth in a series of propositions whose content is as old as the church. These were refined, elaborated, and explicated by Calvin and his followers.

a. God established a covenant with Abraham, the father of all believers. This covenant is the background against which we must see the history of Israel, the ministry of Christ, and the rise of the Christian church. God said:

> "I will establish my covenant between me and thee and thy seed after thee, throughout their generations, for an everlasting covenant, to be a God unto thee, and to thy seed after thee" (Gen. 17:7).

When God called Abraham out of Ur of the Chaldees to a land he would show him and promised to bless him and all the families of the earth through him, the history of redemption began. The first chapters of the book of Genesis are universal history, but with chapter 12 a special group is chosen to be the recipients of special grace, so that they may know the Lord and serve him as a holy community.

b. Little children were included in that covenant community. Circumcision, the sign of the covenant, was given to them as well as to adult members. The seed of Abraham is mentioned in each of the recorded instances in which God gave or repeated the covenant promise (Gen. 12, 13, 15, 17).

> "This is my covenant, which you shall keep, between me and you and your descendants after you: every male among you shall be circumcised. . . . It shall be a sign of the covenant between me and you. He that is eight days old among you shall be circumcised; every male throughout your generations, whether born in your house or bought with your money from any foreigner who is not of your offspring, both he that is born in your house and he that is bought with your money, shall be circumcised" (Gen. 17:10-13).

c. The Christian church, as the successor of Old Testament Israel, is the people of God, the covenant community of this age. When God established his covenant with Abraham he envisioned the eventual inclusion of Gentile nations: in Abraham *all* the families of the earth would be blessed (Gen. 12:3). Writing to Christians in Galatia, Paul recalled that promise:

> It is men of faith who are the sons of Abraham. And the scripture, foreseeing that God would justify the Gentiles by faith, preached the gospel beforehand to Abraham, saying, "In thee shall all the nations be blessed." So then, those who are men of faith are blessed with Abraham who had

faith. . . . Christ redeemed us . . . that in Christ Jesus the blessing of Abraham might come upon the Gentiles, that we might receive the promise of the Spirit through faith. . . . In Christ Jesus you are all sons of God, through faith. For as many of you as were baptized into Christ have put on Christ. There is neither Jew nor Greek. . . . If you are Christ's, then you are Abraham's offspring, heirs according to promise (Gal. 3:7-9, 13, 14, 26-29).

In Romans the apostle uses the figure of an olive tree to teach the continuity—or rather the essential unity—of the old and new covenants. Some branches of the tree, the Jews themselves, were broken off; others, Gentiles, were grafted in. The tree itself, living through both dispensations, is the continuing community of those who know and serve God (Rom. 11:17-24). Jesus' parable of the wicked husbandmen (Matt. 21:33-46) taught this same truth that the Christian church is the successor to Old Testament Israel: "I tell you, the kingdom of God will be taken away from you and given to a nation producing the fruits of it" (vs. 43). That nation—or people, as the word may be rendered—can be none other than the Christian church, which is now God's covenant community. The new covenant, that is, the new form of the old covenant made with Abraham, has been established with it.

In Jeremiah 31:31-34 God promises that he will make a new covenant with the house of Israel and Judah. The author of Hebrews, arguing for the superiority of the new dispensation inaugurated by Christ, quotes this entire passage to teach that that covenant, *promised to Israel,* has been given to the New Testament church (Heb. 8). The only possible conclusion, in his mind, is that Israel, the people of God, is now the New Testament church. This reasoning is borne out by the words with which Jesus instituted the holy supper the night before his crucifixion: "This is my blood of the covenant, which is poured out for many for the forgiveness of sins" (Matt. 26:28). "For this cause he is the mediator of a new covenant" (Heb. 9:15; cf. 7:22; 12:24). Similarly Paul reminds the Corinthians that Christ has made them "ministers of a new covenant" (2 Cor. 3:6). The point is that the biblical writers were perfectly aware that a new covenant had been promised to the house of Israel and Judah, yet they claim with the utmost certainty that it has been given to the disciples of Christ, which means his church. The fact that the church has the new covenant, or New Testament, is proof that it is the Israel of this age.

Paul teaches that the "middle wall" is done away in Christ, so that Gentiles are no longer strangers and sojourners but "fellow citizens with the saints and members of the household of God, built upon the foundation of the apostles and prophets, Christ Jesus himself being the chief cornerstone in whom the whole structure is joined together and grows into a holy temple in the Lord" (Eph. 2:11-22). That temple is the church. A continuous line of spiritual descent runs from Abraham to believers today, so that the Christian church is the Israel of the new dispensation.

d. Infants and children are legitimate members of God's covenant community today, as they were in the days of the Old Testament. The promise is the same: God will be a God to us and our children. As he commanded Abraham and Moses to instruct the children entrusted to them in the way of the Lord (Gen. 18:19; Deut. 6:7), so after the giving of the new covenant, that is, the new form of the covenant of grace God made with Abraham, children continue to be a part of the covenant community. To suppose otherwise would mean that Jewish parents who accepted Christ in the early years of the church would have left a relationship to God in which their children shared for a relationship in which their children would no longer have a share. This never happened because of the continuity of the covenant of grace in both Testaments.

The promise is still to us and our children, as Peter proclaimed on Pentecost (Acts 2:39). The New Testament church regards its children as a heritage of the Lord and presents them to him with no less devotion than Israel did under the old covenant. It hears its Lord say, "Let the children come to me, do not hinder them; for to such belongs the kingdom of God" (Mark 10:14). With Paul, the church recognizes the blessing of covenantal status, acknowledging that, whereas children within the church should otherwise be "unclean," within God's community they are "holy" (1 Cor. 7:14). Calvin writes:

> It is no small stimulus to our education of them in the serious fear of God and the observance of his law to reflect that they are considered and acknowledged by him as his children as soon as they are born (*Inst.*, IV, xvi, 32).

e. As members of the covenant community, children are entitled to its privileges. One of these, the initiatory rite, is the sign of the covenant. Having come in place of circumcision, which was the initiatory rite and sign of the old covenant (Gen. 17:11; Rom. 4:11) given to all future heads of families, Christian baptism is likewise administered to children. Baptism is a sign that one is a member of the covenant people of God (Matt. 28:19f.); circumcision bore the same significance (Gen. 17:10-14). Baptism witnesses to the righteousness which is the believer's by faith (Titus 3:5-7); so did circumcision (Rom. 4:11). Baptism symbolizes cleansing from sin (Acts 22:16; Rom. 6:4; Titus 3:5); so did circumcision (Col. 2:13). So similar are the two rites in significance that Paul equates them in Colossians 2:11f. The Christians at Colossae, he says, were circumcised in Christ "with a circumcision made without hands." And "the circumcision of Christ" was Christian baptism. Baptism has come in the place of circumcision and infants are to be baptized as heirs of the kingdom of God and of his covenant.

The foregoing reasoning is built around the concept of the covenant, which we saw earlier (pp. 26ff.) to be one of the most important teachings in the faith of Israel. Since covenantal theology has become an important part of the faith of the church, especially as it bears on the relationship of children to the church, some additional comments are in order.

In building his church and kingdom, God uses natural means; and infants and children share in the covenantal blessings of the home. As parents rear their children, they play a determinative role in conditioning the spiritual nature and attitudes of those children. God therefore uses Christian parents to mold children's minds and spirits, so that they may come to know, serve, and enjoy him in this life and in the life to come. God uses the intimate relationship of the family as the primary means to bring persons into a saving relationship with himself.

Scripture stresses the importance of communal relationships, first those of the family, then those of wider fellowships, including the local church of which one is a part. No normal person lives only unto himself; rather, he is a person in community. And the immediate community relationship which most determines one's spiritual condition is that of the family. This is why Scripture speaks constantly of the unity and spiritual solidarity of the family. What happens to the spiritual fortunes of one member of a family, particularly a parent, happens to the family as such. This was true of the family of Noah (Gen. 7:1), of Achan (Josh. 7:24), of David (2 Sam. 12:11-15), of the nobleman (John 4:53), of Zacchaeus (Luke 19:9), of Cornelius (Acts 10:2), of Lydia (Acts 16:15), of the Philippian jailer (Acts 16:33), of Crispus (Acts 18:8), of Onesiphorus (2 Tim. 1:16).

Because parents and children are one closely bound spiritual entity before God, they can take vows for the small children for whom they are responsible and represent them before man and God. When even one parent in a family is a believer, the status of a child in that family before God is different from that of a child in a family in which Christ's name is unknown. Before God, the Apostle declares, the child of the covenant is holy (1 Cor. 7:14). In the Ten Commandments God declares that he "will visit the iniquity of the fathers upon the children unto the third and fourth generation of those who hate [him], and . . . show mercy unto a thousand generations of those who love [him] and keep his commandments" (Exod. 20:5). Here is shown "the spiritual solidarity of the family in its successive generations" as well as "the radical kindliness of the covenant of grace."[38]

What holds true for the family relationship is true to a lesser degree in other, wider social relationships. This is especially true within the congregation of the faithful. The members are meant to assist and influence each other. The "communion of saints" which we confess in the creed means that we are responsible for one another. There are occasions such as death or spiritual breakdown in a family when the larger congregational fellowship exercises a special saving function. Both the congregation and the family are involved in covenantal privileges and obligations; and there is the reality and the exercise of spiritual solidarity between them and the individual. That is one reason why baptism is not a private matter but an act of worship in which the whole congregation as well as the family should participate.

For a long time in western culture and the Christian church, the consciousness of social solidarity has been breaking down. This has led to a false understanding of the relationship of persons to each other in society as a whole, as well as in the covenant community which is the church. Within the latter it has led to a misunderstanding of the fundamental relationship of parents to their children and a denial of their essential oneness before God. A more biblical insight recognizes the true order God has created among persons, an order acknowledged by the church in the doctrine of the covenant.

9. INFANT BAPTISM IN THE EARLY CHURCH: HISTORICAL CONSIDERATIONS

Was infant baptism part of the faith and practice of the early church? While there is no direct *biblical evidence* of infant baptism, there is direct historical evidence of that practice within the Jewish community in the days that the New Testament was being written, and there is other evidence to suggest that the early church practiced infant baptism.

The practice of proselyte baptism within Judaism took place when Gentiles wished to become converts to the Jewish faith. This act symbolized their cleansing and identification with the people of God. It was administered to both parents and their children — sons under thirteen and daughters under twelve years of age. Children born to Gentile converts *after* the parents' conversion did not have to be baptized, since they were regarded as sanctified through their parents (an interesting consideration in view of 1 Cor. 7:14).

According to the best authorities on the subject, proselyte baptism is at least as old as Christian baptism.[39] Thus the baptism of infants and of other children was a practice known within the Jewish community from which the Christian church emerged. This is an important consideration in the study of early Christian baptism.

The only other information we have concerning baptism in the first century is the New Testament, which as we have seen offers no evidence for or against infant baptism. What evidence there is from the second century points to the probability of the practice of infant baptism. Concerning the third century there is no question at all. Polycarp was a disciple of the Apostle John. At his death (A.D. 167 or 168 according to Jeremias)[40] Polycarp said that he had served Christ for 86 years, which undoubtedly refers to the time of his baptism. Since we know that he traveled by sea to Rome and back between 157 and 161, an extremely strenuous trip in those days, it is hard to imagine that he had been baptized as a youth and that that trip was made some eighty years later. Then he would also have had to live to be about one hundred years old. His was most probably a case of infant baptism.

A letter from Pliny, written in 112 or 113, speaks of the "very young" who belong to the church along with adults, and says that many "of all ages" have been ensnared by the new faith. Since he believed that the very young as well as the adults should be punished for their faith, this can only mean that these very young children had become full members of the church through baptism. It is reminiscent of Irenaeus' statement that many were "born again to God, infants and children and boys and youths and old men." Since he declares that baptism is "being born to God" and "the power of regeneration unto God," his witness to infant baptism is quite clear.[41]

Origen, born in 185, specifically mentions infant baptism three times, saying that "the church has received the tradition from the apostles to give baptism to little children."[42] He also refers to infant baptism as a "custom of the church." Late in the second century Tertullian objected to infant baptism, but his writings prove that it was the church's practice. He argues that it is not expedient, because it runs the risk that someone who falls away as a young person will lose forever the forgiveness of sins. He does not even hint that infant baptism arose later than the time of the apostles, an argument he surely would have made had he believed it to have been a post-apostolic practice.[43]

At a synod in Carthage in 252 the debate concerning infant baptism revolved around whether infants may be baptized before the eighth day, which is when circumcision was performed. The 66 bishops did not discuss the propriety of infant baptism itself: on that they were all agreed.[44] Augustine often refers to infant baptism in his writings; for example, in one letter he uses phrases like "the firmly established faith of the church," "the firmly grounded practice of the church," and the "perfectly unambiguous apostolical declaration."[45]

Competent Baptist scholars are very cautious about arguing that their position can be identified with that of the early church. One such authority, A. H. Newman, writes: "If the apostolic churches were Baptist churches, the churches of the second century were not. Still less those of the third and following centuries."[46] Note that he does not even claim that the first-century church followed Baptist practice; he merely suggests that it might have.

But if the grounds for the doctrine and practice of infant baptism are adequate, why have difficulties arisen? The problem lies in the area of ecclesiastical and baptismal discipline. The widespread doubts about and rejection of the rite are largely in reaction to a misuse of the sacrament, which in turn is due to a lack of discipline in wide areas of the church. A French pastor who made a careful study of the subject has written that much of the current objection to the biblical practice

> has absolutely nothing to do with baptism itself, but is immediately connected with the *indiscipline* of the church. A church lacking baptismal discipline can no longer be a *Christian* church. It is not a matter of setting up age categories, but of disciplining the administration of baptism in every category, for adults as well as for children. . . . *What is needed is not a suppression of infant baptism, but a restoration of baptismal discipline.*[47]

This lack of discipline results from carelessness and a faulty understanding of the teaching of Scripture concerning the meaning of baptism as a sign and seal of God's covenant of grace for his people. To correct this situation what is needed is proper instruction and a willingness to do things in accordance with the will of God.

> Independently of her lack of discipline the cause of the ineffectiveness of infant baptism is attributable to the unfaithfulness of the church which has too often renounced her vocation to preach the Word *according to the Scriptures.* . . . If the church is to administer baptism faithfully, her preaching must be faithful. She must preach the covenant of grace, salvation by

the outpoured blood of Christ, the necessity of the new birth, regeneration by the Holy Spirit. In the Epistles the Apostles insist on the meaning of baptism and are careful that nothing should rob it of its grace. *Each member of the covenant ought to become what his baptism signifies.*[48]

EXCURSUS: THE MODE OF BAPTISM

The question of whether baptism should be by immersion, pouring, or sprinkling was no problem to the Reformers or, for that matter, in the early church. However, it became an issue of faith subsequently. Some have contended that immersion or submersion of the entire body in water is the only mode which signifies being buried and risen with Christ, and thus that there can be no baptism without it.[a]

A study of Scripture, however, shows that the words "baptize" and "baptism" have a meaning wider than immersion only, and baptism is not restricted to any one mode. Both Old and New Testaments show that the purificatory rites of the Jews used various modes. There was sprinkling of blood and water, but there was also sprinkling of water alone (Num. 19:13, 18, 19, 21). There were pouring, various kinds of washings, dippings, and immersions. The elements used in these rites might be water, blood, or oil. A fair idea of the variety in these acts of ceremonial and religious washings comes from reading such passages as Exodus 28:19-21; Leviticus 8, 14, and 16; and Numbers 19.

There are rites of purification in Scripture other than immersion which are also called baptism or baptizing. In the Old Testament the Hebrew verb *tabal* is sometimes used in the sense of dipping without a complete immersion. A case in point is Leviticus 14:16: in cleansing a leper the priest pours oil into his left hand and, as we read, "shall dip (*tabal*) his right finger in the oil that is in his left hand, and shall sprinkle of the oil with his finger seven times before Jehovah." It is quite impossible to immerse one's finger in oil that is held in the cupped left hand, but immersion is not necessary. All that is required is dipping, and the Hebrew verb *tabal*, translated by both *bapto* and *baptizo* in Greek and by *dip* in English, requires no more than that. In some instances the dipping may have been an immersion; in others it was not.[b]

Having seen that the Hebrew *tabal* need not mean immersion, we turn now to the Greek verbs *bapto* and *baptizo*. An instance in the Greek Old Testament (besides the one given above) where *bapto* cannot mean strictly immersion is Daniel 4:33 and 5:21, where the king is said to be "wet with the dew of heaven." The word in both verses in *bapto*; but the meaning is hardly that the king was immersed, but rather that he was wet, or moistened, with dew.

A text in the Old Testament Apocrypha in which the verb *baptizo* (used only twice in the canonical Old Testament) probably means bathe or wash is Judith 12:7, where it is said that she went out by night and "washed herself at the fountain of water." To insist that the meaning here must be immersion is warranted by neither text nor circumstances.

The New Testament uses the words for baptize frequently. The verbs *bapto* and *baptizo* are found 4 and 76 times respectively, and the nouns *baptisma* and *baptismos*, both meaning "baptism," are used 20 and 3 times respectively. In each case *bapto* is best rendered "dip." In most passages *baptizo*, *baptismos*, and *baptisma* are simply translated "baptize" or "baptism," and nothing can be inferred about the mode. But there are other cases in which the translation "immerse" or "immersion" is obviously not possible, and these throw light on our investigation.

In Mark 7:1-5 the Pharisees accuse Jesus of allowing his disciples to eat with unwashed hands. Verse 3 reads, "For the Pharisees, and all the Jews, do not eat unless they wash their hands, observing the tradition of the elders." In the Greek text a phrase appears which can be translated "with the fist" or alternatively "to the wrist," or, in view of late Greek usage, "to the elbow."[c] The inference is that the Jews had to wash their hands in a very particular manner.[d] Verse 4 continues, "And when they come from the market place, they do not eat unless they purify themselves." The verb here translated "purify" is *baptizo* in most manuscripts, though the Sinaiticus and Vaticanus manuscripts, two of the oldest and best authorities, read *rhantizo* ("sprinkle"). The idea is the same in either instance: that of ceremonial cleansing according to the law, usually effected by sprinkling.

This same tradition lies behind Luke 11:38, the incident when Jesus was entertained in the home of a Pharisee. We read that the Pharisee "was astonished to see that he did not first wash (*baptizo*) before dinner." Murray comments on this passage as follows:

> The important observation is that this tradition is described as baptising oneself (for that is the force of the form *ebaptisthe*) and provides evidence that *baptizo* can be used with reference to an action which did not involve immersing oneself. . . . It is quite unwarranted to insist that on this occasion there must be allusion to the Jewish practice of immersion and that what the Pharisee expected on this occasion was that Jesus should have plunged himself in water. . . . Jewish tradition, it is true, did prescribe immersion in certain cases of uncleanness. . . . But rabbinic tradition prescribed immersion not for the washing and purification which preceded eating, as in this case, but for the uncleanness contracted by such things as leprosy and various kinds of running issue. . . . In other words, there is no evidence which would indicate that the Pharisee expected of Jesus anything more than the washing referred to in Matthew 15:2; Mark 7:3, a washing of the hands as far as the wrist, either by pouring water over them or by dipping them in water. The significant fact is that such washing is referred to as baptising oneself.[e]

The noun *baptismos* in both Mark 7:4 and Hebrews 9 is translated "washing" or "washings." The translation is a good one. Our point is that there are instances where those words are used synonymously. Baptism *is* ceremonial washing, and that washing was done in diverse modes. Hebrews 9 makes that clear. Those who insist on immersion alone recognize that this passage is important for maintaining their position; consequently, they argue that the "various ablutions" (*baptismois*) of 9:10 are not the sprinklings mentioned three times in the context (vv. 13, 19, 21) but refer to immersions supposedly set forth in such passages in the Old Testament as Leviticus 11:32. Throughout Hebrews, however, the author is drawing a contrast between the rites and ceremonies of the old covenant and that which the Christian has in Christ. In this passage he compares the relative ineffectiveness of the "various ablutions," or "baptisms," of the old covenant with the purification effected once for all in Christ. As Murray notes, every rite of washing mentioned in this extended contrast must be included in the "various ablutions" of verse 10.

> In verse thirteen one of these lustratory ordinances is expressly stated to have been performed by sprinkling — "for if the blood of goats and bulls and ashes of an heifer sprinkling the unclean sanctifieth to the purifying of the flesh." When we bear in mind that here a lustratory rite of the old economy is contrasted in respect to its efficacy with the finality and perfection of the blood of Christ and when we remember that it was precisely this thought of relative inefficacy that prompted the reference to "divers baptisms" ["various ablutions"], it becomes exegetically impossible to exclude this rite, or these rites, of verse thirteen from the scope of the "divers baptisms."[f]

Verses 19 and 21 mention sprinkling again, and verses 13, 22, and 23 make clear that these rites were purificatory, so that they indeed fall within the scope of "various ablutions." The conclusion then is that ceremonial sprinkling can be called a baptism as well as any other mode of washing, immersion, or otherwise.

Before leaving this passage we should recall the significance of lustrations by sprinkling frequently mentioned in the Old Testament. These were the holiest rites performed by the Israelite priests. Are we to think, as some claim, that none of these is included in the thought of the writer of Hebrews 9:10? The fact is that the author wants to contrast those most sacred rites under the old covenant with the immeasurably better purification we have in Christ.[g]

Having access to God by "the new and living way which he opened for us through the curtain, that is, through his flesh . . . let us draw near with a true heart in full assurance of faith, with our bodies washed with pure water" (Heb. 10:20ff.). In a doxology the same author says that we are come "to Jesus, the mediator of a new covenant, and to the sprinkled blood that speaks more graciously than the blood of Abel" (Heb. 12:24). In the salutation of his first epistle Peter adopted the same image, so meaningful to the mind of those who knew the Old Testament: "To the exiles . . . chosen and destined by God the Father and sanctified by the Spirit for obedience to Jesus Christ and for sprinkling with his blood" (1 Pet. 1:1f.).

It seems clear then that the sprinkling of blood and of water is the most sacred mode of ceremonial purification, atonement, and consecration to God in the old dispensation. When a priest stood alone before God, in the presence of God and the people, and sprinkled blood or water or a combination of the two on the people and the altar, he was performing the most holy rite which existed in Israel. God Almighty was assuring his people of their cleansing by his grace. Thus in the best-known penitential Psalm the writer pleads, "Purge me with hyssop (sprinkle me), and I shall be clean; wash me and I shall be whiter than snow" (Ps. 51:7).[h] When the Lord, looking forward to the better age that was to come, spoke to a disheartened Israel through his prophet, he said: "Then I will sprinkle clean water upon you, and you will be clean. . . . A new heart I will give you. . . . I will put my Spirit within you" (Ezek. 36:25f.).

From all this some have concluded that sprinkling is the only valid mode of ceremonial lustration for the church today.[i] Calvin's position is more reasonable: "Whether the person being baptized should be wholly immersed, and whether thrice or once, whether he should only be sprinkled with poured water — these details are of no importance, but ought to be optional to churches" (*Inst.*, IV, xv, 19). What is important is the meaning of the rite, not the amount of water used.

The baptism of the Holy Spirit (Matt. 3:11; Acts 1:5; 11:16) on the day of Pentecost is represented as a pouring out (affusion), not as an immersion, in line with the meaning of the symbolism of Pentecost. Christ told his disciples that they would receive power after "the Holy Spirit has come upon you" (Acts 1:8). In his Pentecostal sermon Peter reminded his audience that God had promised that he would "pour out" his Spirit on all flesh (Acts 2:17). The next verse repeats the promise with the same verb, "pour out," and verse 33 does the same. Acts 10:44 and 11:15 speak of the Holy Spirit as falling on persons. The Old Testament passages promising the gift of the Spirit use verbs for pouring or sprinkling (Isa. 32:15; Joel 2:28; Prov. 1:23; Ezek. 36:25ff.). The imagery of this baptism of the Spirit therefore is not that of immersion but of affusion; the latter is thus another valid biblical representation of salvation.

Two other texts should be mentioned. In 1 Corinthians 10:2 Paul writes that Israel was "baptized into Moses in the cloud and in the sea." Immersion seems not to be meant here, for the Israelites crossed dry-shod (Exod. 14:22). Whatever the interpretation, immersion is not taught here.

Finally, a passage often cited by immersionists is Romans 6:1-6, with a parallel in Colossians 2. Paul speaks of the need for Christians to live a redeemed life, because

> all of us who have been baptized into Christ Jesus were baptized into his death. We were buried therefore with him by baptism into death, so that as Christ was raised from the dead by the glory of the Father, we too might walk in newness of life. For if we have been united with him in a death like his, we shall certainly be united with him in a resurrection like his. We know that our old self was crucified with him so that the sinful body might be destroyed, and we might no longer be enslaved to sin (Rom. 6:3-6).

It is incorrect to claim that this passage teaches the mode of baptism — that our "burial with Christ" must be beneath the water, so that we may rise from it into newness of life as he rose from the dead. Paul's point here is not the mode of baptism, but union with Christ; and he uses three metaphors to represent that union: (1) we are buried and risen with him; (2) we are planted together with him; and (3) we are crucified with him. If one of these metaphors is claimed as teaching baptism, it should follow that all teach it, but this is impossible. All three teach union with Christ. Baptismal mode may be taught incidentally, if the apostle was thinking in terms of immersion, but this is not the primary purpose of the passage.[j]

We cannot be certain how persons were baptized in the early church. The earliest statement comes from the *Didache,* probably written between 120 and 160, in which baptism is normally said to be by immersion, with pouring equally valid if there is not enough water available. Baptisms in Rome in the latter half of the second century were by pouring (affusion) with the subject standing in water. Proselyte baptism was by immersion. The recipients were nude, and members of the other sex turned their heads until the baptized were under water. After turning to look the witnesses turned their backs again until the baptized persons were clothed.

If baptism was by immersion in the early church, it would not follow that immersion is indispensable to the sacrament, any more than it is necessary to observe the Lord's Supper in every detail as it was first instituted by Christ. The Supper was first observed at an evening meal in a home as the climax of the annual Passover festival, from which it received important meaning. It was a private gathering of only men, who received bread and wine in a reclining position. These details are not followed in the celebration of Communion today, nor is unleavened bread eaten or footwashing practiced, as was done when the Supper was instituted. Many of those who insist that the validity of the baptismal rite depends on literal precision with respect to mode are unliteral in substituting a nonalcoholic beverage for wine in the Lord's Supper. In neither case is the sacrament invalidated, however, for slavish literalness is not of the essence of the rite. Any mode of baptism which symbolizes the washing away of sin in Christ is acceptable.

Chapter 13

The Freedom of a Christian

A discussion of Luther's contribution to the development of the faith of the church would be incomplete without reference to his insight into the nature of Christian freedom. What he had written on the need for reform, on the gospel, on the sacraments of the church is preparation for this.

Written during the last six months of 1520, *The Freedom of a Christian* is one of Luther's most beautiful writings. Its conciliatory tone is altogether different from earlier polemical tracts in which he attacked papal tyranny and fought for the reformation of the church. Here he sets forth the positive meaning of the gospel in the life of the believer, "the riches and the glory of the Christian life," as he called it. An editor of Luther's writings observes that "in *The Babylonian Captivity of the Church* [Luther] enters and takes [Rome's] central stronghold and sanctuary — the sacramental system by which she accompanied and controlled her members from the cradle to the grave. Only then could he set forth, in language of almost lyrical rapture, *The Freedom of a Christian.*"[1]

Dedicated to Pope Leo X "as a token of peace and good will," *The Freedom of a Christian* sets forth two apparently contradictory theses: "a Christian is a perfectly free lord of all, subject to none; a Christian is a perfectly dutiful servant of all, subject to all."[2] These are taken from 1 Corinthians 9:19 — "For though I am free from all men, I have made myself a slave to all" — and Romans 13:8: "Owe no man anything, except to love one another." Freed by faith from the guilt and power of sin, the Christian is also free to love and to serve his neighbor. This is made possible by the union the Christian has by faith with Jesus Christ his head.

> For this faith is his life, his righteousness and his salvation: it saves him and makes him acceptable, and bestows upon him all things that are Christ's . . . as Paul asserts in Gal. 2[:20] when he says, "And the life I now live in the flesh I live by faith in the Son of God." Although the Christian is thus free from all works, he ought in this liberty to empty himself, take upon himself the form of a servant, be made in the likeness of men, be found in human form, and to serve, help, and in every way deal with his neighbor as he sees that God through Christ has dealt and

still deals with him. This he should do freely, having regard for nothing but divine approval.[3]

The Christian's example is Jesus Christ. Though Lord of all, he took on the form of a servant and was born of a woman, under the law, so that he might fulfil his mission. Quoting extensively from Scripture Luther expands this theme of loving service to show that while there is no justification by works, the Christian, justified by faith, will abound in all good works because he has been united to Christ through whom he has been made good.

> As works do not make a man a believer, so also they do not make him righteous. But as faith makes a man a believer and righteous, so faith does good works. Since, then, works justify no one, and a man must be righteous before he does a good work, it is very evident that it is faith alone which, because of the pure mercy of God through Christ and in his Word, worthily and sufficiently justifies and saves the person. A Christian has no need of any work or law in order to be saved since through faith he is free from every law and does everything out of pure liberty and freely. He seeks neither benefit nor salvation since he already abounds in all things and is saved through the grace of God because in his faith he now seeks only to please God.[4]

In union with Christ the Christian shares the Lord's kingship and priesthood. With respect to kingship, Luther reasons that "every Christian is by faith so exalted above all things that, by virtue of a spiritual power, he is lord of all things without exception so that nothing can do him any harm." All things are subject to him and made to work for him in accordance with God's promise (Rom. 8:28; 1 Cor. 3:21ff.). This does not mean that Christians have physical power or control over things — "a madness with which some churchmen are afflicted" — but they do have great spiritual power. With respect to the priesthood of Christians — "which is far more excellent than being kings" — Luther notes that they may pray for others and teach them the things of God. "Thus Christ has made it possible, provided we believe in him, to be not only his brethren, co-heirs, and fellow-kings, but also his fellow-priests."[5]

Mere historical faith is not enough for one to believe and to live by these truths. Christ must be preached in such a way that "faith in him may be established that he may not only be Christ, but be Christ for you and me, and that what is said of him and what is denoted in his name may be effectual in us."[6]

> [Then] our hearts will be filled by the Holy Spirit with the love which makes us free, joyful, almighty workers and conquerors over all tribula-

tions, servants of our neighbors, and yet lords of all. . . . Just as our neighbor is in need and lacks that in which we abound, so we were in need before God and lacked his mercy. Hence, as our heavenly Father has in Christ freely come to our aid, we also ought freely to help our neighbor through our body and its works, and each one should become as it were a Christ to the other that we may be Christs to one another and Christ may be the same in all, that is, that we may be truly Christians.[7]

His closing words are among the finest statements of Christian devotion:

A Christian lives not in himself, but in Christ and in his neighbor. Otherwise he is not a Christian. He lives in Christ through faith, in his neighbor through love. By faith he is caught up beyond himself into God. By love he descends beneath himself into his neighbor. Yet he always remains in God and in his love, as Christ says in John 1[:51], "Truly, truly, I say to you, you will see heaven opened, and the angels of God ascending and descending upon the Son of man."[8]

Contrary to Luther's detractors, who try to portray him as an unfettered libertine, a Dutch Luther scholar contends that if one word is at the very center of Luther's doctrine and practice, it is "enslavement" rather than freedom.[9] Luther's tract on Christian freedom confirms that judgment. The tract is entitled *The Freedom of a Christian,* but its subject might be described more precisely as Christian service, indicating how a Christian uses his freedom. In obedience to the Lord's precept and in imitation of his example, a Christian honors God and demonstrates his faith by being a Christ to his fellows.

1. THE BIBLICAL BASE

Luther had caught the same vision that had prompted Paul to write to the Galatians: "For freedom Christ has set us free; stand fast therefore and do not submit again to a yoke of slavery. . . . You were called to freedom, brethren; only do not use your freedom as an opportunity for the flesh, but through love be servants of one another" (Gal. 5:1, 13). Like the Apostle, Luther pleads for responsible freedom, a "middle course," as he calls it, between the two extremes of tyranny and license.

Against "the unyielding, stubborn ceremonialists," Luther counsels his readers to "offend them boldly lest by their impious views they drag many with them into error. In the presence of such men it is good to eat meat, break the fasts, and for the sake of the liberty of faith do other things which they regard as the greatest of sins."[10] Against this type Paul would not circumcise Titus when the Jews insisted that he should (Gal. 2:3), and Christ allowed the apostles to pluck ears of grain on the Sabbath (Matt. 12:1-8).

Those weak in the faith who are ignorant of Christian freedom we must not offend, but "yield to their weakness until they are more fully instructed." Their weakness is the fault of pastors who, instead of instructing them, have "taken them captive with the snares of their traditions." The rule for facing these weak Christians is given in Romans 14:21 and 1 Corinthians 8:13: "If food is a cause of my brother's falling, I will never eat meat."

> For this reason, although we should boldly resist those teachers of traditions and sharply censure the laws of the pope by means of which they plunder the people of God, yet we must spare the timid multitude whom those impious tyrants hold captive by means of these laws until they are set free. Therefore fight strenuously against the wolves, but for the sheep and not also against the sheep. This you will do if you inveigh against the laws and the lawgivers and at the same time observe the laws with the weak so that they will not be offended, until they also recognize tyranny and understand their freedom. . . . On the other hand, use your freedom constantly and consistently in the sight of and despite the tyrants and the stubborn, so that they also may learn that they are impious, that their laws are of no avail for righteousness, and that they had no right to set them up.[11]

Luther deplores ignorance and weakness in believers. He abhors the tyranny which violates Christian liberty, and he withstands it because the freedom Christ gives is too great a treasure to allow silence when it is taken away. Paul's letter to the Galatians plots the course, and faithful discipleship requires the Christian to follow Paul's example. When he does this he experiences the incomprehensible "riches and glory of the Christian life":

> It can do all things and has all things and lacks nothing. It is lord over sin, death, and hell, and yet at the same time it serves, ministers to, and benefits all men. But alas in our day this life is unknown throughout the world; it is neither preached about nor sought after; we are altogether ignorant of our own name and do not know why we are Christians or bear the name of Christians. Surely we are named after Christ, not because he is absent from us, but because he dwells in us, that is, because we believe in him and are Christs one to another and do to our neighbors as Christ does to us. But in our day we are taught by the doctrine of men to seek nothing but merits, rewards, and the things that are ours; of Christ we have made only a taskmaster far harsher than Moses.[12]

Luther wanted others to share this life. The impoverished spirituality of his contemporaries saddened him, and he knew that the fault lay at the door of the church, whose rules and regulations obscured the gospel and hid from view God's grace, which alone justifies and sets the sinner free.

Luther's rediscovery of the gospel, his proclamation of salvation and justification by grace through faith in the merits of Christ, and his teaching of Christian freedom constituted a single theme, which found a quick response in the hearts of multitudes. For this central message of Scripture is meant to satisfy the deepest longings of the human spirit, longings present in spite of sin. The desire for acceptance, forgiveness, and freedom is universal. It is the church's privilege and glory to herald the glad news that these are available, and that they are given, freely, to all who repent and believe:

> Ho, every one who thirsts, come to the waters;
>   and he who has no money, come, buy and eat!
> Come, buy wine and milk without money and without price.
> Why do you spend your money for that which is not bread,
>   and your labor for that which does not satisfy?
> Hearken diligently to me, and eat what is good,
>   and delight yourself in fatness.
> Incline your ear, and come to me;
>   hear, that your soul may live;
> and I will make with you an everlasting covenant,
>   my steadfast, sure love for David (Isa. 55:1-3).

During a conversation with some of his contemporaries, Jesus warned against unbelief, telling those who believed on him: "If you continue in my word, you are truly my disciples, and you will know the truth, and the truth will make you free." They responded that they were children of Abraham and had never been in bondage to anyone — an obvious falsehood, for they were at that very time subject to Rome. They wondered why Jesus had said, "You will be made free." Jesus answered: "Everyone who commits sin is a slave to sin. The slave does not continue in the house forever. The Son continues forever. So if the Son makes you free, you will be free indeed" (John 8:31-36).

A sinner, then, is in bondage to sin until set free by Christ. We noted earlier that Luther's response to Erasmus bore the title *The Bondage of the Will*. A person on his own is not free but a slave to sin. In Christ one is set free from unbelief and all other manifestations of sin. In the one who is the truth incarnated we become free to know God and to love and serve him, and to know, love, and serve our fellows. In Christ we are set free from the love of sin and self and from all the hatred this false love entails. In Christ we receive *the ability* to live and love as children of God, for being in Christ means being recipients of his grace.

The self in bondage to sin can no more love and live for God than it can change the color of its skin (Jer. 12:23). Freed by Christ it can do all things (Phil. 4:13; 1 Cor. 3:21f.). Freedom is knowing the truth, Jesus Christ, and being able by his grace to live the life for which one was created, in fellowship with God. As the divine purpose in creation was that God might have a people, so the divine reason for redemption is that this original purpose may be realized. And God's purpose will not be thwarted: "I will accomplish all my purpose. . . . I have spoken, and I will bring it to pass; I have purposed, and I will do it" (Isa. 46:10f.).

The pageant of history is unfolding on the stage of this world. Its last scene will be one of freedom, even for creation itself:

> For the creation waits with eager longing for the revealing of the sons of God; for the creation was subjected to futility, not of its own will but by the will of him who subjected it in hope; because the creation itself will be set free from its bondage to decay and obtain the glorious liberty of the children of God. We know that the whole creation has been groaning in travail together until now; and not only the creation, but we ourselves, who have the first fruits of the Spirit, groan inwardly as we wait for adoption as sons, the redemption of our bodies (Rom. 8:19-23).

2. CALVIN'S AGREEMENT

Luther's discourse on Christian freedom was a lasting contribution to the faith of the church. What he found in the Word of God he gave back to the people of God from whom it had been taken. Calvin took over Luther's argument in its entirety. Discussing freedom in the *Institutes,* he says that it is "a thing of prime necessity. . . . Apart from a knowledge of it consciences dare undertake almost nothing without doubting; they hesitate and recoil from many things; they constantly waver and are afraid" (*Inst.,* III, xix, 1).

Like Luther, Calvin saw freedom as "an appendage" of justification and says that understanding the reality of freedom "is of no little avail in understanding justification's power. Indeed, those who seriously fear God will enjoy the incomparable benefit of this doctrine." While emphasizing the positive usefulness of the law arousing believers "to a zeal for holiness and innocence" (*Inst.,* III, xix, 2) more than Luther did, Calvin agrees that the Christian cannot serve God with joyful obedience unless he is free from the constraint of the law. That is why he believes with Luther in the necessity of justification by faith alone apart from any human merit. The righteousness in which the Christian stands before God is not his own, but Christ's. Aware that the demands of the law have been fully met, so that it has no claims on him, and with a free conscience, the Christian delights to do the will of God. A slave always fears his master, but a child knows that he is loved by his parents. He and his works are accepted even though they are imperfect.

Calvin's argument concerning indifferent things (*adiaphora*) is similar to Luther's in attempting to set forth the sensible, moderate position of Scripture (*Inst.*, III, xix, 4f.). The tyranny of legalism is rejected on the one hand; the "weaker brother" is respected on the other, but Calvin warns the latter not to make a nuisance of himself with his fastidious distinctions. Whether one eats meat or not, whether he does this or that, depending on circumstances, the mature Christian acts in such a way that his conscience remains free (*Inst.*, III, xix, 16).

Chapter 14

John Calvin: Order and the Holy Spirit

Of all those who have played major roles in forming the faith of the church none has provoked a greater variety of interpretation than John Calvin.

Attempts to locate and explicate the central motif of Calvin's theological thinking differ so widely that one is tempted to agree with those who argue that there is no one "basic doctrine" from which the rest can be derived but that Calvin's theology should be described as a *complexio oppositorum*, a set of ideas held together even when logically contradictory because Calvin believed them to be taught in Scripture.[1] "If we want to speak of a 'system' of Calvin," say Bauke, "we must do so with certain reservations, owing to the plurality of themes that imposed themselves simultaneously upon its author's thinking."[2] As interesting and important as this issue may be, we are concerned here with a more limited question. What specifically did Calvin contribute to the body of faith of the church? What did he develop in the understanding of that faith once delivered to the saints?

Calvin's system of doctrine, as Warfield has written, is the Augustinianism common to the whole body of the Reformers, especially Luther and Martin Bucer:

> Many of the very forms of statement most characteristic of Calvin — on such topics as Predestination, Faith, the stages of Salvation, the Church, the Sacraments — only reproduce, though of course with that clearness and religious depth peculiar to Calvin, the precise teachings of Bucer, who was above all others, accordingly, Calvin's master in theology. Of course he does not take these ideas over from Bucer and repeat them by rote. They have become his own and issue afresh from him with a new exactness and delicacy of appreciation, in themselves and in their relations, with a new development of implications, and especially with a new richness of religious content. For the prime characteristic of Calvin as a theologian is precisely the practical interest which governs his entire thought and the religious profundity which suffuses it all.[3]

Calvin did not consider himself an innovator in theology. He felt bound to the ancient faith of the church which was the subject of his exposition. Its restoration in the church was the reason for his prodigious labors as a Reformer, and its apprehension and integration into the lives of believers was his aim as a minister of the Word of God. But if this is so, in what did Calvin's contribution to the faith of the church consist? In our opinion that contribution can best be set forth under the rubric "order and the Holy Spirit." Anyone familiar with the writings of Calvin is aware of his frequent references to order in every area of theological consideration. Josef Bohatec, who has done the most significant work in this area, speaks of Calvin's "passion for order."[4] And Warfield refers to Calvin as "preeminently the theologian of the Holy Spirit."[5] Others have shown the aptness of that description.[6] Studies of Calvin's doctrines of the church, the law of God, and spirituality have demonstrated the importance of our subject in his thinking.[7] I propose that this major theme in his theological writings is also his major contribution to the faith of the church.

1. THE LATE MEDIEVAL OBSESSION WITH ORDER

Calvin's temperament, the training he received in the schools he attended, and the times in which he lived conspired to make order one of his major emphases. The influence of Stoicism on Calvin's thought and the heavy emphasis on order in that philosophy deserve special attention. The importance of Stoic philosophy to the doctrine of the early church has a close parallel in the fifteenth and early sixteenth centuries.[8]

The major reason for the late medieval rise of Stoicism was the disturbances of the times. The crumbling of the empire in the thirteenth century, the anarchy in Italy and the temporary transfer of the papacy to France in the fourteenth century, civil wars, local tyrannies, the glorification of physical power, general immorality, radical individualism, and the dangers of the extant Epicurean spirit drove many to seek a philosophy of consolation. When there is anarchy and little hope for the future, people seek a form of law and order that gives promise of peace, social stability, and hope for the future, and Stoicism offered this. Its identification of God and order; its belief in the unity of the world controlled by reason and in our ability to apprehend that reason and live in harmony with it, thus giving us mastery over turmoil; its conviction that by inner discipline the wise person lives in harmony with the order of nature and learns that such virtue produces happiness; its belief in one human family — *humanitas*, to which all are bound by natural law—all this made the Stoicism of classical authors popular.

In Stoic thought disorder is irrational and contrary to nature. While there are similarities as well as differences between Stoic and Christian concepts and terms—phrases like city of God, fatherhood of God, brotherhood of man, and law of love appear in Seneca, for example—the Stoic "fatalistic ethic of disposition"[9] becomes visible in its lack of correspondence with reality. Cochrane identifies the weakness of Stoic wisdom as its failure "to build a bridge between 'order' and 'process'; one result being that whatever did not fit in with the preconceptions of its ideal order was denied or dismissed as 'unreal.' "[10] Salvation for the Stoic lay in inner retreat, in conforming to the reality manifesting itself in the law of nature, and this is a matter of mental discipline. David Little elaborates on the effect of this orientation in the late Middle Ages:

> While the recovery of classical thinking resulted in important intellectual innovations in the fourteenth, fifteenth, and sixteenth centuries, very little use was made of the revived thought for any genuine social reorientation. In general, humanists such as Erasmus, Bude, and Ficino were much more concerned to retreat into an *arrière-boutique* [safe refuge] to contemplate the essence of universal humanity and to cultivate their inward rational relationship to it than to reform the structure of things. It is one of the striking features of the Renaissance, whose spirit and conclusions were usually in such direct contradiction to the scholasticism of the Roman Catholic Church, that so much intellectual activity went on with so little social effect. . . .
>
> How could it be otherwise when in humanism, as in Stoicism, social life was but a manifestation of the recurring, inexorable *ordo naturae* in fact of which no break, no transformation is possible? As with their Stoic ancestors, the humanists' ethical activity was determined by the way things are.[11]

2. ORDER IN GOD'S CREATION

Although deeply influenced by Stoicism, Calvin's mental and spiritual world was far removed from it. What created the distance was the Reformer's conception of God. In Stoicism God is identified with the world order; for Calvin the world order is created and sustained by God. The difference between Stoicism and Christianity is the difference between pantheism and the Christian faith. Calvin held that the triune God is the archetype of all order in the universe. By order

Calvin meant proper being, correct arrangement, beauty, harmony, things as they ought to be — in a word, perfection, or, as we shall see, the presence of the Holy Spirit.

Creation receives its imprint from its creator. He is perfect — a concept which includes order — and he imparts something of his glory to the world. "It will not suffice simply to hold that there is One whom all ought to honor and adore, unless we are also persuaded that he is the fountain of every good, and that we must seek nothing elsewhere than in him." That strong statement reflects Calvin's belief in the absolute perfection and sovereignty of God, on whom we are utterly dependent.

> Not only does he sustain this universe (as he once founded it) by his boundless might, regulate it by his wisdom, preserve it by his goodness, and especially rule mankind by his righteousness and judgment, bear with it in his mercy, watch over it by his protection; but also . . . no drop will be found either of wisdom and light, or of righteousness or power or rectitude, or of genuine truth, which does not flow from him and of which he is not the cause. Thus we may learn to await and seek all these things from him, and thankfully ascribe them, once received, to him. For this sense of the powers [*virtutum*, perfections] of God is for us a fit teacher of piety, from which religion is born. I call "piety" that reverence joined with love of God which the knowledge of his benefits induces (*Inst.*, I, ii, 1).

God is the archetype of all the perfection, all the order in the universe. To emphasize God's sovereignty over "the order of nature," an expression Calvin frequently uses, he sometimes uses the terms "ordination," "command," "mandate," "counsel," "decree," and "word" of God. Commenting on Psalm 119:91, he writes: "The whole order of nature depends solely upon the command or decree of God. . . . The hidden power of God so supports all things, that in order to remain in their state they must obey his word or mandate." Or again, "Nothing is carried on without God's command, that is, without his decree, and, as they say, without his ordination."[12]

Because God has ordained or decreed it, the universe exists and the course of history is a reality. The most obscure incident happens in accordance with that decree. Wind and storms, accidents and good fortune, sunshine and rain — all are included.[13] All the good in nature and in history is a reflection of God, for he "represents both himself and his everlasting Kingdom in the mirror of his works with very great clarity" (*Inst.*, I, v, 11; cf. I, xiv, 5, 21). There in his works we behold his perfections, a subject about which Calvin can become almost rhapsodic (e.g., *Inst.*, I, v, 10; xiv, 21). Especially man himself, aptly called by philosophers a "microcosm" because he is such a "rare example" of the divine perfections, is "a clear mirror of God's works" (*Inst.*, I, v, 3), a teaching which is elaborated in the discussion on creation (*Inst.*, I, xv).

In one famous passage Calvin extols the magnificent revelatory character of creation, even declaring that a pious person can say "that nature is God." However, "because it is a harsh and improper saying, since nature is rather the order prescribed by God, it is harmful in such weighty matters, in which special devotion is due, to involve God confusedly in the inferior cause of his works" (*Inst.*, I, v, 5). While God bestows his beneficence on all he has made, we are to remember that creation reflects something of the divine splendor only because that splendor resides eternally in him from whom it comes to us as a gift.

Calvin insists that all three persons of the Trinity are involved in the works of creation, providence, and salvation. The Son and the Holy Spirit are active with the Father in all God's external works. As the three are co-essential and co-eternal, so each is directly related to the order established in creation and history.

In Calvin's treatment of the doctrine of the Trinity (*Inst.*, I, xiii), he identifies biblical references to God's spoken word with the eternal Word himself. Creation was effected by God's word: he spoke, and it was done. But this word was no mere bidding or command. The apostles tell us that the world was made through the Son and that God upholds all things by his powerful Word (Heb. 1:2f.). Calvin remarks: "Here we see the Word understood as the order or mandate of the Son, who is himself the eternal and essential Word of the Father." Later, discussing Jesus' words in John 5:17, "My Father and I have worked even to this day," Calvin remarks:

> God has so spoken that the Word might have his share in the work and that in this way the work might be common to both. But John spoke most clearly of all when he declared that that Word, God from the beginning with God, was at the same time the cause of all things, together with God the Father [John 1:1-3]. For John at once attributes to the Word a solid and abiding essence, and ascribes something uniquely His own, and clearly shows how God, by speaking, was Creator of the universe. Therefore, inasmuch as all divinely uttered revelations are correctly designated by the term "word of God," so this substantial Word is properly placed at the highest level, as the wellspring of all oracles. Unchangeable, the Word abides everlastingly one and the same with God, and is God himself.

The argument for the involvement of the Holy Spirit in the work of God from the beginning is similar. Calvin holds with the church fathers that the creation of "the universe was no less the work of the

Holy Spirit than of the Son," though he does not agree with all of their scriptural support for this doctrine (*Inst.*, I, xiii, 15). Nevertheless, he insists on understanding the Spirit as active in creation and mentions his bestowal of "beauty and order":

> Although no mention is made of the Spirit except in the history of the creation of the universe, nevertheless the Spirit is introduced here, not as a shadow, but as the essential power of God, when Moses tells that the as yet formless mass was itself sustained in him [Gen. 1:2]. Therefore it then has become clear that the eternal Spirit has always been in God, while with tender care he supported the confused matter of heaven and earth, until beauty and order were added (*Inst.*, I, xiii, 22).

The Spirit "quickens" all things in creation; "deprived of his vigor" they would "immediately fall" (Comm. on John 5:17). As God created by his Spirit, he sustains creation by that same Spirit.

> For the power of the Spirit is spread abroad through all parts of the world that it may keep [God's creatures] in their state, that he may supply to heaven and earth that vigor we discern, and motion to all living creatures. . . . God, by the wonderful power and impulse of his Spirit, preserves that which he formed out of nothing (Comm. on Acts 17:28).

God's Word and Spirit were likewise archetypes with the Father of all the order and beauty that was one day to appear. Calvin's understanding of the order manifest in creation is therefore thoroughly trinitarian.

3. SALVATION AS THE RESTORATION OF ORDER

At creation then God gave the world the order it has presently, and since then he has sustained it. We shall look closely now at four areas which readily illustrate Calvin's doctrine of order and the Holy Spirit: salvation, the church, the state, and the Christian life.

Calvin saw salvation as the restoration of order (*Inst.*, II, vi). Since humanity lost in the fall of Adam "that original excellence and nobility" which it once had, God "does not recognize as his handiwork" the resultant corruption of sin. "The natural order was that the frame of the universe would be the school in which we were to learn piety, and from it pass over to eternal life and perfect felicity," but this avails no more. Yet sin has not ruined things so completely that there is nothing good left in creation. Even in pagan writers, Calvin insists, there is still an "admirable light of truth shining [to] teach us that the mind of man, though fallen and perverted from its wholeness, is nevertheless clothed and ornamented with God's excellent gifts." Although this may seem to contradict what Calvin had previously said about the effects of sin, he argues for it on the ground that the pious mind must recognize and appreciate the continuing merciful presence of the Holy Spirit in a sinful creation.

> If we regard the Spirit of God as the sole fountain of truth, we shall neither reject the truth itself, nor despise it wherever it shall appear, unless we wish to dishonor the Spirit of God. For by holding the gifts of the Spirit in slight esteem, we contemn and reproach the Spirit himself (*Inst.*, II, ii, 15).

The Reformer appeals to government, science, philosophy, medicine, and arts developed by the "natural man" as proofs that God's Spirit has not deserted the corrupt human race. The Spirit is still with us; hence, instead of the chaos that would otherwise ensue, there is still order. Because of the destructive tendencies of sin, however, a great conflict rages between the Spirit of God and the powers of darkness. The outcome is certain, because God has determined to save the world and overthrow the powers of darkness, as demonstrated by election and the establishment of the covenant, by which God gathers a people unto himself in Christ and re-establishes the purpose he had in creating the world.

> The Holy Spirit declares that all things were created principally for the use of men, that they might thereby recognize God as their father. ... The prophet concludes that the whole course of nature would be subverted, unless God saved his church. The creation of the world would serve no good purpose, if there were no people to call upon God (Comm. on Ps. 115:17).

The call of Abraham, Isaac, and Jacob, of Israel as a nation under God and of the church, and the coming of Christ in whom the purpose of redemption is summed up — all restore order to the world under the guidance of God's Spirit. Commenting on Ephesians 1:10 — "... to unite all things in Christ" — Calvin remarks:

> The meaning appears to me to be, that out of Christ all things were disordered, and that through him they have been restored to order. And truly, out of Christ, what can we perceive in the world but mere ruins? We are alienated from God by sin, and how can we but present a broken and shattered aspect? The proper condition of creatures is to keep close to God. Such a gathering together (*anakephalaiosis*) as might bring us back to regular order, the apostle tells us, has been made in Christ. Formed into one body, we are united to God, and closely connected with each other. Without Christ, on the other hand, the whole world is a shapeless chaos and frightful confusion. We are brought into actual unity by Christ alone.

The only possible way for people and nations to live well, avoiding the confusion and disorder sin brings, is to live in harmony with God's will and the order he has established.

> So long as ungodliness has possession of the minds of men, the world, plunged as it is in darkness, must be considered as thrown into a state of confusion, and of horrible disorder and misrule; for there can be no stability apart from God. . . . No order can be said to prevail in the world, until God erect his throne and reign amongst men. What more monstrous disorder can be conceived of, than exists where the Creator himself is not acknowledged? . . . If God's method of governing men be to form and regulate their lives to righteousness, we may infer, that however easily men may be satisfied with themselves, all is necessarily wrong with them, till they have been made subject to Christ. And this righteousness has not reference merely to the outward actions. It comprehends a new heart, commencing as it does in the regeneration of the Spirit, by which we are formed again into the likeness of God (Comm. on Ps. 96:10).

In these few sample texts emphasizing salvation as the restoration of order, there have been incidental references to the Holy Spirit. But for Calvin no meaningful discussion of the restoration of order can occur apart from a clear understanding of the function of the Holy Spirit in the re-creation of order. It is the Spirit who calls, regenerates, and bestows faith in Christ, who sanctifies and enables believers to persevere. He creates the believing community as the sphere of activity where he saves by his sovereign grace. The proofs of election and faith and the fruits accompanying salvation are from him. Moreover, he bestows a rich variety of gifts for ministry so that the body of Christ may be complete in every way as God uses it to restore order to the world. Milner is correct in saying that "Calvin . . . thinks of the church as the order emerging out of the correlation of the *ordinatio Dei* and the effectual work of the Holy Spirit."[14]

Jesus Christ is the focus of attention in that salvation which is the restoration of order effected by the Holy Spirit. He is the one to whom the Spirit points as fulfilling the covenant. He is the Second Adam, the elect head of redeemed humanity, the obedient servant, the perfect man who has overcome the disorder of sin and reigns over the church and the world. Christ is God manifest in the flesh, the only one through whom we have access to the Father. Any kind of Arianism was anathema to him — for example, the suggestion that in Jesus there was only a "portion of divinity, outflowing from the whole perfection of God" (*Inst.*, II, vi, 4). Those who seek God anywhere but in Christ have no mediator and consequently cannot "taste God's mercy, and thus be persuaded that he [is] their Father." Ignorant of Christ, they can have only a "fleeting knowledge of God," lapse into "crass and foul superstitions," and betray their own ignorance. "So today," he concludes, "the Turks, although they proclaim at the top of their lungs that the Creator of heaven and earth is God, still, while repudiating Christ, substitute an idol in place of the true God."

Recalling that the Holy Spirit is none other than the Spirit of Christ as well as of the Father, we must add that Calvin sees all of this, including Christ's redemptive work, as being accomplished through and within the all-embracing work of the Holy Spirit. He is the one who restores creation, including the covenant community, to its destined end. In our judgment Calvin would agree that the work of the Holy Spirit is more comprehensive than that of the Messiah.[15] I concur with those who question or object to "theological" or "christological" interpretations of the theology of Calvin.[16] A sound interpretation of Calvin does justice to each of the persons of the Godhead. Against those who favor a "christological" interpretation, it must be said that Calvin emphasizes the work of the Father and the Holy Spirit as well as the Son. Against those who see in Calvin an exclusive "theological" orientation, the response must be that the Reformer makes as much of the work of the Son and the Spirit as of God the Father. Against those who would favor an overweighted pneumatological orientation, it must be said that a correct understanding does justice to Calvin's appreciation of the persons and work of the Father and the Son as well as the Holy Spirit.

Only a trinitarian interpretation of the Reformer, which takes into account the person and work of each person in the Godhead, does justice to him. In discussing the Trinity Calvin quotes a passage from Gregory of Nazianzus which "vastly delights" him: "I cannot think on the one without quickly being encircled by the splendor of the three; nor can I discern the three without being straightway carried back to the one" (*Inst.*, I, xiii, 17). Thus Calvin strives to be balanced and faithful in his interpretation of the biblical revelation.

Calvin would not object to a description of his theology as "balanced" (even though that word can be dangerous), for he appreciated balance, in part at least because of his humanist background and interest in Stoicism. But more important to him than balance was biblical fidelity, and Calvin read Scripture in a thoroughly trinitarian manner. He believed that each person in the Godhead is active in all the external works of God and must be honored for who he is and what he does. Salvation is effected by God *in* the person of Jesus Christ and *through* the Holy Spirit.[17]

All of the life and work of Christ must be seen in a pneumatological framework: he is conceived by the Holy Spirit (Luke 1:35), he carries on his ministry in the power of the Spirit (Luke 4:18), offers himself through the eternal Spirit without spot to God (Heb. 9:14), and is shown to be the Son of God in power according to the Spirit of holiness by his resurrection from the dead (Rom. 1:4). All is done in the power of the Spirit. In conceiving salvation as the restoration of order, therefore, we see it effected by the Lord Jesus Christ, indeed, and through the power of the Holy Spirit.

Finally, we must note the instrument the Holy Spirit uses in effecting salvation and restoring order — the Word of God. The broadest meaning of the Word is God's entire disclosure of himself and his purposes, which was mediated through prophets, apostles, and the Lord Jesus Christ. Conceived more personally the Word is Christ himself, the "person of the speaking God," as Calvin puts it (*Inst.*, I, vii, 4). He collates these two usages of the expression "Word of God" in his comments on John 5:17:

> Inasmuch as all divinely uttered revelations are correctly designated by the term "word of God," so this substantial Word is properly placed at the highest level, as the wellspring of all oracles. Unchangeable, the Word abides everlastingly one and the same with God, and is God himself.

Conceived more narrowly and concretely, the Word is the written record contained in the Bible of what God has said and done in the history of salvation. Long in coming to its final fulness, but authoritative and endowed with divine power from its first utterance, the Word is the principle of order used by the Spirit in the formation of the body, the church, and in the nurture and edification of its individual members.

Because of the darkness of the human situation, God "added the light of his Word by which to become known unto salvation."

> Because he saw the minds of all men tossed and agitated, after he chose the Jews as his very own flock, he fenced them about that they might not sink into oblivion as others had. With good reason he holds us by the same means in the pure knowledge of himself, since otherwise even those who seem to stand firm before all others would soon melt away. Just as old or bleary-eyed men and those with weak vision, if you thrust before them a most beautiful volume, even if they recognize it to be some sort of writing, yet can scarcely construe two words, but with the aid of spectacles will begin to read distinctly; so Scripture, gathering up the otherwise confused knowledge of God in our minds, having dispersed our dullness, clearly shows us the true God. This, therefore, is a special gift, where God, to instruct the church, not merely uses mute teachers but also opens his own most hallowed lips (*Inst.*, I, vi, 1).

So that humanity might always be aware of God's revelation and so that there might be a continuing succession of true teaching, God caused that which he gave to the patriarchs to be "recorded, as it were, on public tablets" (*Inst.*, I, vi, 2). Hence no one can have right understanding of heavenly doctrine "unless he be a pupil of Scripture."

Whereas Calvin believed in the necessity of Scripture because of human ignorance caused by sin, he came increasingly to appreciate its importance in the life and faith of the church through his contacts with "fanatics" who abandoned Scripture and appealed directly to the Holy Spirit to support their own opinions. They dismissed Calvin's position as simplistic pursuit of "the dead and killing letter" (*Inst.*, I, ix, 1); Calvin responded to this "devilish madness" by insisting, like Luther and other Reformers, that the Word and Spirit belong together.

> By a kind of mutual bond the Lord has joined together the certainty of his Word and of his Spirit so that the perfect religion of the Word may abide in our minds when the Spirit, who causes us to contemplate God's face, shines; and that we in turn may embrace the Spirit with no fear of being deceived when we recognize him in his own Image, namely, in the Word. So indeed it is. God did not bring forth his Word among men for the sake of a momentary display, intending at the coming of his Spirit to abolish it. Rather, he sent down the same Spirit by whose power he had dispensed the Word, to complete his work by the efficacious confirmation of the Word (*Inst.*, I, ix, 3).

Some argue that "it is not worthy of the Spirit of God to whom all things ought to be subject, himself to be subject to Scripture." Calvin retorts that it is hardly degrading for the Spirit to be consistent with himself and use the Word he had given (*Inst.*, I, ix, 2). So that God's people need not be deceived if "the spirit of Satan should creep in, [God] would have us recognize him in his own image, which he has stamped upon the Scriptures."

> He is the author of the Scriptures; he cannot vary and differ from himself. Hence he must ever remain just as he once revealed himself there. This is no affront to him, unless perchance we consider it honorable for him to decline or degenerate from himself.

If we "want to receive any gain and benefit from the Spirit of God," therefore, we must go to the Word he has given as the only means to restore order to a chaotic world. The thrust of the argument is that, because God is the author of order and peace, his words, spoken through prophets and apostles and personified in Christ, bring about that new arrangement in human existence which alone gives felicity now and in the hereafter. The agent of the Godhead whose power effects the divine will in the restoration of order is the Holy Spirit. Using the Word, he creates a faith which includes the conviction that he is the author of the Word.

This internal testimony of the Spirit is weightier than anything produced by mere reason, and it makes Scripture self-authenticating. It is not right, then, to subject Scripture to demands for other proof since God witnesses to himself clearly in it. "Illumined by his power, we believe neither by our own nor by anyone else's judgment that Scripture is from God" (*Inst.*, I, vii, 5). Thus Calvin's answer to the important and perplexing question of religious authority is twofold: the objective ground for faith is the Word of God, and its subjective cause is the Spirit who brought the Word into being. This further demonstrates the strategic place order and the Holy Spirit occupied in his thinking.

> As God alone is a fit witness of himself in his Word, so also the Word will not find acceptance in men's hearts before it is sealed by the inward testimony of the Spirit. The same Spirit, therefore, who has spoken through the mouths of the prophets must penetrate into our hearts to persuade us that they faithfully proclaimed what had been divinely commanded (*Inst.*, I, vii, 4).

4. ORDER IN THE GOVERNMENT OF THE CHURCH

In looking at Calvin's understanding of salvation as the restoration of order effected by the Holy Spirit, we have briefly noted enough aspects of his doctrine of the church to observe the correctness of Milner's central judgment that "Calvin . . . thinks of the church as the order emerging out of the *ordinatio Dei* and the effectual work of the Holy Spirit."[18] In view of our purpose here we shall limit our discussion to Calvin's doctrine of the government of the church, further substantiating the thesis that his contribution to the understanding of the Christian faith is in the area of order and the Holy Spirit.

It would be difficult to overestimate the importance Calvin ascribed to the government of the church or its impact on his followers in the sixteenth and following centuries.[19] Book IV of his *Institutes*, his *Ecclesiastical Ordinances* of 1541, many references to church government in his commentaries and sermons, and some of his letters prove how important church order was for Calvin:

> There is nothing in which order should be more diligently observed than in establishing church government; for nowhere is there greater peril if anything be done irregularly (*Inst.*, IV, iii, 10).

> As no city or township can function without magistrate and polity, so the church of God ... needs a spiritual polity (*Inst.*, IV, xi, 1).

The ideal was a careful delineation of church polity, for which Calvin believed the pattern had been furnished by God:

> Now we must speak of the order by which the Lord willed his church to be governed (*Inst.*, IV, iii, 1).

> Up to this point we have discussed the order of church government as it has been handed down to us from God's pure Word, and also those ministries established by Christ (*Inst.*, IV, iv, 1).

Calvin's discussion of the government of the early church and its approximation to the divine plan set down in the Bible shows his belief that how the church is run is not arbitrary, but that the directive has been given by God in his Word. Yet, as Ganoczy shows, "in reality he regards the practice of the 'ancient church' as also normative without defining with precision at what moment in history that practice came to an end."[20] Calvin's appeal to the ancient church in his polemic against Rome shows a remarkable flexibility, hardly to be expected in view of his insistence on Scripture as the sole norm for theory and practice.

> I approve only those human constitutions which are founded upon God's authority, drawn from Scripture, and therefore, wholly divine. ... But because he did not will in outward discipline and ceremonies to prescribe in detail what we ought to do (because he foresaw that this depended upon the state of the times, and he did not deem one form suitable for all ages), here we must take refuge in those general rules which he has given, that whatever the necessity of the church will require for order and decorum should be tested against these. Lastly, because he has taught nothing specifically, and because these things are not necessary to salvation, and for the upbuilding of the church ought to be variously accommodated to the customs of each nation and age, it will be fitting (as the advantage of the church will require) to change and abrogate traditional practices and to establish new ones. Indeed, I admit that we ought not to charge into innovation rashly, suddenly, for insufficient cause. But love will best judge what may hurt or edify; and if we let love be our guide, all will be safe (*Inst.*, IV, x, 30).

While he is speaking about minor regulations here, he adopts a similar posture with respect to bishops in the ancient and sixteenth-century churches, hardly a minor consideration.[21] The criterion is the edification of the faithful (*Inst.*, IV, x, 32). This relatively generous attitude is possible because he was convinced that God guides the church by his Holy Spirit and because he believed that he had found the principles which gave him such freedom in Scripture. While he deplored "human invention" in the order of the church, with its resultant confusion (*Inst.*, IV, ii, 12), Calvin was not as inflexible on this point as some have declared. Rather, he found in Scripture the lines along which the order of the church should be drawn, and he believed that these were willed by the Holy Spirit.

a. The head of the church

The head of the church is Jesus Christ. "He alone should rule and reign in the church as well as have authority or pre-eminence in it, and this authority should be exercised and administered by his Word alone" (*Inst.*, IV, iii, 1). But Calvin continues:

> Because he does not dwell among us in visible presence [Matt. 26:11] . . . he uses the ministry of men to declare openly his will to us by mouth, as a sort of delegated work, not by transferring to them his right and honor, but only that through their mouths he may do his own work — just as a workman uses a tool to do his work.

The preaching office and other aspects of the ministry of the church are clearly understood as in essence the ministry of Christ exercised in the midst of his people. Physically the ascended Christ reigns as king in heaven, but his ministry is accomplished in the power of the Holy Spirit through the Word which is his royal scepter. Whatever is done in the church — proclamation of the Word, administration of the sacraments, maintenance of discipline, care of the poor, instruction of youth, visitation of the sick — is effected in the name and by the authority of Jesus Christ. The church accomplishes its ministry by human instrumentality, but the point is that Christ is the effective agent in salvation and in the building of the church.

This for Calvin is the wonder and glory of ministry. Were the Lord himself to speak from heaven, we would be awed at his majesty. But that is not his mode of operation. He gives us an "exercise in humility" when he speaks to us through men, "some of lower worth than we."

> When a puny man risen from the dust speaks in God's name, at this point we best evidence our piety and obedience toward God if we show ourselves teachable toward his minister, although he excels us in nothing. It was for this reason, then, that he hid the treasure of his heavenly wisdom in weak

and earthen vessels [2 Cor. 4:7] in order to prove more surely how much we should esteem it (*Inst.*, IV, iii, 1).

Reflecting on the divine pattern for the church, Calvin stresses the unity and order which have been given it as described by Paul in the fourth chapter of Ephesians. The apostle shows in this passage that the "human ministry which God uses to govern the church is a chief sinew by which believers are held together in one body" (*Inst.*, IV, iii, 2). This ministry is so important that the church's well-being depends on the attitude it adopts towards those to whom it has been entrusted.

Whoever, therefore, either is trying to abolish this order . . . and this kind of government, or discounts it as not necessary, is striving for the undoing or rather the ruin and destruction of the church. For neither the light and heat of sun, nor food and drink, are so necessary to nourish and sustain the present life as the apostolic and pastoral office is necessary to preserve the church on earth.

The importance of human ministry in the church could hardly be emphasized more strongly. Calvin writes at length about the various offices, call to office, qualifications and training, the voice of the people in the selection of those who are to govern them, and ordination. All is to be done in a way which honors the head of the church, so that his approval is assured. This is to include the faithfulness of officers to the churches to which they are bound.

The Reformer's distaste for the confusion in the pre-Reformation church prompted him to insist that "to keep peace in the church, this order [of having persons duly called and ordained] is necessary. . . . This is not of human devising but ordained by God himself." Whoever takes office in church government "should know that he is bound by this law of divine call" (*Inst.*, IV, iii, 7).

b. The four offices

During the three years Calvin spent in Strasbourg after his expulsion from Geneva, he learned much from Martin Bucer, the city's chief Reformer. While Bucer's exact influence on the Genevan reformer is not easy to measure, it is certain that Bucer's emphasis on the Holy Spirit and on church order made a great impression on him.[22] Wendel points to the significance of Calvin's "almost feverish haste" in presenting himself on the very day of his arrival before the Genevan magistrates and demanding that a committee of pastors and advisors be appointed to draft "regulations for the church and consistory."[23] Having seen what Bucer accomplished in Strasbourg, Calvin was determined to do the same now that he was back in Geneva. He wanted to write the new constitution for the church himself, and, given permission to do so, made it his first order of business in the autumn of 1541. Within a week of his return to the city, the project was well underway, and despite expected delays and necessary revisions, final approval was given to the *Ecclesiastical Ordinances* by the city council in two months.

The opening statement reads:

> There are four orders of offices that our Lord instituted for the government of his church. First the pastors, then teachers, after them the elders, and fourthly the deacons. Therefore if we wish to have the church well-ordered and have it maintained in its entirety, we must observe that form of rule.[24]

Calvin described the office of pastor in greatest detail. He considered this office the most important; hence the pastor is called "the minister" (*Inst.*, IV, iii, 6-7, 10-16).[25] His primary functions are to preach the gospel and to administer the sacraments. To these are added the rule of the church, or the necessity of exercising "upright discipline," as Calvin calls it (*Inst.*, IV, iii, 6; cf. IV, xii). Carrying on the work of the apostles, to whose office theirs is similar (*Inst.*, IV, iii, 5, 6), ministers exercise great authority. But that authority is located in the Word of God which they serve rather than in their own persons.

> The only way to build up the church is for the ministers themselves to endeavor to preserve Christ's authority. . . . [The minister] alone is the schoolmaster of the church. . . . Whatever authority and dignity the Spirit in Scripture accords to either priests or prophets, or apostles, or successors of apostles, it is wholly given not to the men personally, but to the ministry to which they have been appointed; or (to speak more briefly) to the Word, whose ministry is entrusted to them. . . . They have [not] been endowed to teach or to answer, except in the name and Word of the Lord (*Inst.*, IV, viii, 2).

Although each minister is bound to a particular church, where he is to exercise his ministry and thus avoid confusion and keep order, he is actually a minister of the whole church. Here again Calvin finds an analogy in the office of the apostles. The ministers or pastors "have the same charge as the apostles" and serve the whole church (*Inst.*, IV, iii, 5-7). In churches which follow Calvin's interpretation of Scripture, ministers are thus ordained by presbyteries or associations of churches, representative of the whole church of Jesus Christ. Since they serve the whole church even while given a local assignment, they may aid other churches when needed and requested, and may meet in a synod as the occasion may require. For when "the pastors of the church in common, invoking Christ's Spirit, agree, [they] will have much more weight than if they come to a decision and act individually" (*Inst.*, IV, ix, 13; cf. iii, 7).

Although Calvin gave the office of teacher special status in the *Ecclesiastical Ordinances* and recognized its worth in the *Institutes* as well, he affirms that "the pastoral office includes all the functions of the teaching office. This includes interpreting Scripture and keeping doctrine whole and pure among believers. Yet in acknowledgment of the special gifts of the Holy Spirit, he held on the basis of Ephesians 4:11 that a separate teaching office is valid and useful for the church. Bucer in fact had placed the office of doctor at the head of his list of ministries in 1536, and having seen it at work in Strasbourg, Calvin wrote it into the Geneva ordinances in 1541.[26] Relieved of responsibilities "of discipline, or administering the sacraments, or warnings and exhortations," the doctors were to give themselves wholly to their task of interpretation and teaching (*Inst.*, IV, iii, 4). As the pastoral office was similar to that of the apostles, Calvin saw the teaching office as similar to the prophetic office (*Inst.*, IV, iii, 5).

The office of elder, rooted in the Old Testament, where the elders of Israel are frequently mentioned, and in the New Testament, is given to rule the people of God. The "senate" of elders, "chosen from godly, grave, and holy men," has jurisdiction over morals and error; with the pastors it is responsible for the spiritual welfare of the congregation (*Inst.*, IV, iii, 8; iv, 1-3; xi, 6).

To the deacons was given the task of caring for material needs, particularly the needs of the poor. Calvin found the origin of their office, too, in Scripture and saw it as highly useful in the life of the church (*Inst.*, IV, iii, 9; Comm. on Acts 6:3). Here again Calvin learned from those who had preceded him: Luther had called for the restoration of the diaconate in 1530 and Bucer had introduced deacons in Strasbourg in 1536. In a sermon on 1 Timothy 3:6f. delivered near the end of his life, Calvin extolled the importance of this office. In the sermon following, on the next verses in the epistle, Calvin spoke of the necessity for each officer in the church to discharge his own duty in accordance with the gift given him and not to try to do the work of another.[27] Thus order would be preserved and the congregation would be edified.

c. The papacy

Calvin's criticism of the papacy further confirms our thesis that his contribution to the faith of the church was in an emphasis on order and the Holy Spirit. The hierarchy of the Roman Catholic Church, he said, perverted good order, thus demonstrating that it did not possess the Holy Spirit. Rome's fundamental problem was neglect of the Word of God, which as we have seen is the principle or instrument of order used by the Spirit to maintain and edify the church. "These dishonest men . . . only allege a continuous order of succession" rather than fulfil their apostolic office (Comm. on Mal. 2:5). "If bishops are made by the Holy Spirit to the end that they may feed the church, the hierarchy of papistry is ridiculous" (Comm. on Acts 20:28). Roman bishops boast in vain that they are ministers of God when they are not "adorned with the gifts of the Spirit which are necessary for the execution of such an office. To pretend to have the inspiration of the Spirit" is in their case "excessively disgusting" (Comm. on Isa. 48:16).

The reasons Calvin gives for such judgments are scattered throughout his writings, so that one quickly recognizes the Reformer's indignation when he reflected on the hierarchy of his day. Chief among his reasons for criticism was the bishops' failure to set a good example and preach and teach the Word of God. Confusion and disorder had displaced the true order willed by Christ and effected by the Holy Spirit if the Word was given its proper place. Instead of being adorned with godliness and learning, Roman bishops appeared "in a theatrical dress . . . as if a horned mitre, a ring richly set in jewels, or a silver cross and other trifles, accompanied by idle display, constituted the spiritual government of a church, which can no more be separated from doctrine than any one of us can be separated from his own soul" (Comm. on 1 Tim. 3:2).

But it was the papacy which was chiefly responsible for the sad condition of the church and its bishops; and Calvin reserved his sharpest attacks for it. "The papacy itself is directly contrary to church order" (*Inst.*, IV, xii, 26), he held, and in seven chapters of the *Institutes* (IV, v-xi) Calvin offers biblical, historical, theological, and moral grounds for this judgment. In the light of prevailing conditions the claims of the papacy are so "utterly ridiculous and stupid" that he will leave "unsaid how much difference there is between the pope's chancery and a right ordering of the church" (*Inst.*, IV, vii, 26). The difference, in a word, is that between the machinations of the Evil One and the order of the Holy Spirit.

Calvin is baffled at the attempt "to bind Christ, the Holy Spirit, and the church to a place [Rome], so that whoever may rule there, even if he is a devil, is still considered the vicar of Christ and head of the church because it was once Peter's see." To Calvin this is "not only impious and insulting to Christ, but extremely absurd and alien to common sense." For, he reasons, "the Roman pontiffs either have for a long time been quite devoid of religion or have been its greatest enemies" (*Inst.*, IV, vii, 29). He assumes that the details of the degradation of the papacy are common knowledge, so he devotes his effort to answering the papal claims on the basis of Scripture and history. The papal usurpation of authority

> amounts to nothing less than an assault against heaven itself. It is an arrogance which hurls "Christ down from his heavenly throne," "robs God of his honor," and "disorders the whole symmetry of the church."
>
> The ordinary ministry which has been conceded to Rome, then, proves to be only a masquerade; her "order" is no longer to be regarded as a "lawful order." In her degeneration, we are once again presented with the "horrible and fearful spectacle" of a church in "filthy waste and lamentable dissipation." The decadence of Rome, no less than that of Jerusalem, induces in Calvin a revulsion which is very nearly physical.[28]

So certain is Calvin that a break with Rome is necessary if he is to remain faithful to Christ that the charge of being a schismatic does not bother him. He must leave the Roman fold in obedience to the Holy Spirit whom Christ has sent to give insight and comfort in the Word. Calvin believes that he is called to restore true order to the church and to point out the causes of confusion and disorder that are evident in the old ecclesiastical system.

> When we resist the papal priests, we do not violate God's covenant, that is, it is no departure from the order of the church, which ought ever to remain sacred and inviolable. We do not then, on account of men's vices, subvert the pastoral office and the preaching of the word; but we assail the men themselves, so that true order may be restored. ... We therefore boldly attempt to subvert the whole of the papacy, with the full confidence that we minimize nothing of true doctrine. ... Indeed, the order of the church, the preaching of the truth, and the very dignity of pastors, cannot stand unless the church is purged of its defilements and its filth removed.[29]

Calvin feels called to assist in that purging, and he is confident that the one who is effecting it is the head of the church through his Holy Spirit.

5. ORDER IN THE STATE

Throughout his adult life, from the time he wrote his commentary on Seneca's *De Clementia* in 1532 until his deathbed expression of hope for the Republic of Geneva in 1564, Calvin displayed a profound concern for civil government in both theory and practice. "It would be difficult or impossible," says McNeill, "to name another eminent theologian whose correspondence is so fraught with references to contemporary political issues," a fact often overlooked by readers interested only in theological or ecclesiastical data.[30] Most of the material in the chapter on civil government in the 1559 edition of the *Institutes* is in a similar chapter in the first edition of 1536, which indicates the consistency of Calvin's attention to the subject. As we noted, Fairbairn judges that Calvin was "greater as a legislator than a theologian" and that his politics was a "more perfect expression of the man than his theology." Elaborating on that he says:

> While [Calvin's] theology was less original and effective than his legislation or polity, yet he so construed the former as to make the latter its logical and indeed inevitable outcome. . . . [The theology and polity were] so organically connected that each lent strength to the other, the system to the church and the church to the system.[31]

A reading of Calvin to assess his emphasis on order, one aspect of which is ecclesiastical and civil government, leads to a similar judgment. There is indeed a "passion for order," evidenced by the Reformer's writings on civil government.[32]

a. The foundation of civil government

In seeking to build a holy community, a quest he viewed as obedience to the will of God, Calvin believed that both church and state are means ordained to that end. While the church has priority inasmuch as it deals with the inner, spiritual life and speaks God's word to the magistrate, the state is also God's instrument to create a decent society, indeed, a Christian civilization. These two governments are not antithetical but exist to serve God with the same end in view. Ministers of the Word of God serve the one government, but princes too are "ministers of God. . . . The Lord has declared his approval of their offices." Indeed, says Calvin, God has ordained them as well as the offices of the church, for "there are no powers except those ordained by God."

> No one ought to doubt that civil authority is a calling, not only holy and lawful before God, but also the most sacred and by far the most honorable of all callings in the whole life of mortal men (*Inst.*, IV, xx, 4).

Those who deny that the foundation of civil government in the ordination of God is compatible with Christ's teaching betray their ignorance and devilish arrogance. They would bring ruin to society if their views prevailed (*Inst.*, IV, xx, 5). Because all power is from God and every magistrate is ordained by God, resistance to or rejection of the magistrate is rebellion against God. Even wicked magistrates must be accepted as God's judgment on his people and not resisted, for the greatest of tyrannies still maintains some semblance of order in society (*Inst.*, IV, xx, 24-26; Comm. on Rom. 13:1-4). The only exception is if the ruler commands disobedience to God.

Ronald Wallace has shown Calvin's heavy emphasis on the divine command to render to all their due. In all human relationships this is the very order of nature ordained by God. "Mutual communication and subjection within the order of nature" are built into society in its creation and its re-creation after the Fall. Wallace cites dozens of passages from the commentaries and sermons to demonstrate the Reformer's unusual concern in this matter. No order is more important to human welfare than the state. Since God accomplishes his purposes with respect to the state through princes or magistrates who have received whatever gifts they have from the Holy Spirit, they are to rule as "God's deputies," as "ordained protectors of public innocence, modesty, decency, and tranquility," as "ministers and representatives of God" who "have their authority solely from him" (*Inst.*, IV, xx, 6, 22, 25; Comm. on Ps. 101). Mueller's list of Calvin's titles for rulers is impressive: "These titles, most of which Calvin traces to the Scriptures, suggest to him the divine ordering of magisterial and royal authority or, for that matter, of any other authority."[33]

b. The purpose of civil government

There are three reasons for civil government, according to Calvin: the fact of sin, God's goodness and grace, and the preservation of humanity.[34] If sin had not disrupted the original order, civil government would not have been necessary.

Had we remained in the state of natural integrity such as God first created, the order of justice would not have been necessary. For each would then have carried the law in his own heart, so that no constraint would have been needed to keep us in check. Each would be his own rule and with one mind we would do what is good and just. Hence, justice is a remedy of this human corruption. And wherever one speaks of human justice let us recognize that in it we have a mirror of our perversity, since it is by force that we are led to follow equity and reason.[35]

So absolutely necessary is government to curb disorder and maintain at least a semblance of the present "divinely established order" that Calvin calls those who "furiously strive to overturn it . . . insane and barbarous men" (*Inst.*, IV, xx, 1). The function of government "is no less than that of bread, water, sun, and air; indeed, its place of honor is far more excellent."

> For it does not merely see to it, as all these serve to do, that men breathe, eat, drink, and are kept warm, even though it surely embraces all these activities when it provides for their living together. It does not, I repeat, look to this only, but also prevents idolatry, sacrilege against God's name, blasphemies against his truth, and other public offenses against religion from arising and spreading among the people; it prevents the public peace from being disturbed; it provides that each man may keep his property safe and sound; that men may carry on blameless intercourse among themselves; that honesty and modesty may be preserved among men. In short, it provides that a public manifestation of religion may exist among Christians, and that humanity be maintained among men (*Inst.*, IV, xx, 3).

Calvin thus sees a multiple purpose in government: it serves to promote religion and to maintain order in society. The state benefits Christians and others even though a true understanding of the state is limited to Christians.

> The exact knowledge of the nature of the state is a part of faith. The state is not the object of natural knowledge but of revealed knowledge. Undoubtedly this is the reason that all the catechisms and confessions of faith edited by Calvin or inspired by him contain one or more paragraphs devoted to the state.[36]

Only the Christian rightly understands the state; yet it exists for all. McNeill comments, "Calvin the humanist survives in Calvin the theologian."[37]

c. Forms of civil government

As a realist, Calvin rejected the "false and foolish" notion that a modern state could be run under "the political system of Moses" rather than "the common law of nations" (*Inst.*, IV, xx, 14). Nor did he suppose that one form of government might serve the needs of all humankind.

> Divine providence has wisely arranged that various countries should be ruled by various kinds of government. For as elements cohere only in unequal proportion, so countries are best held together according to their own particular inequality (*Inst.*, IV, xx, 8).

One who takes God's will seriously is content with whatever form of government God has set over him. Kings, princes, queens, magistrates — all alike are ordained of God and are to be honored. It is an "idle pastime" for private citizens to debate the pros and cons of various types of governments, since they can do nothing about it anyway. Rather, they should submit themselves to the ordinance of God under which they are called to live. It is not easy to decide which form of government is best. A king may be bad, but a ruling clique may be worse, Calvin reasons, and rule by the people may lead to sedition. Nevertheless, human weakness makes it safer to have a number of people ruling rather than just one, so that there may be mutual admonition, help, and correction.[38] In the end Calvin is most comfortable with aristocracy, or a system which mixes aristocracy and democracy; this "far excels all others."

McNeill observes that the phrase "compounded of aristocracy and democracy" was set in the *Institutes* the year in which Calvin helped with the revision of the constitution of Geneva.

> By this constitution the four syndics who were the chief magistrates of the city were elected by the General Council of all citizens, but they were not nominated by it. A list of eight names was prepared by the Little Council and presented to the General Council which by vote elected four of the eight. As for the Little Council, it filled its ranks by co-optation, subject to the approval of the Council of Two Hundred, whose membership was also nominated by the Little Council. This is "aristocracy compounded with democracy," Geneva style.[39]

Calvin's ideal, as McNeill writes, is "an aristocracy of excellence, not of lineage, checked by the democracy of popular election. 'The best' men are chosen by popular vote from a restricted list of names selected by their experienced predecessors in office."

d. The limitations of the state: the right of rebellion

Nothing in Calvin's discussion of civil government is more startling than his position on resistance to tyranny. His abhorrence of disorder and his conviction that rulers hold office by the ordinance of God lie behind the many admonitions to accept one's political lot in life whatever that may be. But the obedience due rulers is not absolute like God's authority. Obeying a ruler must never lead to disobeying God. Christians owe such obedience to God that they should be ready to "suffer anything rather than turn aside from piety" (*Inst.*, IV, xx, 32).

Godlessness for Calvin means lawlessness, and lawlessness means disorder. Godless rulers therefore are guilty of disorder and should be removed. This is not the responsibility of ordinary citizens but of the lesser magistrates. Indeed, if the latter "wink at kings who violently fall upon and assault the lowly common folk . . . their dissimulation involves nefarious perfidy, because they dishonestly betray the freedom of the people, of which they know that they have been appointed protectors by God's ordinance" (*Inst.*, IX, xx, 31). Ordinary citizens must revere and obey their rulers, except when obedience to God is threatened. When occasion requires, they may beseech God for help. They are not to take things into their own hands, however, and resist even unjust rule. God will hear them; as he "delivered the people of Israel from the tyranny of Pharaoh through Moses; from the violence of Chusan, king of Syria, through Othniel; and from other servitudes through other kings or judges," he can deliver them today through those charged to watch the rule of kings.

Those "sent by God's lawful calling to carry out such acts, in taking up arms against kings, did not at all violate that majesty which is implanted in kings by God's ordination; but, armed from heaven," they did God's will (*Inst.*, IV, xx, 30). Thus God uses lesser magistrates and princes to overthrow tyranny and restore order to the state. "Let princes hear and be afraid," Calvin adds (*Inst.*, IV, xx, 31). Whatever their gifts, they have them from the Spirit of God, by whom they are obliged to use them in accordance with the divine intention.

6. ORDER IN THE LIFE OF THE CHRISTIAN

Calvin's conception of salvation as the restoration of order extends to an emphasis on order in the life of the Christian. Since sin is disorder, a sinful life apart from Christ is a disordered life. In Christ and through the Holy Spirit one can overcome disorder and be restored to what God intended for the world and those whom he has put into it to rule over it as his deputies.

a. The guidance of the Word

As his life is restored to order, the Christian is born of the Word of God and redirected by it. We saw that the Word is the principle of order God uses in the restoration of the world; thus it is the guide for the believer seeking to live for Christ and carry out God's will in daily life. By the work of God's Spirit in his heart the Christian comes to love and treasure the Word, allowing it to inform the mind, cleanse the affections, and strengthen the will. Even though we are at first adverse to the Word and want to follow our own way, the Spirit's influence enables us as Christians to let the Word mold our life. In his study, *Calvin's Doctrine of the Christian Life,* Wallace begins a section on "Discipline Under the Word" as follows:

> The Christian life is for Calvin a life lived under the influence and guidance of the Word of God. A Christian is one who gives himself up in a spirit of utter docility to the teaching of the Word, to be ruled and disciplined by its precepts, even though its teaching and discipline is alien to our own corrupt nature. Whether or not we subject ourselves thus to the Word of God is the sure test of whether or not we fear God himself.[40]

To despise God's Word, Wallace shows, is to despise God himself. Thus Calvin argues for the absolute necessity of Scripture as the blueprint of what life reshaped and restored to order by the Holy Spirit should be.

The Spirit for Calvin does not substitute for or supplement the Word, but rather authenticates it. The Word has no power in itself, unless the Spirit makes it efficacious so that it accomplishes God's purpose in the believer's life. Calvin stressed the work of the Holy Spirit much more than Luther; but both Calvin and Luther would agree that to separate his work from the Word of God would be dangerous and heretical "enthusiasm" which would add to the disorder in the world rather than correct it.

b. Life in the presence of God

Directed by the Word, the Christian makes God the center of life and seeks to live in his presence (*coram Deo* — to use the Reformers' familiar Latin phrase). The Word and the Spirit who gives it life function to make one conscious of God, so that like the Psalmist he meditates on God day and night. Living before the face of God comes naturally when Word and Spirit have their rightful place in the heart, and when life is reshaped by them.

I have shown elsewhere that the conception *coram Deo* is fundamental in the religious thought of Calvin, running through most of his thinking.[41] He always felt himself to be standing before the living God, so that whatever he did had religious significance. Nothing is remote from the Creator; every area of life was of concern to him. That is the meaning of providence, of the creation of humanity in the divine image, of Christian calling, daily blessings, prayer, the struggle against temptation, suffering, spiritual exercises, especially the hearing of the Word and the celebration of the sacraments, and, indeed, of salvation itself. The Spirit irradiates life and, relating its every aspect to the God who sustains it, gives it meaning and order.

c. The law of God

The Spirit gives life meaning and order through the Word; and the Word viewed as an expression of God's will is law. Law has a variety of meanings for Calvin, as Hesselink has shown — sometimes commandment, sometimes decalogue, but often much more. Calvin frequently equates law with covenant, using the two concepts "almost interchangeably."[42] Occasionally, law signifies the whole revelation of God.

> God is Lord and therefore the rule of his law is manifest everywhere — in providence, in the secret work of his Spirit in the reprobate, in the calling of his children, in their sanctification and restoration to his image, in his governance of nations, and finally in the coming of his kingdom. The scope of the work of the law is as broad as the activity of God himself. The law is not the gospel, but it serves the gospel; it is an indispensable part of the gospel. In a sense, it is prior to and more comprehensive than the gospel, for it was the mode of God's relationship to man prior to and apart from sin.
>
> The meaning of the law is thus not to be found in individual commandments, not even in the ten commandments, where the essence and sum of the law is expressed. The idea behind its accommodated form as it has come to us in the decalogue is that God might be preeminent. "We must not play with God!" is the constant reminder provided by the law. This was true of Adam before the fall. It is true of the man who has been reconciled to God in Christ. For the law was given on the one hand that God might maintain the right due to himself, and on the other hand that man might know that God ruled over him.[43]

Calvin distinguishes three "uses" of the law — pedagogical, political, and as a guide in the life of the Christian. But his "particular accent on the third use . . . has become a hallmark of Reformed theology,"[44] and plays a striking role in his understanding of order in the life of the Christian.

Saved from sin and reconciled to God, the grateful Christian desires to do the will of his heavenly Father. That will is expressed in myriad ways in Scripture and is made intelligible and appealing through the work of the Holy Spirit in the believer's heart. Thus while some see God's law as a burden cramping their life-style and dampening desire,

Calvin sees it as a blessing. What some resent as an uplifted finger of
the law with countless warnings, Calvin sees as the good counsel of
a friend. Some would shrug off the commandments of God as fetters
depriving them of freedom; Calvin says that this only subjects them
further to the bondage of sin and drives them further from the freedom
they want.

Given the human situation, Calvin argues that this natural resent-
ment towards the law of God is not strange, for God's law expresses
his will for human life, and our wills collide with that. It seems easier
to follow our own inclinations, more pleasant to give way to our own
desires. But a life of real tranquillity requires that we heed Scripture
when it calls upon us "to resign ourselves and all our possessions to
the Lord's will, and to yield to him the desires of our hearts to be
tamed and subjugated" (*Inst.*, III, vii, 8).

Human laws may limit us and take away some of the joy of living,
but God's law is through and through a blessing, protecting against
the onslaughts of evil and pointing out the way of peace and happiness. Thus Calvin understands the law as a positive help to the Christian pilgrim journeying through life. "Calvin seems to find it impossible
to find encomiums extravagant enough to describe the law. Like the
Psalmists he revels in describing its sufficiency and majesty, its simplicity and beauty, its profundity and power."[45]

While this "third use of the law" is the most pertinent for discussing
order in the life of the Christian, Calvin does not always neatly distinguish between the various functions of the law. Hesselink shows
that Calvin's appreciation for the comprehensiveness and the particulars of the law is so great that it is often difficult to discern the exact
usage the Reformer has in mind. Sometimes there appears to be a
combination of meanings, as in his discussion of the establishment of
the covenant at Sinai when God gave his people the law. "In the
deliverance of his people, God did not act the part of a beneficial
father merely for a day, but in the promulgation of the law he also
established his grace, that the hope of eternal life might continue
forever in the church" (Comm. on Ps. 111:9). Hesselink notes that
immediately after this statement Calvin "warns his readers that he is
not speaking here of the commandments abstractly conceived, for 'the
Holy Spirit refers especially to the promises which are in Christ, by
which God in gathering his chosen people to himself, begot them
again to eternal life.' "[46]

Calvin's reference to the Holy Spirit in the promulgation of the law
and its function in the life of Israel is not unusual. Hesselink demonstrates that for Calvin the law, like Scripture as a whole, is a dead

letter without the Holy Spirit.[47] With the Spirit, however, the law is mighty to convict of sin and to assist believers in the way of righteousness, so that they may be renewed according to the image of God.

> Newness of life consists in *knowledge* — not as though a simple and bare knowledge were sufficient, but he [Paul] speaks of the illumination of the Holy Spirit, which is lively and effectual, so as not merely to enlighten the mind by kindling it up with the light of truth, but transforming the whole man. And this is what he immediately adds, that we are *renewed after the image of God*. Now, the *image of God* resides in the whole of the soul, inasmuch as it is not the reason merely that is rectified, but also the will. Hence, too, we learn, on the one hand, what is the end of our regeneration, that is, that we may be made like God, and that his glory may shine forth in us; and, on the other hand, what is the image of God . . . , the rectitude and integrity of the whole soul, so that man reflects, like a mirror, the wisdom, righteousness, and goodness of God. . . . There is nothing more excellent at which the Colossians can aspire, inasmuch as this is our highest perfection and blessedness — to bear the image of God (Comm. on Col. 3:10).

d. The right use of this present world

As Calvin saw it, the world to come should ever be before our minds, and the meaning of this life is preparation for the next. "There is no middle ground between these two; either the world must become worthless to us or hold us bound by intemperate love of it" (*Inst.*, III, ix, 2). But although Calvin sets his eye on the world to come, he is deliberately inconsistent in his argument, adopting a moderate position in the end. Whereas "many" would "seek an excuse for the intemperance of the flesh in its use of external things, and . . . would meanwhile pave the road to licentious indulgence," others are "far too severe" in their negative attitude towards material goods (*Inst.*, III, x, 1). Calvin's position between these two extremes is based, he believes, on sound biblical principles outlined in two chapters in the *Institutes* (III, ix, x).

The most striking feature of Calvin's doctrine is his simultaneous renunciation and acceptance of the world. There are frequent reminders that this world and all that is in it has been affected by sin. He calls this world a sepulcher, a prison, misery, a place of exile which should be despised and trampled under foot. This is not our eternal home, though its glitter and tinsel easily blind us to eternal verities and give us a false sense of values. While it might thus appear that "contempt for the present life" (an expression Calvin uses with approval) is his position, we must bear in mind that these negative assessments are repeatedly said to be by "comparison with the life to come." And Calvin's recognition that this world is God's creation, already redeemed in Christ and in which his Spirit is operating, gives him a positive attitude towards the world. The Christian is called to keep in tension a renunciation of the world and an acceptance of and dominance in it.

In accepting the world as God's good gift, Calvin stimulated an active and aggressive temper which seeks to dominate the world and use its resources. The contempt believers feel for this present world should not beget hatred of God's magnificent creation. Although it abounds in misery, it has many exquisite blessings, and unless we see God's goodness in these we are ungrateful. The idea that we must limit our use of creation to only those things which are necessary Calvin calls "far too severe" (*Inst.*, III, x, 1). God is also the giver of those things which bring pleasure.

> The use of God's gifts is not wrongly directed when it is referred to that end to which the Author himself created and destined them for us, since he created them for our good, not for our ruin. . . . Now if we ponder to what end God created food, we shall find that he meant not only to provide for necessity but also for delight and good cheer. Thus the purpose of clothing, apart from necessity, was comeliness and decency. In grasses, trees, and fruits, apart from their various uses, there is beauty of appearance and pleasantness of odor? What? Did he not so distinguish colors as to make some more lovely than others? What? Did he not endow gold and silver, ivory and marble, with a loveliness that renders them more precious than other metals or stones? Did he not, in short, render many things attractive to us, apart from their necessary use? Away, then, with that inhuman philosophy which, while conceding only a necessary use of creatures, not only malignantly deprives us of the lawful fruit of God's beneficence but cannot be practiced unless it robs a man of all his senses and degrades him to a block (*Inst.*, III, x, 2, 3).

Moderation with thanksgiving is the manner in which God's people should avail themselves of his gifts. The constant danger is self-indulgence.

> Where is your thanksgiving if you so gorge yourself with banqueting or wine that you either become stupid or are rendered useless for the duties of piety and of your calling? Where is your recognition of God if your flesh boiling over with excessive abundance into vile lust infects the mind with its impurity so that you cannot discern anything that is right and honorable? Where is our gratefulness toward God for our clothing if in

the sumptuousness of our apparel we both admire ourselves and despise others, if with its elegance and glitter we prepare ourselves for shameless conduct? Where is our recognition of God if our minds be fixed upon the splendor of our apparel? For many so enslave all their senses to delights that the mind lies overwhelmed. Many are so delighted with marble, gold, and pictures that they become marble, they turn, as it were, into metals and are like painted figures. The smell of the kitchen or the sweetness of its odors so stupefies others that they are unable to smell anything spiritual (*Inst.*, III, x, 3).

e. Sanctification and the glory of God

The key to the right ordering of life is self-denial and longing only for the blessing of God. To deny oneself is not only a negative attitude and practice but a positive giving of oneself to God and one's fellows, inasmuch as the Christian does not belong to himself but to his Lord. Longing only for the blessing of God curbs wrong ambition and teaches the Christian to accept his lot in life with patience, tranquillity, endurance perhaps, and joy. Dakin comments on how this doctrine took effect in church history: Calvin's teaching "was not a whit behind Stoicism in inculcating fortitude, but in addition it had the dynamic of faith in the living God, a faith possible even to the common man. It was thus no aristocratic ethic but a system of life which could be made to run in the highways and byways of the workaday world."[48]

The purpose of such disciplined living was growth in grace, an emphasis for which Calvin and the churches influenced by him have been noted. Calvin's overriding concern is the glorification of God, and this is best effected when his children become molded into his image. The prominence Calvin gives the doctrine of sanctification is matched in no other major writer of his time. Prayer, meditation on the future life, cross-bearing, the proclamation of the Word in preaching, teaching, and the sacraments — all are intended to serve the end of growth into the likeness of Christ.

The key to understanding Calvin's discussion on the Christian life in Book III of the *Institutes* — the place where one is best able to read the heart of Calvin — is the doctrine of the Holy Spirit. It is the Spirit who takes the things of Christ and makes them known to God's children, fashioning them according to his will by his almighty power.

The beginning of right living is spiritual, where the inner feeling of the mind is unfeignedly dedicated to God for the cultivation of holiness and righteousness. But no one in this earthly prison of the body has sufficient strength to press on with due eagerness, and weakness so weighs down the greater number that, with wavering and limping and even creeping along the ground, they move at a feeble rate. Let each one of us, then, proceed according to the measure of his puny capacity and set out upon the journey we have begun. No one shall set out so inauspiciously as not daily to make some headway, though it be slight. Therefore, let us not cease so to act that we may make some unceasing progress in the way of the Lord. . . . Let us look toward our mark with sincere simplicity and aspire to our goal; not fondly flattering ourselves, nor excusing our own evil deeds, but with continuous effort striving toward this end: that we may surpass ourselves in goodness until we attain to goodness itself. It is this, indeed, which through the whole course of life we seek and follow. But we shall attain it only when we have cast off the weakness of the body and are received into full fellowship with him (*Inst.*, III, vi, 5).

We have seen how Calvin's interest in the dual theme of order and the Holy Spirit is important for understanding his theology and his contribution to the faith of the church. That dual theme often becomes one, for Calvin points to order as a gift of the Spirit and sometimes offers it as evidence of the Spirit's presence.

Appearing near the beginning of a new period in history, Calvin took up the concept of order, which had inspired and dominated medieval thought from Augustine to Bernard to Aquinas to late medieval humanism, and made it a "fundamental category" of his system.[49] Through sin the "whole order of creation was inverted" (Comm. on Eph. 4:24); by the grace of the Holy Spirit order is restored. This, in sum, is Calvin's view of history. He contended against both the Anabaptists and Rome because of the disorder that he believed they had brought into the church. What he labored to achieve is a church and society in which that which ought to be, as he understood it, would become a reality.

There is nothing wholly new in Calvin's theology except his remarkable ability to see things clearly and to put them together well. He would have been the last to claim that he was teaching new doctrine: it was the ancient faith of the church, the faith of Christ and his disciples, that he expounded. No innovator, Calvin was rather able to "integrate . . . and synthesize the ideas of his predecessors, and draw out their implications, with a systematic precision which in the world of Reformation theology was entirely new, and proved extraordinarily fruitful."[50]

We might illustrate our thesis further by elaborating some of Calvin's particular doctrines, or his views on church discipline, or his belief that there should be order in theology. But we shall instead reiterate Calvin's striking emphasis on the Holy Spirit, an emphasis often explicitly associated with order and always implicit when he mentions order. The prominence of the Holy Spirit in Calvin's writings leads John Dillenberger to call the Spirit "the pivot upon which everything turns."

> For Calvin every apprehension of God depends upon the activity of the Spirit, upon the way in which God becomes alive and lively to the depths of man. At the edges and limits of Calvin's thought, the Spirit takes over. The Spirit is so self-evidently the pivot of his apprehensions that it frequently operates as a *deus ex machina*.[51]

Whether Calvin is justified in his emphasis on order and the Holy Spirit can be determined only by an appeal to Scripture. That task is beyond the limits of our purpose. Calvin's emphasis on the Holy Spirit might soon appear justified in view of the extensive biblical materials on the subject. His constant use of the category of order might appear to be an imposition on the scriptural revelation, but this is an involved question and not easily answered. It is sufficient for us to note Calvin's use of the concept and its incorporation into the faith of the church. Its earlier use does not detract from the significance of his contribution, for his association of order with the Holy Spirit was an emphasis the church had not clearly seen before, which would become part of the legacy of a large part of the people of God.

Chapter 15

Experiential Christianity

A major task of the sixteenth-century Reformation and Counter-Reformation was defining the faith of the church. Fresh study of Scripture and of earlier doctrinal tradition was fundamental in this endeavor. Debates between the confessions provided the atmosphere and motivation for an abundance of theological activity such as the world had not seen even during the fourth- and fifth-century christological controversies. The recent invention of printing made it possible for the Reformers and their opponents to disseminate their tracts rapidly and widely. Some of Luther's writings were reprinted several times in the year of their appearance.

The quantity and quality of sixteenth-century theology has given it a pride of place which has been both bane and blessing to the church in later generations. The creeds of the church — to mention only one type of theological writing — summarized the faith of the believing community and became a rich legacy which gave guidance and inspiration to multitudes in succeeding generations. But the excellence of the Reformation literature and the normative place given it served to inhibit further creative labor and endowed that writing with a prestige which rivaled that normally ascribed to the Word of God.

Even the most tradition-bound adherents of the confessions, however, acknowledge the need for continuous theological endeavor. No creed or theological treatise says the last word. John Robinson's oft-quoted remark, "The Lord has more truth yet to break forth out of his holy Word," was made in response to the situation of churches of the Reformation in the seventeenth century. The Lutherans failed to advance "beyond what Luther saw," said Robinson, "while the Calvinists stick fast where they were left by that great man of God, who yet saw not all things." And in the late nineteenth century Abraham Kuyper remarked that the Reformed churches did not err when they wrote confessions, but when they stopped writing them. So at the desk, in the lecture hall, and in the pulpit theological activity continued.

Moreover, the faith is challenged in every period. So while the Reformation remains the greatest period of theological productivity in the history of the church, it did not in fact quash all further effort. Creeds and other Reformation writings were honored, but the church continued to reflect on its faith and develop it further; and if its efforts were not as spectacular as those of Luther and company, they were no less important. To be sure, part of the post-Reformation story is one of retrogression rather than progress, but there were also significant areas which received their richest treatment in this period, and we shall focus on two of these. The first, Christian experience, has as much to do with how the faith is apprehended as with specific doctrine; the second, eschatology, we have already touched on in connection with Augustine, but it deserves further attention because of new insights worked out in the twentieth century.

1. RELIGIOUS EXPERIENCE

The biblical account of God's dealings with his people is a story of religious experience. Scripture is the telling of that tale. In the Old Testament Abraham is called a friend of God (Isa. 41:8); the Lord "used to speak to Moses face to face, as a man speaks to his friend" (Exod. 33:11); David communed with God and was said to be "a man after God's own heart" (1 Sam. 13:14); the prophets claimed to be spokesmen for God; indeed, Israel's entire history is set forth as the experience of the chosen people with the living Lord. He had drawn them into covenant with himself in order that he might bless them as a nation and make them a blessing to others. That is the story of the Old Testament.

The New Testament completes the story of the Old. It tells of the personal visitation of God with humanity in human flesh. In the person of Jesus Christ God became man, as truly man as anyone can be. The reason for his incarnation was the salvation of humankind through the revelation he brought, the atonement he offered for sin, and his triumph over death and the powers of darkness. In Jesus Christ humanity has had the most intimate conceivable relationship with God.

To those earliest Christians whose experience we read in the New Testament, this is the fact which makes all else in life meaningful. But that experience was not limited to Christ's earthly sojourn; it continued after the ascension. That is the meaning of Pentecost, the fulfilment of Christ's promise to be with his disciples "always, to the close of the age" (Matt. 28:20). The New Testament demonstrates that the disciples' "experience of the risen Christ was just as real as their experience of the historical Christ, and it never occurred to them to distinguish between the two."[1] This is the secret of the boldness of Peter and John (Acts 4:13); of the ministry of Paul (Gal. 2:20); of the strength of the church in every age. Before his ascension Jesus had told his friends that he would not leave them alone and desolate, but that he would return to them after his departure in the person of the Holy Spirit (John 14:16-18). They were to remain in Jerusalem until they had received the gift of the promised Spirit (Acts 1:4), and then they were to begin their witness to the world.

The story of the church since the apostolic age is not materially different from that which preceded it. It is still the story of the risen Lord in the midst of his church, saying "Fear not" (Rev. 1:17, 20). This fellowship with Christ strengthened the martyrs, comforted the discouraged, and made the faith real to multitudes. One reads of broad Christian experience in the *Confessions* of St. Augustine, in Bonaventura's seraphic vision, in the religious orders, and in the sects and mainstream of the church. It lies behind the ringing challenge of the youthful Athanasius in *The Incarnation of the Word of God,* and behind the ecstasy which made Aquinas lay down his pen with the remark, "All that I have written seems to me like so much straw compared to what I have seen and what has been revealed to me." It accounts for Luther's escape from despair and Wesley's strange heart-warming on Aldersgate Street. In every age men and women have been touched by God in experiences which have shaped or altered their lives.

But if Christian experience is so important in its ramifications, and indeed so fundamental for an adequate apprehension of Christian faith, it has received slight attention in most theological writing. For the most part, experience is recognized, and that is all. And much mainline theology does not even do that: it avoids experience altogether except for the intellectual dimension of it. The leading theological traditions of the West, where most theology has been written, are almost exclusively intellectual, thus narrowing the range of experience drastically. Augustine might be suggested as counterevidence to this general rule, but for all the appeal of his writing, it too is an exercise in reason.

That is not strange, for theology by definition is rational discourse about God, which means that reason must be given a functional priority. But what happens when reason is not limited to functional priority but is given priority, period? Even more, what happens when reason is the only human faculty in which theology seems to be interested and to which it makes its appeal? Then theology becomes intellectualistic or rationalistic, and it does not do justice to the people or faith it seeks to serve. Theology sells itself short when it concerns itself with only a part of human experience instead of the whole.

The theologians of the church took over Aristotle's employment of sense and reason as the instruments for apprehending reality. Their thinking was greatly influenced by his conception of man as a rational animal. Aquinas' acceptance of Aristotle's theory of knowledge eventually had a determining effect on theological method. Moreover, the heavy rationalism of Descartes' philosophical method confirmed and intensified the way the faith of the church was conceived, written, and taught.[2]

Even Calvin, who sought to do justice to the whole person in his theology, tended to intellectualize the faith. To be sure, he affirmed that the act of faith "is more of the heart than of the brain" and insisted that "the Word of God is not received by faith if it flits about in the top of the brain" and does not take "root in the depth of the heart" (*Inst.*, III, ii, 8, 36). He struggled to avoid arid scholasticism, and his biblical-practical method was intended to do justice to the whole person and to all of human existence. But others could later use Calvin's strenuous mental activity and the well-organized body of doctrine he bequeathed to the church to intellectualize the life of faith and thereby delimit the range of experience believers might otherwise enjoy.

Beginning with Theodore Beza, Reformed theology after Calvin exhibited increasing tendencies towards intellectualism and rationalism, which produced imposing systems of theology and spiritually impoverished believers. A theological method prevailed which reveled in logic and speculation; and this theology penetrated into congregational life, so that in pulpit and classroom people were fed a steady diet of right doctrine framed in carefully reasoned propositions which fit into a system that was logically correct. The exalted place given reason and the widespread fear of mysticism drove feeling under a shadow, and multitudes left the church. Nor did Lutheranism escape these tendencies. Luther himself had repudiated rationalistic late medieval scholasticism, but his church, under the influence of Melanchthon and others, soon moved back in the direction of rationalism.

Other trends have been at work in the church, however; and one of these is the desire to enrich spiritual life by recognizing and ministering to a broader range of human experience than reason alone. This can be seen in post-Reformed Puritanism and Pietism, in Methodism and movements within the Roman Catholic Church, in the Evangelical awakening and Existentialism, and in the Liberation Theology of our day.

2. MYSTICISM AND ACTIVISM

Cotton Mather is an example of American Puritanism who was highly gifted intellectually (he graduated from Harvard College at 15 and was a prodigious author) and also unusually sensitive to God's presence in all of human experience. God was more relevant to Mather than breathing. Not surprisingly, one finds in his work an emphasis on the place of the Holy Spirit in the life of the Christian. He accepted without question predestination, the work of Christ, justification, and other doctrines of the objective side of the faith, but his accent was on "experiential religion," the Christian's spiritual states.

While Scripture was the norm of all Puritan religion, the attention to personal piety and the work of the Holy Spirit in Mather's ministry was so great that he can be said to have "led an emotional life that swung unevenly between conventional piety and direct encounters with the Holy Spirit," even though he resisted Quakerism.[3] Assent to orthodox doctrine was insufficient in Mather's view; there must also be daily communion with God and evidence in one's life of the transforming power of the Holy Spirit. Thus Mather carried Calvin's insistence on pure doctrine, discipline, and a godly life one step further; in addition, there had to be visible proof of the possession of faith.[4] None could be members of the church "except such as were visible subjects of our Lord Jesus Christ."[5]

Mather combined in himself two well-defined streams of experiential Christianity: one which emphasized mystical fellowship with God, contemplation, inwardness, prayer, spiritual elation, and joy in the Lord, and the other which stressed the desirability of doing God's will in all of life. Both the mystical and activistic strain sought to bring the human will and feeling as well as the intellect to the surface in experience, even though the accents differed. The longest and most thorough development of these was in the Netherlands.

The antecedents of the mystical strain of Dutch Reformed experiential theology lay earlier than the Reformation. A representative is Jean de Taffin, chaplain of William the Silent, Prince of Orange. Taffin had no disagreements with the creeds and theology of the church, but he insisted that these were only means to experience walking with God from day to day. One should "feel" the reality of fellowship with God through the Holy Spirit. It is good to know the creeds; it is better to have an experiential knowledge of God, to "feel that he loves us," as he put it.

F. Ernest Stoeffler says that for Taffin "the main source of ultimate certainty was not a series of reasoned convictions gathered from the

Word, as it was to some of the Puritans. Nor was it a theologically based trust in a divine act of the imputation of the righteousness of Christ to the sinner. It was founded upon the experience of 'holy affections and desires.' " Stoeffler quotes Taffin: "If we have these motions, these holy affections and desires before mentioned, let us not doubt that we have the Holy Spirit dwelling in us and consequently that we have also faith."[6] It would be mistaken to regard this as pure subjectivism, inasmuch as Taffin appeals constantly to Scripture; but his real interest is the testimony of Scripture confirmed in experience.

As might be expected, some carried the emphasis on feeling too far. For them intense religious experience of an emotional or of a mystical nature became the desired goal. They sought *gelukzaligheid* and *godzaligheid* — untranslatable Dutch words to describe the state of bliss experienced when one is caught up into fellowship with God. Those so favored, it was said, feel the perfect contentment, joy, and peace that God gives his children in this life as a down payment of what is to come in heaven. For God has already raised us up with Christ and "made us sit with him in heavenly places, that in the ages to come he might show the immeasurable riches of his grace toward us in Christ Jesus" (Eph. 2:7). "What no eye has seen, nor ear heard, nor the heart of man conceived, what God has prepared for those who love him, God has revealed to us through the Spirit" (1 Cor. 2:9).

This revelation through the Spirit, which involves the whole person, is the greatest proof that God is a gracious father to his children. Through self-denial, the mortification of the flesh, and rigorous spiritual discipline the believer can rise above this world and enjoy fellowship with God. But the attempt to rise above this world led to a difficulty for Dutch pietism. S. Van der Linde has shown that a weakness of leading spirits of the Dutch experiential theology was their negative attitude towards this world. In D. G. à Brakel, A. Comrie, and the later writings of W. Teellinck we find a one-sided emphasis on the spiritual life. Creation is considered unimportant, hardly worthy of being taken up in the service of the Creator. Such thinking led these persons to associate creation with sin, as though God has deserted this world and we have to find him apart from it.[7] While this movement claimed all of life for God, many of its leaders forgot that God's spirituality and holiness do not make him stand over against his creation. By encouraging world rejection, at least in some degree, the Dutch "later Reformation" furthered secularization.

The activistic stream of Dutch experiential theology stressed *doing* the will of the Lord. Great attention was given to the law as an expression of that will, and piety was conceived of as thinking, saying, and doing what is right before God. This emphasis came to be known as "precisionism," and its ideal is eloquently expressed in the funeral eulogy of a Reformed divine:

> He was a righteous or upright man, who possessed a large measure of the image of God. He did what was right, for the right reasons, according to the right rules, in a right manner, and towards the right end.[8]

A representative of this tendency was William Ames, who left England in 1609 to teach in the Netherlands. There he wrote his *Marrow of Theology,* whose first sentence defines theology as "the teaching of living for God," an idea he had inherited from Calvin.[9] Ames tries to show that theology should not be as concerned with statements *about* God as with knowledge of how to live for him. Contemporary orthodoxy, which Ames encountered in his colleagues J. Maccovius and S. Lubbertus at the University of Franeker as well as in F. Gomarus and others at Leiden, held that the task of theology is to make correct statements about God and salvation. Logic and speculation were seen as important sources for theology, and theology had come to seem remote from life. Ames went back to Calvin, whose interest he saw as practical and existential living for God.

In developing his thought, Ames sought to meet the needs of his day. In doing so he became anti-intellectualistic, anti-metaphysical, and anti-speculative. True religion, he held, is not found at the end of a syllogism but it must be based on Scripture alone and found in Jesus Christ. Clever reasoning and speculation are repudiated: the devil is the greatest metaphysician. Ames scorned the philosophical proofs for God's existence. He held that since natural theology is impossible, reason must be guided by faith, which gets its materials from revelation alone.[10] Similarly for ethics: in Scripture one finds the norm by which to live. Philosophical attempts to find that norm are ridiculous and lamentable. Convictions arrived at by natural reason must be validated by Scripture if they are to be normative in the life of the Christian. From Scripture we learn that our goal is not to live comfortably or happily but well, that is, according to God's will.

To live well, Ames argued, is to live as a Christian. This is possible solely by grace. Sin has so weakened the will and corrupted human nature that the Holy Spirit alone can liberate and move the will rightly, inducing it to accept God's grace and enabling us to understand Scripture spiritually instead of only literally. These two kinds of knowledge, literal and spiritual, differ in kind, not only in degree.[11]

Ames sees theology as consisting of two parts, faith and observance. Faith he defines (much like Calvin) as a "resting of the heart on God."[12] Faith exceeds human capacities: it is a decision made possible by the Holy Spirit. Presupposing a knowledge of the gospel, faith "is by no means a mere act of the intellect." Rather, it embraces the whole person including the will.[13] It is choosing to trust God and to live one's whole life for him.

This accent on the importance of the will in making a decision to live for God Ames carries out consistently. It is reflected in his understanding of what theology is: "Since this life is the spiritual work of the whole man, in which he is brought to enjoy God and to act according to his will, and since it certainly has to do with man's will, it follows that the first and proper subject of theology is the will."[14] The will is involved in conversion; it is found "first and most appropriately" in sanctification; and it is "the principal subject of observance" or "obedience," which is the crucial thing commanded by God.[15] Ames' treatment of observance includes such matters as conscience, temptation and its resistance, prayer, and one's duty to God and man. Ames differed from the more mystical pietists in his insistence that while love includes joy and satisfaction, the emphasis is on doing God's will.[16]

While we may thus distinguish the mystical and activistic streams of experiential theology, the two were frequently seen in the same persons as aspects of a more fundamental desire for godliness. Taffin stressed joy in the Lord but without intending to neglect precisionism. Ames was chiefly concerned with the latter: his practical, antimetaphysical inclination led to a moral activism. Others reveled in the contemplation of the beauty, being, and grace of God. In Cotton Mather or his Dutch contemporary William à Brakel, there is such a combination of the two that it is difficult to tell where the heavier emphasis lies. But whatever the emphasis, these persons believed heartily that the Christian faith was relevant to the whole range of human experience and that theology should speak not only to the intellect but also to the affections and the will.

Jonathan Edwards, the Wesleys and Methodism, the Otterbein/Brethren tradition in Germany and America, Schleiermacher, Kierkegaard, modern existentialism, the charismatic movement — all are witnesses to the legitimacy of experiential Christianity. If extra-rational experience has a rightful place in theology, the Heidelberg Catechism and Utrecht's first professor Gijsbert Voetius were right to stress the utilitarian, experiential character of the faith.[17] The Tennents and Frelinghuysen were correct in their abhorrence of formal religion and "presumptuous security" in the churches of the American middle colonies.[18] Coleridge did not err in rejecting the mere intellectual acceptance of dogma.[19] Revivalism was not all bad.

All these would have agreed with Ames: "it is self-evident that theology is not a speculative discipline but a practical one."[20] Reason was not denied — all those mentioned in the preceding paragraph were intellectuals — but it was believed to be only one aspect of the total human experience, and experience was seen to be greater than any intelligible formulation of it. We are not only thinking beings; we are believing, acting, willing, doubting, suffering, loving, fearing, and rejoicing beings. In order to perceive this "wider field," Richard Niebuhr argues, "we must awaken to it" in our total experience.[21] He cites Paul's appeal to his "busy and disputatious parishioners" in Corinth that they not live "restricted" lives, but that they "widen" their hearts (2 Cor. 6:11-13).[22]

Paul's advice that the Corinthians broaden their concerns was no isolated injunction. He had informed them that the best things in life are revealed by God's Spirit (1 Cor. 2:4-16) and that they should be wary about the pretensions of human wisdom (1 Cor. 1:18 – 2:5). He had mentioned their joy, their grief, hope, faith, pride, generosity, sense of decency and shame, integrity, sympathy, friendship, anxiety, and spiritual gifts. His eulogy of love (1 Cor. 13) makes his appreciation of extra-rational experience even clearer.

What Paul wrote to the Corinthians, he wrote to others also, demonstrating his belief that the totality of human experience is the field of operation for the Spirit of God. Paul had learned that from the Old Testament and the revelation which he received from his Lord. No event involving persons is insignificant, but each has a place in the eternal purpose God has worked out in his Son (Eph. 3:11), a purpose so comprehensive and personal that even birds and flowers and grass are included in it. Because this is so, God's children may rest assured that their heavenly Father cares for them in all of life (Matt. 6:26-34). Aware of that teaching of Jesus, Paul drew out its implications for receiving, comprehending, and proclaiming the faith.

Chapter 16

Eschatology: The Kingdom, the Spirit, and the End

The faith of the church has always included a belief that certain events will come to pass in the future. The future is connected with the past and the present as a part of the framework of time God created for the drama of redemption. Eschatology and history therefore are correlative from the biblical perspective. Augustine gave this issue special treatment in *The City of God,* written soon after the Goths under Alaric sacked and occupied Rome in A.D. 410. Augustine argued for a long view of history which discerns God at work in it, shaping events, redeeming history, and leading it forward to that day when Christ will appear as judge and make history's meaning clear to all.

The faith that God is the Lord of history and that the future belongs to him has been the comfort of the faithful down the centuries and is written into the creeds and liturgy of the church. But although this area of doctrine was rather thoroughly thought through by the early church, there has been a new understanding and appreciation for eschatology in the twentieth century. After a period of drought during which the major theologies gave little attention to the subject and important aspects of eschatological doctrine were denied or treated as myths to be cast off, interest was suddenly revived about the time of World War I. Eschatology became the central concern for many.

The trauma of the war put an abrupt end to earlier optimism and gave rise to a sense of crisis in which churchmen felt themselves confronted here and now by ultimate issues, by God in mercy and in judgment. One sees this in the early writings of Karl Barth and in much post-war literature.[1] The "Theology of Crisis" was born out of this new mood. What is the meaning of history? Is there a divine purpose in history? What does the future hold? The depression, the rise of the totalitarian states, the "revolution of nihilism," and World War II heightened interest in these questions.

The consequence of all these assaults on earlier certainties was that a large volume of fresh literature on eschatology was produced and the meaning of the word was radically altered. No longer did eschatology refer to a "short and harmless chapter" at the conclusion of Christian dogmatics, as Barth described the earlier treatment; it now came to mean God's mighty shaking of the foundations of our social, political, economic, and ecclesiastical as well as personal lives. Eschatology presents the themes of the ever-present Christ, reigning, judging, and coming in the fulness of his power and Holy Spirit. Nineteenth-century liberal theology had understood the kingdom of God as a social and ethical value which came in the heart of the individual believer; now it was seen as the dynamic rule of him who was dead and is alive again and whose second coming will mean the end of present world history. Eschatology no longer meant distant future, but our confrontation with ultimate issues here and now.

1. THE COMING OF THE KINGDOM

The present realities of Christ, the Holy Spirit, the powers of evil, and heaven and hell are always before us in the Bible. Since God appeared in the person of Jesus Christ, who accomplished redemption, a new age has dawned. With the atonement, resurrection, and ascension of Christ, and the giving of the promised Holy Spirit, the kingdom of God has come and the powers of the new age are here. We are living in the last days, says the New Testament (Acts 2:17).

When John the Baptist announced that the kingdom of God was at hand (Matt. 3:2) and Jesus went through Galilee with his disciples teaching and preaching the gospel of the kingdom (Matt. 4:23; 13:11; Luke 8:1; 9:2), the expressions "kingdom," "kingdom of God," and "kingdom of heaven" were not new to the covenant community. Daniel had used such language in interpreting Nebuchadnezzar's dream: the image of gold, silver, iron, and clay which was destroyed by the stone "cut out by no human hand" was a succession of world kingdoms. The stone was "a kingdom which shall never be destroyed"; set up by God, it "shall stand forever" (Dan. 2:36-44). In a later dream of his own Daniel saw "one like a son of man" come with the clouds of heaven and stand before the "Ancient of Days":

To him was given dominion and glory and kingdom,
That all peoples, nations, and languages should serve him;
His dominion is an everlasting dominion which shall not pass away,
And his kingdom one that shall not be destroyed (Dan. 7:13f.).

The concept dramatized in these visions reached back into Israel's history beyond the time when the people demanded a king so that they might be like the nations around them. With the establishment of visible monarchy the king was to represent God, but the dismal reality was that most kings failed miserably to reflect this theocratic ideal. Pious souls awaited a better day when God would intervene directly to establish a new order marked by his reign among his people. Even during the dark days of captivity this hope was not quenched. Kept fresh by prophets and the miserable circumstances in which the people found themselves, it was quickened and developed into the messianic expectation so notable in late Old Testament Judaism.

The coming of the kingdom in Christ was the "kingly self-assertion of God, of his coming to the world in order to reveal his royal majesty, power, and right."[2] It meant that "the initial stage of the great drama of the history of the end" had begun;[3] that the Messiah had appeared (Matt. 3:11; 16:16); that Satan and his kingdom had been overthrown (Matt. 12:28; Luke 11:20); that salvation has come (Luke 1:69; 2:3ff.; 3:6; 4:21; 19:9); that judgment has entered into the world (John 5:22, 27; 9:39; 12:31; 16:8); that the law has been fulfilled (Matt. 5:17; Rom. 8:4); that the church has been established as a sign of the kingdom (Matt. 16:18f.);[4] that the end of history has already come proleptically in Jesus Christ;[5] and that the Holy Spirit has been given as the first-fruits and guarantee of the salvation eventually to be realized fully (Rom. 8:23; 2 Cor. 1:22; 5:5; Eph. 1:14).

The blessings attending the coming of the kingdom are so great that the "least in the kingdom of heaven" is greater than any prophet of the old covenant, including the greatest of them all, John the Baptist (Matt. 11:11). For the knowledge of redemption in Christ and the other gifts imparted with the coming of the Spirit gave the disciples a privileged status unknown before. Now that the Messiah has come, the "ruler of this world [has been] cast out" (Matt. 12:31), and the kingdom of God has been established. Those who are subject to him have been made "a kingdom and priests to God" and are promised that they shall reign on earth (Rev. 5:10; cf. 1:6).

2. ANTICIPATION OF THE END

Theology has come to see that when the New Testament ascribes the "end" to Christ, this is a very important eschatological consideration. In the Old Testament the "end" as that which gives meaning to the whole was always future: Israel looked ahead to the day God would redeem his people. The coming of Christ changed that: the "end" in the sense of redemptive history is Jesus Christ, who has already appeared. Oscar Cullmann remarks that "what Paul says in Rom. 10:4 concerning the law, that Christ is its 'end,' may be applied to all features of the redemptive process; its 'end' is the Christ who died on the cross and rose. While the 'end' was previously only expectation, it is now acknowledged as fulfillment."[6] In the vision of John, Christ announces that he is the Alpha and the Omega, the first and the last, the beginning and the end (Rev. 21:6; 22:13). Paul describes the warnings against immorality in Israel as written for the benefit of his contemporaries "upon whom the end of the ages has come" (1 Cor. 10:11).

The early Christian community was convinced that in Jesus Christ and his Spirit the meaning of the world and human existence has been revealed. The world which Christ created and redeemed and human existence which he sustains do *not* have meaning in themselves. They exist for Christ; he is their purpose, their "end." From the beginning God had a purpose which was to be realized in Christ (Eph. 1:4-12; 3:11). In his eternal purpose God has determined the "end," Jesus Christ, the "lamb without blemish or spot," who "was destined before the foundation of the world but was made manifest at the end of the times" for the sake of believers (1 Pet. 1:20). After his life on earth Christ sent the promised Spirit, whose coming was a pledge that at some time yet to come he would complete the redemption which had already been achieved.

Paul, who repeatedly mentions the guarantee of the Spirit, tells the Philippians that he is sure that "he who began a good work in you will bring it to completion at the day of Jesus Christ" (Phil. 1:6), that is, at the end of history when Christ will judge all. Even now the Holy Spirit is the first-fruits (Rom. 8:23) or guarantee (2 Cor.1:22; 5:5; Eph. 1:14) of what is yet to come. As salvation has been achieved in Christ and is also a future inheritance "to be revealed in the last time" (1 Pet. 1:5), so the kingdom of heaven is a present reality whose full manifestation will occur in the future (Luke 21:31). "The one great kingdom of the future has become present," Ridderbos writes; "the future, as it were, penetrates into the present."[7]

Cullmann writes similarly:

> It is already the time of the end, and yet is not *the* end. This tension finds expression in the entire theology of Primitive Christianity. The present period of the Church is the time between the decisive battle, which has already occurred, and the "Victory Day." To anyone who does not take clear account of this tension, the entire New Testament is a book with seven seals, for this tension is the silent presupposition that lies behind all that it says. This is the only dialectic and the only dualism that is found in the New Testament. It is not the dialectic between this world and the Beyond; moreover, it is not that between time and eternity; it is rather *the dialectic of present and future.*[8]

3. THE END AS THE DETERMINATION OF THE PRESENT

The unprecedented theological interest in the "end" has led to some startling and far-reaching eschatological developments in our time. Of first importance here is the Dutch theologian A. A. van Ruler. He defined the kingdom, which he took to be a fundamental category in Scripture, as the "infinite and saving activity of God with the world," and "that which God does with the world for its salvation from out of his future."[9] This notion of God coming out of his future is taken literally.

Theology which is informed and determined by Scripture, says van Ruler, bears an eschatological character. This means more than a mere interest in the end or a mere confession that we are now living in the last days. Eschatological theology means rather that God is coming to us out of his own predetermined future. If we are to understand him and his saving activity, we shall have to begin with the end.

> In the light of the Word of God everything is directed towards his determined end; it is ordered and formed therefrom and can only be understood from it. Therefore in dogmatic thinking we must begin with the end and look backwards from there. Rather, we must *walk* backwards — it is a movement and indeed a movement backwards — to the cross, and — yet further back — to the beginning of creation and the fall. We move in the action of God which can only be understood from out of the end.[10]

Such an understanding of theology does not leave us immobile. Led by God's Spirit we move into his future, at whose center is his kingly rule. Besides embracing the church, its sign, this kingly rule includes the state, culture, indeed all of creation. Because God loves his creation he saves it and wills to use his people in it. Withdrawal from the world is thus wrong. Nor should we speak of Christ as the king of the church when he is in fact king of the world including the church. If we begin our thinking about the reign of Christ and the kingdom with the church, we never really get outside the church, and the secularization of life is thus hastened.[11] Since it belongs to God, all of life, including everyday life, is sacred. To find the meaning of the everyday life of God's kingdom, we must begin with the ordinary things of which Jesus is king. This includes demonic powers, but that is precisely where Christ wills to reign. Everything is included in God's eternal purpose and moves towards that predestined end which he has ordained.

To those who object that an emphasis on the kingdom as embracing the world and culture might not give the church the attention it deserves, Van Ruler responds that the church exists for the sake of the world. The idea that the world exists for the sake of the church he calls a Gnostic fantasy. Scripture declares that God created the world; and while the church is elect, the world will be glorified. Indeed, God has in Christ already glorified his creation in principle. The church is not glorified; it disappears! "The world is the real thing; the church is only an intermezzo."[12]

Expounding the relation of the church to the world within the overarching kingdom of God, Van Ruler insists that the church must ever be turned to the world so that it may serve it in accordance with the will of God. Its first service is to inform the world that God has saved it and will continue that saving action as he directs it towards the end. This is the reason for the existence of the church; it is God's mission in the world.[13] There is a place for this eschatological vision of mission in the theological system, Van Ruler holds, if we begin with eschatology and thus follow the apostolic vision. With eschatology as our point of departure, we study God's plan for his world and learn the place of mission in it. Mission is the bridge between the ascension and second coming of Christ; it binds the beginning and the end together historically as God comes from out of the future to lead his creation to its destined end.

Van Ruler's conception of mission is so broad and fundamental that only an eschatological framework is sufficient to hold it. It is not enough to enclose mission within Christology or make it a part of ecclesiology. Jesus Christ is indeed the center of God's redemptive activity in the world, but that activity, carried out by God's Spirit, is more comprehensive than the life of Christ.[14] Van Ruler speaks about the "relative independence" of the doctrine of the Spirit in developing a theology of salvation and mission.[15] Mission understands apostolic office as grounded in the kingdom as well as the church. It sees Christ and the covenant community, but beyond Christ and the community it beholds God and his entire created world. Van Ruler emphasizes the need to rethink all of theology with an eye to the trinitarian, eschatological, and historical considerations of creation, man, time, and history with which Scripture confronts us as we contemplate service to God.

Contemplating that service, theology sees that "the essence of the mission of the church is not that the church goes out, witnesses, and stands in the world, but that it is used." God uses the church in his engagement with the world; and he is busy with the world in ways far broader than the apostolic church could imagine. For God uses more than his church; he wrestles with every human heart and is a

concerned participant in the attempts of nations to give social, political, economic, and cultural form to life. The church stands modestly
in the midst of all this: "In this great world process, which should be
understood as a divine drama, the church is used by God. That is the
essence of her mission, and, therefore, mission is also her essence."[16]

The church may be seen as an instrument or a vehicle to carry the
Word of God to people and nations, but these metaphors are inadequate. Mission, for example, is customarily conceived as a vehicle, a
caboose on the train, an appendage to the church, one thing among
the many that the church has to do. Van Ruler would rather speak of
the mission of the church as its essence. He prefers the metaphor of
the church as a candle which burns; it gives light, then disappears.[17]
In the most profound sense, the church is not what it *is*, or what it
has, or what it *does*, but that *for which it is used* in God's purpose.
It has been called, justified, and sanctified for the glory of his name
as his kingdom comes and his will is done on earth. Thus God's great
historical, eschatological intention for the world, of which predestination is the very heart, is fulfilled.[18]

In its comprehensiveness Van Ruler's eschatology is similar to the
theology of the contemporary German Wolfhart Pannenberg and to
the school of process theology. Like these other schools of thought,
Van Ruler speaks of the future as belonging to the divine essence.[19]
While such language indicates how seriously he takes his eschatological stance, it does not compromise God's sovereignty for him, and
Van Ruler binds his eschatology to the doctrine of predestination.[20]
Whether Pannenberg and process theology are adequate here is less
certain.

Pannenberg stresses history as the fundamental category of reality
so strongly that he writes about *reality as history* and of God as
coming to be. So overwhelming are the evidences of God's revelation
in history that only sinful obstinacy prevents the confession of that
truth. The meaning of history is given in Jesus Christ, in whom the
end of history has appeared proleptically. Christ is God with us, Son
of God and Son of Man, the "final measure of all subsequent history"[21]
whose predestination is the center of God's plan for history. In him
alone can the unity of history be understood.[22]

The obsession with history leads Pannenberg to reject traditional
incarnational theology "from above" in favor of doing theology "from
below."[23] Thus one should not speak of the pre-existent Logos coming
to dwell among men but of the man Jesus whose person and works
revealed him to be God and man. In the history of Jesus' life the
crowning event was his resurrection. That stupendous act, in which

God's final victory over sin was anticipated, was "not only constitutive for our perception of his divinity, but it is ontologically constitutive for that divinity."[24]

God also is ontologically constituted in history: "In a restricted but important sense, God does not yet exist. Since his rule and his being are inseparable, God's being is still in process of coming to be."[25] Pannenberg holds that the idea of the future as an attribute of God still needs development and must be associated with the concepts of the kingdom and lordship of God.

> Is not God God only in the accomplishment of his lordship over the world? This is why his deity will be revealed only when the kingdom comes, since only then will his lordship be visible. But are God's revelation of his deity and his deity itself separable from each other? The God of the Bible is God only in that he proves himself as God. He would not be the God of the world if he did not prove himself to be its Lord. But just this proof is still a matter of the future according to the expectations of Israel and the New Testament. Does this not mean that God is not yet, but is yet to be?[26]

Although these statements must be understood as indications of a method of historical investigation which seeks to do justice to historical reality, they do seem to preclude an adequate ontology. Pannenberg does not mean to compromise the transcendence and sovereignty of God, but to stress that the lordship of God has not yet been revealed and will only be revealed at the end, from which the present gets its meaning and which has already appeared in Jesus Christ, the prolepsis of the future.[27]

The question has been raised whether Pannenberg's "eschatological ontology" is a viable one.[28] His insistence on the importance and the universality of history is on the mark, but this need not be done in a way that compromises the doctrine of God. In any case, the language he uses is unhappy; it may be exaggerated or misleading and does not lead to understanding.

Pannenberg's approach might be regarded as one type of process theology, radical in its historico-eschatological method, but seeking nevertheless to do justice to the central affirmations of the faith of the church. That is less true of other adherents of process theology. Charles Hartshorne affirms that "becoming" rather than "being" is the basic form of reality and that God is in process of becoming. To conceive of God abstractly as "immutable being" is an unreal, meaningless exercise; rather, he should be seen as "the eminent form of becoming."[29] Process alone is real.

Alfred North Whitehead had said this earlier, but his thought did not make an impact on theology until the concept of "event" came into its own. Now Hartshorne can write:

> It is beings which decay or are destroyed, not happenings. These can do neither. Try to destroy a past event. How would you go about it? Events are immune to destruction. Try to corrupt or impoverish a past event. All you can do is tell historical lies. You do nothing to the event. Events, once they have occurred, are absolutes, impassible in the old theological sense.[30]

Because events are the stuff of reality, God too is caught up in them. He is not to be conceived as eternally the same but, in the words of Hartshorne, "as perpetually growing in content by virtue of additions from the world, each addition being strictly permanent, once for all." If this conception of God is true, as Hartshorne believes, "the ever-growing sum of realities and goods can be real and good for someone, for one personal consciousness. From this consciousness, the process version of omniscience, nothing is ever subtracted, but to it all novelties are added."[31] Thus the "divine self-fulfillment" is achieved and our own "transience" is surmounted. "In the long run," Hartshorne writes, "we are nothing, except as God inherits reality and value from our lives and actions."[32]

Process theology sees this as an inspiring eschatological conviction. We are co-creators with God "though in a humble, local, more or less blind and faltering way."[33] We are all artists, enriching reality at each moment with something not previously there.

> What we create is primarily, and first of all, our own experiences, each of which is a more or less harmonious, beautiful and in its final concrete quality, free response to the myriad stimuli and memories playing upon us at the moment. Indirectly these experiences contribute to those of other creatures, and finally, all contribute to God.[34]

The appeal in this line of thought is that it takes history seriously. The commonplace is invested with sacred significance and given a place in the echatological drama being played. And process theology indeed speaks to many traditional Christian convictions. But it goes awry in failing to distinguish God from the process. Not to conceive of God as the Lord of history, prior to and independent of creation, *in* history but transcendent over it, is to abandon the biblical view for something less than the historic Christian position. There are of course differences among process theologians, but those who have been most prominent are influenced by A. N. Whitehead's denial of the transcendence of God and his affirmation that God and the universe are interdependent.[35]

One of the spokesmen of process theology has expressed surprise that there is not a surge of interest today in the doctrine of the sovereignty of God. If he "were not committed to the contrasting view," he writes, he would be "very much inclined to explore this alternative."[36] Process theology and the Christian church indeed have "contrasting" views in fundamental doctrine. Only the doctrine of God taught by the prophets and apostles can give the church the strength it needs to accomplish its task. That doctrine came alive in Jesus Christ.

The new eschatology has been a contribution to the faith of the church. Never before have the people of God seen so clearly the direction of history or the significance of its end. Never before has there been so full an understanding of the coming of the kingdom as that which is already present but not yet complete. Never before has there been such appreciation of the Holy Spirit as the first-fruits and guarantee of our eternal inheritance, and the giver of spiritual gifts and graces, ministries and equipment for service.[37]

The new eschatology and a new appreciation for the work of the Holy Spirit have developed together. This development has led to a new interest in the mission of the church to proclaim the gospel and to apply that gospel to society with its many needs.[38] In the latter task the relevance of the social gospel has been rediscovered,[39] some of its most visible interpretations being the various theologies of nature and of liberation that mark our time. All of this points to the doctrine of Christian vocation. Faith and action, theology and ethics belong together. The people of God are called to exert themselves in service, to work while it is yet day. To this the new eschatology summons them.

Chapter 17

The Relevance of the Faith

To identify what kind of world one lives in is a matter of serious consequence, whether that be the world of pre-Christian Rome, of Aquinas and the age of faith, of the Reformation, or of today. For our understanding of the world enables us to address ourselves to it in one way or another. For the Christian this means the possibility of comparing it with God's intention for the world and ministering to it in his name.

Ours is not the world that our parents and grandparents conceived it to be. Totalitarianism in a Europe once baptized, rising crime rates and the abandonment of Christian morality, crises of belief in God and in the influence of organized religion are only a few — if potent — evidences of that. We no longer take certain mores for granted. We do not go to war to make the world safe for democracy; we hope we can retain it for ourselves. Disillusionment, pessimism, and even cynicism are evident in all sectors of society. Little wonder that ours is being called a post-Christian era.

Our purpose in this brief concluding chapter is to focus on the relevance in such a world of Christian theology and the faith of the church. By Christian theology we mean the attempt to understand, articulate, and defend the faith. By the faith of the church we mean that revealed religion inscribed in the Bible which confesses Jesus Christ as Savior of the lost world and the Holy Spirit as God's gracious presence in the world, preserving and renewing it for complete restoration at the next appearance of Christ.

The doctrines of the sovereignty of God and of sin and grace lie at the center of this conception. There is only one remedy for this world's ills: God himself in the person of Christ, God-become-flesh, who has effected redemption and opened the way to reconciliation and blessing. That faith, the message of salvation proclaimed by the apostles, and the theology which studies and articulates it, are as relevant today as ever. It is well to remind ourselves of this, especially in the face of the numbing barrage of bad news which tends to make us lose our nerve and to dim that vision of the coming kingdom which Christians need from day to day. It is not so much new ideas with which the church deals, then, as an appreciation of old ideas and their relevance in the world today.

1. THE NEED FOR CHRISTIAN FOUNDATIONS

The first idea that needs to be recovered is that of Christian foundations in every intellectual discipline, but particularly in the humanities and in the social sciences. Both those branches of learning concerned with human culture and those dealing with the institutions and functioning of organized human community are based on some foundation. That foundation consists of presuppositions which come out of one's view of life as a whole — one's *Weltanschauung* as the Germans call it, a subject dealt with exhaustively by Herman Dooyeweerd.[1]

These foundations are the unproved assumptions, the fundamental attitudes and concepts which determine how we "see" a given body of knowledge. They provide us with the glasses through which we view a piece of literature, an economic scheme, or a doctrine of the state. This is important because how we see a body of knowledge determines how we may use it. To take a familiar example, the Marxist doctrine of man is different from the doctrine of man in a Christian frame of reference. Marxism views man primarily as economic man, while Christianity sees him primarily as God's creature made for fellowship with God. Economic interests are important, to be sure; but Christianity sees them as only one set of interests among others equally or more important.

Another example is the state. Christians understand the state as derived from God and consisting of people who have inalienable rights given them by God. Others, like the philosopher Hegel, see the state as the ultimate revelation and reality achieved by Spirit. The state is the actuality of the ethical idea. It is the ethical mind knowing and thinking itself — the closest that Hegel gets to the idea of God. The human person does not find freedom in his natural state of being, but only within the civil state, which has the supreme moral right over against him. The supreme duty of the individual is to be a member of the state; the right of the world spirit, manifested in the state, surpasses all special privileges.[2]

So great is the difference in views here that Augustine, comparing thought similar to Hegel's with Christian faith, claimed that, whereas the latter came from God, the former can only be ascribed to demons. The infinite distance between the city of Christ and that of the devil means that even though they now appear together, after the resurrection they shall be apart forever. In his study *Christianity and Classical Culture*, Charles N. Cochrane has demonstrated that, on Augustine's presuppositions, he was right in his judgment of non-Christian thought. Rome's error

> may be summarily described as a failure to identify the true source of power and, therewith, its true character and conditions. The error thus indicated is original, and to it may be ascribed the whole tissue of fallacies which frustrate the secular aspirations of men. These fallacies Christianity explodes in a sentence: all power comes from on high.[3]

This difference in foundations — God *or* Caesar — remains today, and the failure to discern this is evidence of and a contributing factor to the malaise of our time. A brilliant example of such a failure is Walter Lippmann's *A Preface to Morals*. Lippmann exposes the serious ethical situation when "the acids of modernity" have eaten away the old foundations on which life has been built. But after his impressive diagnosis, the cure he offers is nothing more than warmed-over Stoicism. The foundation Lippmann would lay for a moral order is disinterestedness, maturity, freedom from tension, unperturbedness, the ability to live above pain and fear — as though the world were, like Lippmann, ninety-nine percent pure intellect and living comfortably in America! His concluding description of the ideal person reveals this fundamental philosophy:

> Since nothing gnawed at his vitals, neither doubt nor ambition, nor frustration, nor fear, he would move easily through life. And so whether he saw the thing as comedy, or high tragedy, or plain farce, he would affirm that it is what it is, and that the wise man can enjoy it.[4]

But evidently Lippmann was dissatisfied with his proposed foundation of mere Stoicism. Later he would lament the confusion caused by inability to agree on educational goals and values:

> There is no common faith, no common body of principles, no common body of knowledge, no common moral and intellectual discipline. Yet the graduates of these modern schools are expected to form a civilized community. They are expected to govern themselves. They are expected to have social conscience. They are expected to arrive by discussion at common purposes. When one realizes that they have no common culture, is it astounding that they have no common purpose? That they worship false gods? That only in war do they unite? That in the fierce struggle for existence they are tearing Western society to pieces? They are the graduates of an educational system in which, though attendance is compulsory, the choice of the subject matter of education is left to the imagination of college presidents, trustees, and professors, or even to the whims of the

pupils themselves. We have established a system of education in which we insist that while everyone should be educated, yet there is nothing in particular that an educated man must know.[5]

A gifted observer of and commentator on the passing scene, an intellectual leader in the western world, Lippmann was typical in his confusion about the foundation needed in social life, especially in the intellectual disciplines of the humanities and the social sciences. Much of his criticism was on target, for the typical European or American college or university is indeed as Lippmann described it, with departments operating in isolation from each other and none interested in establishing a common foundation and common goals to make the whole meaningful. Economics is taught the way the particular department or teacher wants to teach it; history is taught by professors who arbitrarily sort out the facts they like; the natural sciences are taught as ends in themselves; the arts are taught for art's sake; and scholarship is pursued for its own sake.

What prevails in higher education is true of society as a whole. No wonder there is widespread uncertainty and dissatisfaction. What is needed is what Christian theology has to offer: a knowledge of the faith and its relevance for a true understanding of life, something Lippmann failed to achieve. James Truslow Adams has said, "Unless we can agree as to what the values of life are, we clearly can have no goal in education, and if we have no goal, the discussion of methods is futile."[6] Christian theology claims to know what those values are. It knows the foundation, for "no other foundation can any one lay than that which is laid, which is Jesus Christ" (1 Cor. 3:11). The society of the future will be determined by the response to that Pauline observation.

2. THE CRITICAL FUNCTION OF THEOLOGY

A theological foundation enables a person to exercise his critical faculties, so that the process of building may be done aright. This points to another important theological task which makes theology's relevance in the world today clearly evident. The work of theological commissions and Christian action commissions in various denominations indicates that this task is not being ignored today. But simply assigning the particular function of criticism of this idea or of that movement to special commissions suggests a general reluctance on the part of the "average Christian" to become involved in the critical assessment of culture.

By criticism I do not mean destructive carping but the kind which is motivated by benevolence and has improvement as its goal. Why should Christians not engage in critical reflection on anything and everything from the point of view of the biblical revelation?[7]

There is too much uncritical acceptance of this program or that leadership in our time. People grow weary and quit the game; often the loss is by default. This spirit inside and outside the church allows for disaster. Within the church the excuse one sometimes hears is one which reveals the bad side of certain kinds of pietism—a retreat from the world and a failure to grapple with its problems. Or the church may degenerate into a mutual admiration society, afraid to measure its own performance by the Word of God, much less to look critically at anything outside its walls. Staff and members go around telling each other, "I'm OK — You're OK," and there is strong insistence that the whole atmosphere be one of affirmation, positive thinking, and cheer. If the church is to regain the prophetic stance which has characterized Protestantism in its heroic periods, it cannot take this easy road but will "test everything, hold fast what is good, [and] abstain from every form of evil" (1 Thess. 5:21).

We say that we do not like a lot of what is going on in the world: the failures of socialism and the excesses of capitalism, the dehumanization and exploitation of the underprivileged, corruption and crime, national chauvinism, greed and selfishness, class strife and hatred. The question is: why not?

This is the question which bothered Karl Barth, and because he had the capacity to ask it vigorously and critically he became a great prophet. Barth recorded his reaction to the tragic events at the time of the beginning of World War I:

> For me personally one day at the beginning of August [1914] . . . stamped itself as the *dies ater* [black day]. It was that on which ninety-three German intellectuals came out with a manifesto supporting the war policy of Kaiser Wilhelm II and his counselors, and among them I found to my horror the names of nearly all my theological teachers who up to then I had religiously honoured. Disillusioned by their conduct, I perceived that I should not be able any longer to accept their ethics and dogmatics, their biblical exegesis, their interpretation of history, that at least for me the theology of the nineteenth century had no future.[8]

Refusing to be caught up in German chauvinism, the young Swiss pastor struggled, from an increasingly firm foundation, to interpret and evaluate the social and political situation. Later National Socialism would drive him to such reflections again. The answer he gave then is found in the Barmen Declaration: Jesus Christ is the Good Shepherd, and the sheep hear his voice and not the voice of a stranger.

The world situation today may not be so obviously shocking, but it is fundamentally the same. By what criteria do we judge our own country's role in international affairs? What is going on in Africa or the legislature? How do we evaluate it? By what criteria do we assess the hatred in the Middle East? Do we make our judgment on the basis of the maxims of a Kantian ethic or of some other humanistic ethic or of humanitarian concern? These are not adequate to bear the weight of the problem; indeed, the fact that many have no more than this is a large part of the world's problem. We need more than "the arm of flesh" to lean upon.

As an essential part of its theological task the church must speak to the world about any and all issues, setting forth the great scriptural principles on the basis of which men and nations should seek to make decisions and live. To think critically and theologically about the current gambling craze is not only to raise prudential considerations but to point out how gambling seriously compromises Christian principles. The theologically critical motive behind a struggle to maintain the purity of our natural environment ten or a hundred years hence is that the earth is the Lord's, and he has told us that we must love our neighbor—including those who come after us. Again, in the international debate with Marxism why don't Christians make more of the weaknesses in the Marxist doctrine of man, which make it incapable of comprehending the heights and depths of the human spirit. The Marxist estimate of man as an economic animal allows for no true freedom of the spirit; nor is it able to understand forgiveness or the depths of sin.

Concerning sin Marxism is utterly naive in failing to see why, when economic, physical, social, and recreational needs have been provided for, there should still be dissatisfaction, crime, and bitterness of spirit. Concerning forgiveness, a Czech theologian, who knew Marxist socialism as well as anybody, has written:

> The real meaning of life is the awareness that we live on the basis of the forgiveness of sins, granted as a gift of the sovereign grace of God. We can find no just relationship with the people around us if we do not realize that we need the forgiveness of others and that we are called to forgive. Theology fails to reach its true depths if it does not grasp this ultimate truth in all its historical and literary, dogmatic, and liturgical studies. What is involved is a mystery—in the genuine sense of the word—free of any mythical or irrational speculations. It is a mystery in the sense that no

scientific or philosophical category is sufficient to explain this relationship, and that the same is true of the most profound psychological or sociological studies. Whoever thinks that it is possible to — and that he can — explain the ultimate realities of sin and forgiveness by means of reason, ethics, or psychology, remains far from what is decisive in human life, from what is the real dynamic in the relationship between man and God, between man and his neighbour. The understanding of other men goes well beyond the mere level of social — or even the most noble-minded ethical — conventions.

From this we can also understand why theology and confessions of faith have so long talked of the Creator Spirit (*Creator Spiritus*). By this they did not mean some sort of mystical influence which miraculously intervenes in our lives. What they really meant to say was that truly to understand man, to understand his existential relationship to God and to other men, a much more profound and penetrating method is needed than that of science with its reason, ethical conventions with their norms, its clever intuitions, or its careful studies of natural and psychological processes. It is on this deep level that we encounter what we call "love" or "joyful hope" — that which does not surrender even at times of the worst failure or of unavoidable misfortune.[9]

That is what is meant by exercising the critical function of theology in today's world.

Christians must show the relevance of their work and witness. The faith with which they are entrusted gives them the materials needed to evaluate and decide. Motivation, illumination, and insight come from the Holy Spirit, who is God with us in the struggle. Christians dare not keep silent, for Christian theology has been called to give light for the way. This is not only a matter for the seminary classroom or learned volumes; in ten thousand pulpits and millions of homes the Word of the Lord must sound: "This is the way; walk in it." And all have to listen and to obey. Perhaps the church has been too modest in its exercise of this responsibility.

The church has often been too modest in using its prophetic voice to assess the complex social, political, economic, and cultural situation of today. If it is a watchman set on the walls of our civilization, however, it cannot remain silent but it must set before all people everywhere that Word of God over against which, and with which, decision will be made.

3. THE UNIVERSAL NATURE OF THEOLOGY

The reason theology must exercise its critical function in and for the sake of society at large is its universal nature. The message which gives it life is for all people, not only for the church, even though it is only the church that listens. Because the message is from God, it has universal relevance; and if it has universal relevance it is wrong to keep it from others. An ancient proverb said that one who has what the world needs is a debtor to the world. What does the world need more than a word from God? That is why the theological task is relevant and why the science of theology is universal in nature.

The early church sensed that in its contest with the gods of Rome. The Savior of the world was Jesus Christ, not Caesar or some voiceless pagan deity; and the church, in its faith, had a word for all people. That is why Justin Martyr could speak so boldly about the change Christ had effected in the lives of believers, a change he would accomplish in any who would confess his name and go to him for grace.[10] That is why apologists and theologians could challenge the old order in God's name. That is why Augustine had the courage to lift up others as he joyfully preached and taught and wrote about the good news in the midst of "a rotten, disintegrating world."[11]

Since the time of Augustine theology has been aware of its nature as a universal science with a message for all men and women everywhere. One sees this during the age of faith in Thomas Aquinas' *Summa Contra Gentiles.* It is evident in Calvin's dedication of his works addressing them to persons in all walks of life. It lay behind Abraham Kuyper's and A. A. van Ruler's range of interests and their conviction that theology has an important message for every aspect of life. And it comes out in the contemporary emphasis of Wolfhart Pannenberg on "the universal meaning of the history of Jesus."[12] To quote only from Pannenberg: whereas historical statements "set forth the specific individuality of the event with which they are dealing," dogmatic statements have "universal meaning." The specific individuality of Jesus and his universal meaning "are so intertwined that the process of acquiring knowledge of this always passes from one to the other." Pannenberg is insistent on the universal nature of theology:

> The historical individuality of Jesus is rightly understood only in knowing its universal meaning—ultimately, in fact, only through personal trust. Conversely, all dogmatic statements about his universal meaning constantly require grounding in and confirmation by the historical particularity of the message, way, and figure of Jesus.
>
> Concretely, to say that the dogmatic statement possesses universality means above all that it takes account of the earthly way of Jesus together with his resurrection from the dead as an act of God. Statements about God refer essentially to the totality of reality and imply an understanding of this whole insofar as we can speak meaningfully about God only by

speaking of him as the creator of the universe. The statements about Jesus which speak about God's act and God's revelation in him correspond to a view of the whole of reality as a history effected by God, in other words, to the biblical-Israelite view of reality.[13]

Pannenberg's very proper insistence on theology's universal character is no new idea. It is profoundly Calvinistic; and no Calvin scholar has shown this motif in Calvin's own thinking better than André Biéler, who laments the fragmentation of life which the church and theology have permitted and their retreat from the battle for the whole of life into a safe zone where politics and economics are left alone. What is needed is a

> rediscovery of the biblical realism which encompasses the totality of existence. It is necessary to make again, in every age, the discovery that had made the Calvinistic reformation. It had discerned that the Word of God is concerned about the togetherness of human activity and it had resolutely decided to allow itself to be guided by it. It belongs to each new generation to make anew this discovery in maintaining a reckoning of the change of the historical situations always in evolution.
>
> May this past example of the presence of the church in the world in its totality... help Christians in the search for a truth which will set them free from the mortal antagonism of the contemporary ideologies so that they may find again the realism of a biblical theology incarnating itself in the new affairs of our time.[14]

Because God is God the science which seeks to understand him and his will is the fundamental science, the science which imparts meaning to the rest of life. It is universal in that all of humanity needs its service. We should think of it not so much as the "queen of the sciences," as a servant eager to serve. It could help other sciences see their rich meaning and true role in a universe created and sustained by God, and the futility of work undertaken in isolation from him. For what does it profit if one gains the whole world of knowledge about this or that and loses his own soul? To put the matter more philosophically, what satisfaction is there in knowing one small segment of the world of knowledge if one fails to know something of the whole, or how that little piece is related to others? Theology, in its universal nature, has a word of wisdom here.

4. THE TRUE HUMANISM

The final thought in our case for the relevance of theology is that only theology and the Christian faith it articulates make possible the development of a true humanism. Every school of thought claims a devoted interest in humanism, of course; it would take someone less than human to oppose it. Yet definitions — where they exist at all — vary. Not all are willing to state clearly their doctrine of man.

How do we define man? As a social being? A rational animal? A sportsman or playboy? As a power-thirsty egomaniac? A workhorse? An American, or German, or African? A Communist party member? If anywhere, the humanisms of the world show their inadequacy here, in their understanding of man. Is man only a rational animal? Then kill him if he gets in the way! Is he only an economic being? Then give him a job and forget him! Is he a mere playboy? Leave him alone; he will be a disillusioned and bitter cynic tomorrow. If man is no more than any of these — or all of them put together — there is little reason for the human struggle. All talk about "human rights" is non-sense. One political system is as good as another, and in the struggle for success nothing is wrong. Transcendence disappears, and life means only what we make of it. Beyond that there is nothing. With many embracing — consciously or unconsciously — that sort of philosophy, it is no wonder that pessimism and hopelessness are on the upswing and crime rates rise.

But is this the true man? Biéler writes:

> The man whom we moderns know . . . is not the authentic man. He is only a pale shadow, a counterfeit, a caricature of man. This man has no hope whatever of reaching anything. In spite of his marvelous gifts which still witness in him to the majesty of the work of God, everything that the man of today undertakes is devoted to death and ends in death. . . . Although not intending to do so, . . . idealists deceive natural man by having him believe that merely imagining what a man wishes to become actually changes him into what he wants to be![15]

Pessimism, however, does not have the last word for the Christian. There is a humanism that is unwilling to denigrate God's lieutenant, to rob him of his birthright, to see him as a beast of the field. This is the true humanism, which sees man as a creature of God, a *child* of God, and a brother and sister of God's Son, the new Adam, who shows what humankind is destined to be. This humanism insists that man may not be exploited, liquidated, dismissed from thought, forgotten. In the Old and New Testaments even the stranger must be cared for and the enemy loved and forgiven. Why? One passage which talks about these requirements offers the ultimate reason: because Christians must be perfect, even as their Father which is in heaven is perfect (Matt. 5:48). As children of God it is their calling and destiny to *live* as children of God. That does not mean that they regard themselves as better than others, but that they minister to others just as God ministered to them.

This is the true humanism, a view of man which sees him, though full of contradictions, as a creature made by and meant for God. As Blaise Pascal put it:

> What a chimera then is man! What a novelty! What a monster, what a chaos, what a contradiction, what a prodigy! Judge of all things, imbecile worm of the earth; depositary of truth, a sink of uncertainty and error; the pride and refuse of the universe!
>
> Who will unravel this tangle? Nature confutes the sceptics, and reason confutes the dogmatists. What then will you become, O men! who try to find out by your natural reason what is your true condition? You cannot avoid one of these sects, nor adhere to one of them.
>
> Know, then, proud man, what a paradox you are to yourself. Humble yourself, weak reason; be silent, foolish nature; learn that man infinitely transcends man, and learn from your Master your true condition of which you are ignorant. *Hear God (Pensées,* 434).

Notes to Chapter 1

1. John Calvin, *Institution of the Christian Religion*, translated and annotated by Ford Lewis Battles (Atlanta: John Knox, 1975), p. 35.

2. Emile Doumergue, *Jean Calvin: Les Hommes et les choses de son temps* (Lausanne: Georges Bridel, 1910), IV, 361.

3. E.g., Gustaf Aulén, a Lutheran, makes the point that Christian faith is "entirely theocentric. ... God is the sole object of faith." *The Faith of the Christian Church* (Philadelphia: Muhlenberg, 1960), p. 20.

4. N. P. Williams, in *The Study of Theology*, ed. Kenneth E. Kirk (London: Hodder and Stoughton, 1939), pp. 13f.

5. On Scripture's witness to itself, see Benjamin B. Warfield, *Revelation and Inspiration* (New York: Oxford U. P., 1927).

6. The most famous such instance was the declaration by the Council of Trent on April 8, 1546, that the truth of God is "contained in the written books and the unwritten traditions, ... seeing that one God is the author of both — as also the said traditions, as well those appertaining to faith as to morals, as having been dictated, either by Christ's own word of mouth, or by the Holy Ghost, and preserved in the Catholic Church by a continuous succession." Quoted in Philip Schaff, *The Creeds of Christendom* (New York: Harper, 1890), II, 80.

7. Although Brunner writes that Christian doctrine and faith are true "in so far as this doctrine and this faith agree with the teaching of the Bible," he says later that "the Word of Scripture is not the final court of appeal, since Jesus Christ himself alone is this ultimate authority. ... Scripture remains the sole *source* of our knowledge of revelation ... but it is in no way the norm of our knowledge and our doctrine." *The Doctrine of God* (Philadelphia: Westminster, 1950), pp. 44, 47f.

8. Barnabas Nagy, in *Biblical Authority for Today*, ed. Alan Richardson and Wolfgang Schweitzer (Philadelphia: Westminster, 1951), p. 84.

9. Among twentieth-century writers Karl Barth (in his *Church Dogmatics*) and Thomas F. Torrance (in his *Theological Science*) have shown this very clearly.

10. Cf. Georgia Harkness, *Foundations of Christian Knowledge* (New York: Abingdon, 1955), pp. 42ff. On the scientific character of theology, see also E. Ashby Johnson, *The Crucial Task of Theology* (Richmond: John Knox, 1958); Abraham Kuyper, *Encyclopedia of Sacred Theology* (New York: Scribner's, 1898), pp. 56-228; Karl Barth, *Church Dogmatics*, I/1, 1ff.; Benjamin B. Warfield, *Studies in Theology*, esp. pp. 49ff. and 91ff.

11. Warfield, *Studies in Theology*, p. 95.

12. Brand Blanshard, *The Nature of Thought* (London: Allen & Unwin, 1948), I, 654.

13. Cf. George Ernest Wright, *God Who Acts* (London: SCM Press, 1952), pp. 109, 116, *et passim*.

14. "Of the Laws of Ecclesiastical Polity," III, viii, 4.

15. See my "The Experiential Theology of Early Dutch Calvinism," *The Reformed Review*, XXVII/3 (Spring 1974), 180-89; James R. Tanis, *Dutch Calvinistic Pietism in the Middle Colonies* (The Hague: Martinus Nijhoff, 1967); F. Ernest Stoeffler, *The Rise of Evangelical Pietism* (Leiden: E. J. Brill, 1965).

16. T.L. Haitjema, *Dogmatiek als Apologie* (Haariem: De Erven F. Bohn N. V., 1948), p. 107 (italics his).

17. For a modern Roman Catholic statement on the importance of experience in the formulation of Christian doctrine see Avery Dulles, *The Survival of Dogma* (Garden City, N.Y.: Doubleday, 1971), esp. chapters 10-12.

18. Quoted by Reinhold Seeberg, *Text-book of the History of Doctrines,* tr. Charles E. Hay (Grand Rapids: Baker, 1952), II, 224.

19. *LW,* XLIV, 200f.; XLV, 337ff.

20. Herman Bavinck, *Gereformeerde Dogmatiek* (Kampen: J. H. Kok, 1908), I, 647ff.

21. *Ibid.,* p. 652.

22. *Ibid.,* pp. 662f. Ronald Gregor Smith has written: "Faith demands to be understood. And as soon as this demand is honestly faced, the traditional doctrines play their part: not as normative, not as a substitute for faith, but as servants in the house of faith. Faith without doctrine is a wildly swaying weathercock, driven around by every gust of the arbitrary imaginative or speculative power of men. Doctrine without faith is a sullen and joyless taskmaster, the slave-driver with the whip. There is no immutable doctrine; but the reality of the doctrinal tradition keeps faith from fantasy. The two must go together; but the greater of the two is faith." *The Doctrine of God* (Philadelphia: Westminster, 1970), pp. 47f.

23. Cf. Luther's address, "To the Christian Nobility of the German Nation," in *LW,* XLIV, esp. p. 205.

24. Cf. the essays by John Marsh, "History and Interpretation," and James Muilenburg, "The Interpretation of the Bible," in *Biblical Authority for Today,* pp. 181-218.

25. Herbert Butterfield, *Christianity and History* (London: G. Bell and Sons, 1950), p. 2. Cf. Ronald Gregor Smith, *The Doctrine of God,* chapters 4ff.

26. Pannenberg, *Theology and the Kingdom of God* (Philadelphia: Westminster, 1969), p. 56.

27. "Process Philosophy as a Resource for Christian Thought," in *Philosophical Resources for Theology,* ed. P. LeFevre (Nashville: Abingdon, 1968), p. 45. Cf. his essay "Philosophical and Religious Uses of 'God'," in *Process Theology: Basic Writings,* ed. E.H. Cousins (New York: Newman, 1971), p. 115.

28. See Hugh Ross Mackintosh's discussion, *Types of Modern Theology,* (London: Scribner's, 1939), esp. pp. 66-68; Bultmann, *History and Eschatology* (New York: Harper, 1957), p. 155: "Do not look around yourself into universal history, you must look into your own personal history. Always in your present lies the meaning in history, and you cannot see it as a spectator, but only in your responsible decision." See also James McConkey Robinson, *Das Problem des Heiligen Geistes bei Wilhelm Herrmann* (Marburg: Karl Gleiser, 1952), pp. 79-100. Richard R. Niebuhr shows that in "existentialist introspection . . . the objective past is wholly unimportant." *Resurrection and Historical Reason* (New York: Scribner's, 1957), p. 59; cf. pp. 7ff.

29. *Op. cit.,* p. 68.

30. Quoted by Owen Chadwick, *From Bossuet to Newman: The Idea of Doctrinal Development* (Cambridge: The University Press, 1957), p. 17. Bossuet's position is reminiscent of the opinion of Vincent of Lerins that church

teaching develops "in the same doctrine, in the same understanding, and in the same opinion." Cf. Avery Dulles, *The Survival of Dogma*, pp. 186, 225.

31. Chadwick, *op. cit.*, p. 19.

32. On the influence of liberal German theology on Newman, see Chadwick, *ibid.*, pp. 102-19.

33. John Henry Cardinal Newman, *An Essay on the Development of Christian Doctrine* (Westminster, Md.: Christian Classics, Inc., 1968); see also his *A Grammar of Assent* (New York: Longmans, Green and Co., 1947).

34. Chadwick, *op. cit.*, p. 149.

35. On Newman's willingness to use the category of feeling, see Chadwick, *ibid.*, p. 152.

36. Nor, for that matter, do they meet the test described in the *Commonitorium* of Vincent of Lerins: "This we may hold, that which has been believed everywhere, always, and by everyone." Quoted by Philip Schaff, *History of the Christian Church*, III, 613.

37. E.g., Hans Küng, *The Church* (New York: Sheed and Ward, 1967); *Infallibility: An Inquiry* (Garden City, N.Y.: Doubleday, 1971); Avery Dulles, *The Survival of Dogma*. An older study of church infallibility from the Protestant perspective is George Salmon, *The Infallibility of the Church* (Grand Rapids: Baker, 1951).

38. Dulles writes: "In principle, every dogmatic statement is subject to reformulation. . . . It may be necessary to discard the human concepts as well as the words of those who first framed the dogma." *The Survival of Dogma*, p. 161. He suggests the need to "reconceptualize" dogma from a "present point of view" (p. 162), and later contends for a position "which affirms the doctrinal infallibility of the church while allowing for reformulation in terminology and concept" (p. 194). What infallibility means is not clear in the discussion. He is probably correct that "almost certainly the confusing term 'irreformable' would be omitted" today (p. 198).

39. E.g., T.F. Torrance has shown the misunderstanding concerning the doctrine of grace that entered the teaching of the church soon after the apostolic age. *The Doctrine of Grace in the Apostolic Fathers* (Edinburgh: Oliver and Boyd, 1948).

40. James Orr, *The Progress of Dogma* (London: Hodder and Stoughton, 1902), p. 30.

41. *Ibid.*, p. 23.

42. *Ibid.*, p. 21.

Notes to Chapter 2

1. T.C. Vriezen, *An Outline of Old Testament Theology* (Oxford: Basil Blackwell, 1958), p. 2.

2. *Ibid.*, p. 149.

3. On God's revelation, see, e.g., Walther Eichrodt, *Theology of the Old Testament* (Philadelphia: Westminster, 1961-67), II, 15-92; Vriezen, *An Outline of Old Testament Theology*, pp. 162, 232-69.

4. Vriezen, *op. cit.*, pp. 257-61.

5. *Ibid.*, p. 261.

6. Eichrodt, *op. cit.*, I, 36ff.

7. Gottlob Schrenk, *Gottesreich und Bund im älteren Protestantismus* (Darmstadt: Wissenschaftliche Buchgesellschaft, 1967), pp. 36-49; Hans Heinrich Wolf, *Die Einheit des Bundes* (Neukirchen: Buchhandlung des Erziehungsvereins, 1958), pp. 19-24. For an assessment of the place of the covenant in the thought of Calvin see my "Calvin on the Covenant," *Reformed Review*, XXXIII/3 (Spring 1980). See also Charles S. McCoy, "Johannes Cocccius: Federal Theologian," *Scottish Journal of Theology*, XVI (1963), 352-70; Everett M. Emerson, "Calvin and Covenant Theology," *Church History*, XXV (1956), 136-44.

8. Cf. Eichrodt, *op. cit.*, II, 104, esp. n. 3.

9. Donald M. Mathers, *The Word and the Way* (Toronto: United Church Publishing House, 1962), pp. 20f.

10. George S. Hendry, *Theology of Nature* (Philadelphia: Westminster, 1980), p. 14.

Notes to Chapter 3

1. Vriezen, *An Outline of Old Testament Theology*, p. 176.

2. W. Sanday, quoted by B. B. Warfield, "The Biblical Doctrine of the Trinity," in *Biblical and Theological Studies*, ed. by Samuel G. Craig (Philadelphia: Presbyterian and Reformed, 1952), p. 32.

3. Cf. A. Harnack, *History of Dogma* (New York: Russell and Russell, 1958), III, 40ff.; J.N.D. Kelly, *Early Christian Doctrines* (New York: Harper, 1958), pp. 115ff.

4. Warfield, "The Spirit of God in the Old Testament," *Biblical and Theological Studies*, pp. 127-56.

5. As Gustaf Aulén calls it, in *The Faith of the Christian Church*, p. 227.

6. *TDNT*, V, 243ff.

7. Emil Brunner, *Doctrine of God*, p. 117.

8. Eichrodt, *Theology of the Old Testament*, I, 206.

9. *Church Dogmatics*, II/1, 330.

10. *Ibid.*, p. 325.

11. Stephen Charnock, *The Existence and Attributes of God* (Grand Rapids: Kregel, 1958).

12. A modern theologian who shared the nominalist conviction was Friedrich Schleiermacher: "All attributes which we ascribe to God are to be taken as denoting not something special in God, but only something special in the manner in which the feeling of absolute dependence is to be related to Him." *The Christian Faith* (Edinburgh: T. & T. Clark, 1928), I, 194.

13. James Orr, *Side-Lights on Christian Doctrine* (London: Marshall Brothers, 1909), pp. 11f.

Notes to Chapter 4

1. Kelly, *Early Christian Doctrines*, p. 139.

2. Harnack, *History of Dogma*, III, 14ff. James Orr refers to the Alogi

as an "obscure party," to whom Harnack gave "a quite unmerited importance." *Progress of Dogma*, p. 90.

3. Harnack, *op. cit.*, pp. 40ff.; Kelly, *op. cit.*, pp. 115ff., 140; Orr, *op. cit.*, pp. 99ff.

4. Kelly, *op. cit.*, p. 141.

5. *Ibid.*

6. Harnack, *op. cit.*, I, 252.

7. Kelly, *op. cit.*, p. 141. For a description of the philosophy of Gnosticism, see pp. 22-28.

8. Orr, *op. cit.*, p. 97.

9. Harnack, *op. cit.*, II, 357; Kelly, *op. cit.*, pp. 128ff.; Orr, *op. cit.*, pp. 110f.

10. Kelly, *op. cit.*, pp. 224-26.

11. *Ibid.*, p. 227; cf. Jaroslav Pelikan, *The Christian Tradition: A History of the Development of Doctrine* (Chicago: Univ. of Chicago Press, 1971), I, 194f.

12. *Ibid.*, p. 173.

13. Quoted by Orr, *op. cit.*, pp. 109f. Cf. also Donald M. Baillie, *God Was in Christ* (New York: Scribner's, 1948), pp. 69f.

14. Schaff, *The Creeds of Christendom*, II, 60.

15. Kelly, *op. cit.*, p. 297.

16. Schaff, *The Creeds of Christendom*, II, 62f.; italics added. It is a curious historical fact that whereas the western (Latin) version of the creed reads "*in* two natures" just before the four italicized adverbs, the present Greek text reads "*from* two natures," making possible a Eutychian reading here, even though the text as a whole runs counter to that teaching. Schaff is of the opinion that the original Greek version also read "in two natures" and that it was altered in the interests of Eutychianism.

Birger Gerhardsson writes: "The synoptic tradition was transmitted and written down in the context of a church which did not believe Jesus to be a mere earthly teacher. It believed him to be the Messiah: Christ, the Son of Man, the Servant of the Lord, the Son of God, the Lord—to mention only a few of the messianic epithets. This high Christology cannot be disconnected from the impression made by Jesus on his disciples, and furthermore it must have some original connection with Jesus' own view of his work, of his position, and of himself. The opinion expressed by so many scholars, that the Christology of the N. T. is essentially a creation of the young church, is an intelligent thesis, but historically most improbable." *Memory and Manuscript* (Uppsala: Almquist & Wiksells, 1961), p. 325.

For further details on the development of christological dogma, see A. Grillmeier, S. J., *Christ in Christian Tradition*, Vol. I (Atlanta: John Knox, 1975).

Notes to Chapter 5

1. R.P.C. Hanson, *Tradition in the Early Church* (Philadelphia: Westminster, 1962), pp. 35ff., 96, 130.

2. Pelikan, *The Christian Tradition*, p. 116; the quotation within the quotation is from Irenaeus. Kelly remarks: "Admittedly there is no evidence for

beliefs or practices current in the period which were not vouched for in the books later known as the New Testament. But there is equally nothing to suggest, and general probability makes it unlikely, that Christian teachers had these books specifically in mind on the majority of occasions when they referred to the apostolic testimony. It is much more plausible that they were thinking generally of the common body of facts and doctrines, definite enough in outline though with varying emphases, which found expression in the Church's day-to-day preaching, liturgical action and catechetical instruction, just as much as in formal documents. It is a commonplace that the New Testament writers themselves presupposed, and on occasion quoted summaries of, this outline message or 'kerygma,' which apparently existed in various forms." *Early Christian Doctrines*, pp. 33f.

3. Gerhardsson points to a "commonplace which we recognize from elsewhere in Antiquity: an attitude of scepticism to the written word. . . . What can be learned from the written page cannot be compared with that which may be learned from the lips of a living person. The consummate knowledge is to be found in oral teaching, in which the pupil receives not only texts, but also interpretation." *Memory and Manuscript*, pp. 196f.

4. Hanson, *op. cit.*, p. 235.

5. *Ibid.*, p. 217.

6. *Ibid.*, p. 188; cf. Kelly, *op. cit.*, p. 58.

7. *Op. cit.*, p. 187; cf. W.C. van Unnik, "De la Règle," *Vigiliae Christianae*, III (1949), 1-36. For further discussion of the setting of the New Testament canon see A. Souter, *Text and Canon of the New Testament* (London: Duckworth, 1954); E. Flesseman-Van Leer, *Tradition and Scripture in the Early Church* (Assen: Van Gorcum, 1954); F.F. Bruce, *Tradition: Old and New* (Grand Rapids: Zondervan, 1970); B.F. Westcott, *The Canon of the New Testament* (London: Macmillan, 1896).

8. Cullmann writes: "The difference established between apostolic and post-apostolic tradition is not arbitrary, but . . . it is the difference which the Church itself made, at the decisive moment in the second century, by formulating the principle of an apostolic canon and an apostolic summary of belief." *The Early Church* (Philadelphia: Westminster, 1956), p. 96.

9. Schaff, *The Creeds of Christendom*, II, 80, 82.

10. Concerning Christian interpretation of the Old Testament, Harnack writes that the church "had to demonstrate the agreement between the two testaments, in other words, to christianize the OT completely, to discover prophecy everywhere. . . ." *History of Dogma*, III, 199.

11. See Kelly, *op. cit.*, p. 56, for locations.

12. *Ibid.*

13. Gerhardsson notes "the distinctiveness of the Christ-tradition" in this respect: "There is no equivalent to this in the accounts of any Rabbi; still less can such matters be regarded as standing at the centre of the Rabbinic tradition. This in turn implies that Jesus was regarded as the eschatological mediator of revelation, the *'only' teacher* in the most qualified meaning of the word." *Tradition and Transmission in Early Christianity* (Lund: C.W.K. Gleerup, 1964), p. 41.

14. Kelly, *op. cit.*, p. 66.

15. *Ibid.*, p. 61; Bavinck, *Gereformeerde Dogmatiek*, I, 423f.

16. *Ibid.*, pp. 473f.; cf. G. C. Berkouwer, *Holy Scripture* (Grand Rapids: Eerdmans, 1975), pp. 170-94.

17. CO, LIV, 292.

18. For a discussion of the history of the problems of the inspiration, interpretation, and authority of Scripture see Jack B. Rogers and Donald K. McKim, *The Authority and Interpretation of the Bible: An Historical Approach* (New York: Harper & Row, 1979).

Notes to Chapter 6

1. Harnack writes: "The two great types of thought . . . did not evolve themselves in the controversy. They gained in clearness and precision during its course, but both arose, independently of each other, from the internal conditions of the church. We can observe here, if anywhere, the 'logic' of history. There has never, perhaps, been another crisis of equal importance in church history in which the opponents have expressed the principles at issue so clearly and abstractly." *History of Dogma*, V, 169.

2. *On Grace and Free Will*, 6, in NPNF, Vol. V.

3. See the evidence in Kelly, *Early Christian Doctrines*, pp. 346ff.

4. *De Principiis*, I, vii, 4; II, viii, 3, 4 *(ANF, Vol. IV)*.

5. *On Marriage and Concupiscence*, II, 30 (NPNF, Vol. V).

6. *On the Forgiveness of Sins, and Baptism*, II, 36 (NPNF, Vol. V); *City of God*, XIII, 20; XIV, 11 (NPNF, Vol. II).

7. *On Rebuke and Grace*, 32, 33; *On the Forgiveness of Sins, and Baptism*, I, 2 (both NPNF, Vol. V); *Enchiridion*, 105 (NPNF, Vol. III); *City of God*, XII, 21; XIII, 20.

8. *On the Soul and Its Origin*, I, 6; II, 4, 7-9; IV, 18-20, 38 (NPNF, Vol. V); *De Quantitate Animae*, in Migne, *Patrologiae Latinae* (Paris, 1865), XXXII, 1035ff.

9. *On the Soul and Its Origin*, I, 27; IV, 5; *De Quantitate Animae*, I, 2.

10. Orr, *The Progress of Dogma*, p. 146.

11. *Against Two Letters of the Pelagians*, I, 57; *On Grace and Free Will*, 3 (NPNF, Vol. V).

12. *Contra secundum Juliani Responsionem imperfectum opus*, in Migne, *op. cit.*, XLV, I, 78. Harnack calls this statement of Julian "the key to the whole mode of thought; man created free is with his whole sphere independent of God. He has no longer to do with God, but with himself alone. God only re-enters at the end (at the judgment)." *Op cit.*, V, 200 n. 3.

13. *On the Grace of Christ*, I, 2 (NPNF, Vol. V).

14. *Op. cit.*, V, 62ff.; cf. Orr, *op. cit.*, p. 146.

15. *Against Two Letters of the Pelagians*, III, 24.

16. *On the Grace of Christ*, I, 5 (NPNF, Vol. V); cf. Pelagius, *The Christian Life and Other Essays*, tr. F.L. Battles (Pittsburgh, 1972), p. 61.

17. *Ibid.*, I, 28, 38. Elsewhere Augustine writes that in Pelagianism the only grace which is not given according to merits is forgiveness. *On Grace and Free Will*, 15.

18. *Enchiridion*, 27, 45-48; *On the Forgiveness of Sins, and Baptism*, I, 8-16.

19. *Enchiridion*, 11-15.

20. *On Marriage and Concupiscence,* I, 9ff.

21. *Against Two Letters of the Pelagians,* III, 22.

22. *On the Grace of Christ,* I, 25; *On Rebuke and Grace,* 45, 13-25; *On the Spirit and the Letter,* 5, 21, 34; *On Nature and Grace,* 4, 62; *On the Predestination of the Saints,* 34-37 (*NPNF,* Vol. V).

23. *On Grace and Free Will,* 15.

24. *Ibid.,* 20.

25. Canons of the Synod of Dort, III, 2, in Schaff, *Creeds of Christendom,* III, 588.

26. Harnack, *History of Dogma,* V, 258ff.; cf. Pelikan, *The Christian Tradition,* p. 329. Harry J. McSorley notes that "from the tenth to the middle of the sixteenth century. . . , theologians seem to have been completely unaware of the existence of the Council of Orange and its teachings. Only at the time of the Council of Trent were they recovered and reaffirmed. Since Trent they have been restored to their rightful place as important witnesses of the tradition of the ancient Church in Catholic treatises on grace." *Luther: Right or Wrong?* (New York: Newman Press, 1969), pp. 118, 121f.

27. Examples are the bull *Cum Occasione* of Innocent X in 1653, reaffirmed by Alexander VII in 1665, and the bull *Unigenitus Dei Filius* of Clement XI in 1713. An example of Pelagian teaching in a contemporary Roman Catholic theological text is the popular symposium *The Teaching of the Catholic Church,* ed. George D. Smith (New York: Macmillan, 1949), where, in the discussion on sin (I, 331ff.), the Pelagianism leaps from the page.

28. *On the Predestination of the Saints,* 7.

29. *Ibid.,* 16, 10, 15, 19.

30. *Ibid.,* 9.

31. *Ibid.*

32. Besides *On the Predestination of the Saints,* he wrote a second treatise, *On the Gift of Perseverance;* cf. also *On Rebuke and Grace,* 20-25; *Enchiridion,* 100ff.; *City of God,* XV, 1.

33. *On the Gift of Perseverance,* 35.

34. *On the Predestination of the Saints,* 30f.; cf. *On the Gift of Perseverance,* 67.

35. *On the Predestination of the Saints,* 34.

36. *On Rebuke and Grace,* 17.

37. *On the Predestination of the Saints,* 19.

38. Finding its biblical base in 1 Cor. 12:6, Luther often uses the expression "God works all in all." Althaus comments that Luther "expands the sense of this passage far beyond Paul's meaning in its original setting." *The Theology of Martin Luther* (Philadelphia: Fortress, 1963), p. 274.

39. "The Bondage of the Will," in *LW,* XXXIII, 37.

40. The "American Edition" of *Luther's Works* softens and corrupts Luther's language in translation here. Instead of his strong "God foreknows and wills all things" (*praesciat et velit*), it reads: "God foreknows all things." The omission of "and wills" misses the very point of Luther's argument. Luther says that without this confidence that God knows *and wills* all things one cannot "believe his promises and place a sure trust and reliance on them. For when he promises anything, you ought to be certain that he knows and is able and willing to perform what he promises. . . . Christian faith is entirely

extinguished, the promises of God and the whole gospel are completely destroyed, if we teach and believe that it is not for us to know the necessary foreknowledge of God and the necessity of the things that are to come to pass." *Ibid.*, pp. 42f.

41. *Ibid.*, p. 293.

42. Althaus is correct that "in spite of all appearances to the contrary" Luther's theology of predestination is "completely untheoretical and pastoral" while Calvin works out "a theoretical doctrine of double predestination." *The Theology of Martin Luther*, p. 286.

43. The common belief that the Synod of Dordt taught "limited atonement" is based on the statement that the "saving efficacy" of the work of Christ is for the elect alone (II, viii). In its sufficiency (II, iii), availability (II, v), God's desire and the sincerity of the offer (III, viii, ix), there is no limitation whatever. Cf. Harold Dekker, "Redemptive Love and the Gospel Offer," *The Reformed Journal*, Jan. 1964, pp. 8ff.; "Telling the Good News to All Men," *RJ*, March 1964, pp. 15ff.; "Limited Atonement and Evangelism," *RJ*, Dec. 1964, pp. 22ff.; James Daane, "What Doctrine of Limited Atonement?" *RJ*, Dec. 1964, pp. 13ff.

44. Francois Wendel, *Calvin: The Origins and Development of His Religious Thought*, tr. Philip Mairet (New York: Harper & Row, 1963), p. 268.

45. E.g., "The Eternal Predestination of God" and "A Defense of the Secret Providence of God," *CO*, VIII, 249-366. Cf. Wendell, *op. cit.*, p. 269.

46. For a summary of recent criticism see K. Runia, "Recent Reformed Criticisms of the Canons," in P.Y. De Jong, ed., *Crisis in the Reformed Churches* (Grand Rapids: Reformed Fellowship, 1968). Barth says that Remonstrant thought "should be interpreted in the light of the persistence of medieval Pelagianism." *Church Dogmatics*, II/2, 67. See also L. Knappert, *Geschiedenis der Nederlandsche Hervormde Kerk Gedurende de 16e en 17e Eeuw* (Amsterdam: Meulenhoff, 1911), I, 128.

47. For evidence that the threat of this brand of Unitarianism was not imaginary, see Scott, *The Articles of the Synod of Dort and Its Rejection of Errors* (Utica, N.Y.: William Williams, 1831), pp. 29, 36f., 42ff., 73f.; H. John McLachlan, *Socinianism in Seventeenth Century England* (London: Oxford U.P., 1951), pp. 30ff.; Cornelis Van der Woude, *Sibrandus Lubbertus* (Kampen: J.H. Kok, 1963), pp. 157, 181-84, 576; William Cunningham, *Historical Theology* (Edinburgh: T. & T. Clark, 1863), II, 375ff.; G.P. van Itterzon, *Franciscus Gomarus* (The Hague: Martinus Nijhoff, 1930), pp. 189-99,294.

48. At his trial J. van Oldenbarneveldt, a member of the Remonstrant party, said that he did not consider the doctrinal questions one-tenth as important as "the authority of the States to pass ecclesiastical laws and ordinances." He is also reported to have said, "My Lords, the States-General, are the foster-fathers and natural protectors of the church, to whom supreme authority in church matters belongs." Henry E. Dosker, "John of Barneveldt, Martyr or Traitor?" *The Presbyterian and Reformed Review*, IX (1898), 314, 318.

49. Wendel, *op. cit.*, p. 182. Cf. Calvin, *Inst.*, III, xxiii, 12.

Notes to Chapter 7

1. Oscar Cullmann, *Christ and Time*, tr. F.V. Filson (Philadelphia: Westminster, 1950), p. 135.

2. *Ibid*., pp. 144ff.; see also William Manson, "Eschatology in the New Testament," in *Eschatology: Four Papers* (Edinburgh: Oliver and Boyd Ltd., n.d.).

3. G.W.H. Lampe, "Early Patristic Eschatology," in *Eschatology: Four Papers*, p. 29.

4. Oscar Cullmann, *Early Christian Worship* (London: Henry Regnery, 1953), p. 116.

5. Charles Norris Cochrane, *Christianity and Classical Culture* (New York: Oxford U.P., 1944), p. 483.

6. Marcus Dods, in the "Translator's Preface" to *City of God*, NPNF, II, xii.

Notes to Chapter 8

1. Orr, *The Progress of Dogma*, pp. 209f.

2. See Robert S. Franks, *A History of the Doctrine of the Work of Christ in Its Ecclesiastical Development* (New York: Hodder and Stoughton, n.d.), I, 11-163.

3. *Ibid*., pp. 34-51.

4. *Ibid*., pp. 51-62.

5. *The Incarnation of the Word of God*, 4, 6, 7 (NPNF, 2nd series, Vol. IV).

6. *Ibid*., 8.

7. *Ibid*., 9.

8. *Ibid*., 20.

9. *Ibid*., 29f.

10. This expression is used repeatedly, e.g., 7, 45. The rational cast of the treatise is also seen in the frequency of the expressions "fitting," "unfitting," "unfittingness," "incongruity," "unsuitable," "unworthy," "consonant," "unthinkable," as well as the statement in the opening paragraph: "There is inconsistency between creation and salvation."

11. *Great Catechism*, 26 (NPNF, 2nd series, Vol. V).

12. *Second Oration on Easter*, XXII (NPNF, 2nd series, Vol. VII).

13. Cf. Franks, *op. cit*., I, 128.

14. *Cur Deus Homo*, I, 1, in *St. Anselm: Proslogium; Monologium; Cur Deus Homo?* tr. S.N. Deane (LaSalle, Ill.: Open Court, 1951).

15. *Ibid*., I, 9, 10.

16. *Ibid*., I, 10.

17. *Ibid*., I, 11.

18. *Ibid*., I, 12.

19. *Ibid*., I, 20.

20. *Ibid*., I, 20, 21.

21. *Ibid*., I, 12.

22. *Ibid*., I, 13.

23. *Ibid.*, I, 21.
24. *Ibid.*, II, 5.
25. *Ibid.*, II, 6.
26. *Ibid.*, II, 10, 11.
27. *Ibid.*, II, 18b.
28. *Ibid.*, II, 14.
29. For assessments of Anselm's doctrine see Franks, *op. cit.*, I, 164ff.; II, 81, 106: Harnack, *History of Dogma*, VI, 54ff.
30. Cf. Franks, *op. cit.*, I, 193ff.
31. J.A. Dorner, *A System of Christian Doctrine* (Edinburgh: T. & T. Clark, 1880), IV, 22f., quoted by Orr, *op. cit.*, pp. 234f.
32. Franks, *op. cit.*, I, 301ff.
33. Harnack writes correctly: "Socinianism has no ground in its own premises for recognizing the Godhead of Christ." *Op. cit.*, VII, 146.
34. A. Ritschl, *The Christian Doctrine of Justification and Reconciliation*, as quoted by Orr, *op. cit.*, p. 236.
35. A. Mitchell Hunter, *The Teaching of Calvin* (London: James Clarke, 1950), p. 111.
36. On this see Wendel, *Calvin: The Origins and Development of His Religious Thought*, pp. 127ff.
37. For Luther's strong emphasis here see Althaus, *The Theology of Martin Luther*, pp. 208ff.; and Gustaf Aulén, *Christus Victor* (London: SPCK, 1931). Aulén's thesis, that this is Luther's line of thought in opposition to Anselm and the Latin type of atonement teaching, is shown by Althaus to be a "significant misinterpretation of Luther" (pp. 218ff.).
38. See, e.g., Luther on Gal. 3:13; *Lectures on Galatians* (*LW*, XXVI, 276ff.).

Notes to Chapter 9

1. Schaff, *History of the Christian Church*, VII, 1.
2. *Ibid.*, V, 156 n. 1.
3. Quoted by E. Gordon Rupp, *The Righteousness of God* (London: Hodder and Stoughton, 1953), pp. 103f., 111.
4. Heiko Oberman, *The Harvest of Medieval Theology* (Cambridge: Harvard U.P., 1963), p. 132. Cf. Biel's sermon, "The Circumcision of the Lord," in Oberman's *Forerunners of the Reformation* (London: Lutterworth, 1967), pp. 169ff.
5. *Harvest of Medieval Theology*, p. 133.
6. McSorley, *Luther: Right or Wrong?* pp. 218ff., 224ff., 228ff. McSorley, a Roman Catholic, challenges Luther's condemnation by Leo X in 1520.
7. *Ibid.*, p. 294.
8. Harnack, *History of Dogma*, VII, 203. Luther remarks that Erasmus' position is worse than that of the Pelagians (*LW*, XXXIII, 268, 280).
9. *The Bondage of the Will* (*LW*, XXXIII, 206-11, 262ff., 270ff.
10. *Ibid.*, pp. 288f.

Notes to Chapter 10

1. This distinction between the meritorious and formal causes of justification, which predated the Council of Trent (1545-63), was continued after the council. See quotations in William Cunningham, *Historical Theology*, II, 19f.
2. Quoted in Schaff, *The Creeds of Christendom*, II, 99.
3. *Ibid.*, p. 92.
4. *Op. cit.*, II, 12. Cunningham claims that there were "two or three rash and incautious expressions of Luther . . . which . . . the Council did not scruple" to use in order to prejudice the case against the Reformers.
5. Quoted by Althaus, *The Theology of Luther*, p. 224.
6. *Ibid.*, p. 225.
7. *LW*, XXXIV, 336ff.
8. *Ibid.*, XXVI, 133.
9. This medley of comments is taken from the *Lectures on Galatians (LW*, XXVI, 152, 159, 160, 161, 167, 168).
10. Orr, *Progress of Dogma*, p. 251.
11. *LW*, XXVI, 140.
12. Orr, *op. cit.*, p. 253.
13. Quoted by James Buchanan, *The Christian Doctrine of Justification* (Grand Rapids: Baker, 1955), p. 129.

Notes to Chapter 11

1. Cf. his letters in *ANF*, Vol. 1: *Smyr.* 8; *Trall.*, 2; *Phil.*, 4.
2. For Roman Catholic statements see McSorley, *Luther: Right or Wrong?;* Joseph Lortz, *The Reformation in Germany* (New York: Herder and Herder, 1968).
3. Althaus, *The Theology of Luther*, p. 287.
4. *LW*, XLI, 143.
5. *Ibid.*, p. 144.
6. Althaus, *The Theology of Luther*, p. 298; cf. his *Communio Sanctorum* (Munich: Kaiser, 1929).
7. Althaus, *The Theology of Luther*, p. 298.
8. *Ibid.* Attacking the usual view of the saints and treasury of merits, Luther writes: "The merits of the saints cannot act as a treasury for us since the saints themselves considered them deficient; unless someone should think that they are a treasure for us, not because they are surplus merits, but because the church is a communion of saints in which each one works for the other, as members one of another. But the saints did this during their lifetime, and if they were to do it now, it would be accomplished by intercession rather than by the power of the keys." *LW*, XXXI, 216.
9. Althaus, *op. cit.*, p. 305.
10. *Ibid.*, pp. 305f.
11. *Ibid.*, pp. 308ff.
12. *Ibid.*, pp. 302f.
13. *LW*, XXXI, 318.

14. Schaff, *History of the Christian Church,* VII, 182.

15. *LW,* XXXIX, 65-72.

16. *Ibid.,* p. 101.

17. Theodore G. Tappert, ed., *The Book of Concord* (Philadelphia: Muhlenberg, 1959), p. 315.

18. *LW,* XLI, 148. Luther complained against the Zwichau prophets' denigration of the Bible in the interests of personal experience. "The Bible means nothing" to them, he laments. The Zwickau prophets said, "It is Bible—Booble—Bable," as they derided Luther's insistence on Scripture. *LW,* XL, 50.

19. *LW,* XLI, 151ff.

20. *Ibid.,* pp. 166ff., 173. Luther denounces Canon Law as a "stinking and filthy book."

21. *Ibid.,* pp. 223ff.

22. *Ibid.,* p. 199.

23. *Ibid.,* pp. 199f.

24. *Ibid.,* pp. 211 (cf. 126ff.), 217, 232.

25. *LW,* XL, 383ff.

26. *Ibid.,* pp. 7ff.

27. *Ibid.,* pp. 36f.

28. *Ibid.* Seeberg cites three instances where Luther writes: "Therefore upon whomsoever the office of preaching is laid, upon him is laid the highest office in the church." *Text-book of the History of Doctrines* (Philadelphia: Lutheran Publication Society, 1905), II, 294.

29. *LW,* XL, 269ff.

30. A major theme of Luther's tract *To the Christian Nobility of the German Nation (LW,* XLIV, 127ff.; cf. XXXIX, 151ff., 234ff.).

31. *LW,* XL, 34.

32. *Ibid.*

33. *Ibid.*

34. Where bishops were retained in Lutheran lands, as in Pomerania, in 1525, it was decided: "Bishops shall continue and remain: not anointing-bishops, nor ordaining-bishops, but such as preach and teach and expound the pure Word of God and preside over the church." G.D. Henderson, *Presbyterianism* (Aberdeen: The University Press, 1954), p. 34. Henderson relates Beza's decided influence against hierarchy in the Reformed churches: "At Geneva Calvin had indicated, and the Council without hesitation agreed, that Beza should be his successor in the unofficial leadership of ecclesiastical affairs; but when the matter came before the Compagnie des Pasteurs, Beza, who had been acting as moderator in Calvin's place during his illness, proposed that they go back to annual appointment. He set forth the risks of a pre-eminence that might re-introduce pre-Reformation abuses, and might set a bad example for other Reformed Churches. Beza was elected, but only for the year, re-elected, however, after that annually till his death. Parity had become a dogma" (p. 47).

35. *CO,* X, 23f.

36. Cf. Winthrop S. Hudson, *The Great Tradition of the American Churches* (New York: Harper & Brothers, 1953), pp. 19ff.

Notes to Chapter 12

1. The crude mentality of church officialdom in Berengar's time is shown in the oath extracted from him in 1059, "that bread and wine, which are placed on the altar after consecration, are not just a sacrament but are also the true body and blood of our Lord Jesus Christ, and not only sacramentally but in truth are handled and broken by the hands of the priests and are chewed by the teeth of the faithful." J.P. Whitney, *Hildebrandine Essays* (Cambridge: The University Press, 1932), p. 179.

2. Epp. 138, 7 (*NPNF*, 1st series, I, 483).

3. Cf. *On the Sacraments of the Christian Faith*, ed. Roy J. DeFerrari (Cambridge, Mass.: Medieval Academy of America, 1951).

4. Schaff, *Creeds of Christendom*, II, 119.

5. *Ibid.*, pp. 120ff., 176.

6. *LW*, XXXVI, 18.

7. *Ibid.*, p. 29.

8. *Ibid.*, pp. 36ff.

9. *Ibid.*, pp. 47f.

10. *Ibid.*, p. 124.

11. *LW*, XXXVII, 29.

12. *Ibid.*, p. 53.

13. A.M. Fairbairn, in *The Cambridge Modern History* (Cambridge: The University Press, 1934), II, 345f.

14. In *The Library of Christian Classics: Zwingli and Bullinger* (Philadelphia: Westminster, 1953), XXIV, 181f.

15. *Ibid.*, pp. 254ff., 176ff.; *LW*, XXXVII, p. xii; cf. Frank Hugh Foster, "Zwingli's Theology, Philosophy, and Ethics," in Samuel Macauley Jackson, *Huldreich Zwingli* (New York: Putnam, 1901), pp. 365ff.

16. *Library of Christian Classics*, XXIV, 258, 259.

17. *LW*, XXXVII, 55, 57, 63f., 65, 210, 214, 229.

18. *Ibid.*, pp. 215f.

19. Althaus, *The Theology of Luther*, p. 392. Cf. J.L. Neve, *A History of Christian Thought* (Philadelphia: Muhlenberg, 1946), I, 249ff., 302ff. Neve writes that in the final Lutheran settlement in the *Formula of Concord* it is held that "Christ's Body and Blood are truly and essentially present and are received with the bread and wine. It is not, however, a 'physical or earthly presence'. ... It takes place in a supernatural, incomprehensible, heavenly way" (p. 306).

20. Seeberg, *Text-book of the History of Doctrines*, II, 320.

21. Hunter, *The Teaching of Calvin*, p. 182.

22. Calvin, *Tracts*, II, 244-579.

23. *Ibid.*, p. 384.

24. *Ibid.*, p. 502.

25. *Ibid.*, p. 576.

26. *Ibid.*, p. 577.

27. *Ibid.*, pp. 89ff.

28. *Letters of John Calvin*, ed. Jules Bonnet (New York: Burt Franklin, 1972), III, 82.

29. Hunter, *op. cit.*, p. 185.

30. *Ibid.*, p. 186. For evidence that Luther did not feel the antipathy to-

wards Calvin's doctrine of the eucharist that he felt towards Zwingli's, see Schaff, *History of the Christian Church*, VII, 659f.

31. Cf. Seeberg, *Text-book of the History of Doctrines*, I, 332.

32. Schaff, *Creeds of Christendom*, II, 87f.

33. *The Catechism of the Council of Trent*, tr. T.A. Buckley (London: George Routledge and Co., 1852), Part II, Ch. II, Q. 41.

34. Cf. *The Holy and Blessed Sacrament of Baptism (LW*, XXXV, 29-43).

35. Cf. Althaus, *The Theology of Luther*, pp. 356ff.; Seeberg, *op. cit.*, II, 284.

36. Seeberg, *op. cit.*, pp. 283ff. Luther's "Small Catechism" gives a clear statement of his position. Schaff, *Creeds of Christendom*, III, 85ff.

37. Seeberg, *op. cit.*, II, 316.

38. Pierre Marcel, *The Biblical Doctrine of Infant Baptism: Sacrament of the Covenant of Grace* (London: James Clarke, 1953), p. 118.

39. E.g., Joachim Jeremias, *Infant Baptism in the First Four Centuries* (London: SCM Press, 1960), pp. 26, 28, 37ff.; A. Oepke, in *TDNT*, I, 535; W. Brandt, in *Hastings' Encyclopedia of Religion and Ethics* (New York: Scribner's, 1928), II, 408; Strack-Billerbeck, *Kommentar zum Neuen Testament aus Talmud und Midrasch* (München: C.H. Beck'sche Verlagsbuchhandlung, 1922), I, 103.

40. Jeremias, *Infant Baptism in the First Four Centuries*, pp. 60-63. Cf. *The Martyrdom of Polycarp*, ix (*ANF*, I, 41).

41. Irenaeus, *Against Heresies*, II, xxii, 4; III, xvii, 1 (*ANF*, I, 391, 444).

42. Cited by Jeremias, *op. cit.*, p. 65.

43. Tertullian, *Homily on Baptism*, tr. and ed. Ernest Evans (London: SPCK, 1964), p. 39.

44. Cf. Joachim Jeremias, *The Origins of Infant Baptism* (London: SCM Press, 1963), pp. 65ff.

45. *NPNF*, 1st series, Vol. I, p. 157n.

46. A.H. Newman, *A History of Anti-Pedobaptism* (Philadelphia: American Baptist Publication Society, 1897), p. 3.

47. Marcel, *The Biblical Doctrine of Infant Baptism*, p. 235.

48. *Ibid.*, pp. 236ff. An able statement against infant baptism is Paul K. Jewett's *Infant Baptism and the Covenant of Grace* (Grand Rapids: Eerdmans, 1978).

NOTES TO EXCURSUS: The mode of baptism

a. So, e.g., Alexander Carson, *Baptism in its Mode and Subjects* (Philadelphia: American Baptist Publication Society, 1860), pp. 119ff., 163.

b. Lexicographers list "dip" and "moisten" as meanings for *tabal*; so, e.g., Brown, Driver, Briggs, *Hebrew and English Lexicon of the Old Testament* (New York: Houghton, Mifflin, 1906); Edward König, *Hebräisches und Aramäisches Wörterbuch zum alten Testament* (Leipzig: Dietrich, 1931); Solomon Mandelkern, *Veteris Testamenti Concordantiae Hebraicae atque Chaldaicae* (Leipzig: Margolin, 1925); see also the commentary by A. Dillmann, *Die Bücher Exodus und Leviticus* (Leipzig: Hirzel, 1880), pp. 423, 517.

c. H.B. Swete, *Mark* (London: Macmillan, 1898), *in loco*.

d. See Strack-Billerbeck, *Kommentar zum Neuen Testament*, II, 691-704, for supporting rabbinical evidence.

e. John Murray, *Christian Baptism* (Philadelphia: Committee on Christian Education of the Orthodox Presbyterian Church, 1952), pp. 16f.

f. *Ibid.*, p. 21.

g. Murray comments: "What immersions, prescribed in the Old Testament, are directly pertinent to the precise thought of this passage and will satisfy the description 'divers baptisms?' " *Ibid.*, p. 22. Cf. Moses Stuart, "Is the Manner of Christian Baptism Prescribed in the New Testament?", *Biblical Repository*, April 1833, pp. 370ff.

h. The meaning of the second clause is the same as the first, in accordance with the rule of parallelism in Hebrew poetry. Purging, sprinkling with hyssop, *is* washing to the Psalmist.

i. So, e.g., John R. Church, *Why Baptize by Sprinkling?* (Louisville: Herald Press, n.d.).

j. Against the argument that this passage teaches immersion, Warfield states that Paul "labors to make his readers connect their baptism with the death and resurrection of Christ by the aid of another mediating thought; viz., that their baptism was with respect to Christ's death for their sins. He repeats the heavy clause, 'through baptism unto death' (Rom. 6:4) in order to prevent them from missing a point which, if baptism in its very mode symbolized burial and resurrection with Christ, they could not in any event miss." *The New Schaff-Herzog Encyclopedia of Religious Knowledge* (Grand Rapids: Baker, 1949), I, 449. Cf. Murray, *op. cit.*, p. 31.

Notes to Chapter 13

1. *LW*, XXXVI, 5.
2. *LW*, XXXI, 344.
3. *Ibid.*, p. 366.
4. *Ibid.*, pp. 361f.
5. *Ibid.*, pp. 354f.
6. *Ibid.*, p. 357.
7. *Ibid.*, pp. 367f.
8. *Ibid.*, p. 371.
9. W.J. Kooiman, *Luther: Zijn Weg en Werk* (Amsterdam: Ten Have, 1954), p. 46.
10. *LW*, XXXI, 373.
11. *Ibid.*, p. 374.
12. *Ibid.*, pp. 344, 368.

Notes to Chapter 14

1. E.g., E. Doumergue, *Jean Calvin* (Lausanne: Georges Bridel & Cie, 1910), IV, 37-39, makes the honor and sovereignty of God Calvin's fundamental emphasis. Cf. E. Troeltsch in "Calvin and Calvinism," *Hibbert Journal*, VIII (1909/10), 106; and Benjamin B. Warfield, *Calvin and Calvinism* (New

York: Oxford U.P., 1930), p. 354. W. Niesel, *Theology of Calvin*, tr. Harold Knight (Philadelphia: Westminster, 1956), p. 247, sees Jesus Christ as determinative of both the form and content of Calvin's theology, and offers a summary of various other positions (pp. 10-20). Benjamin Charles Milner, Jr., *Calvin's Doctrine of the Church* (Leiden: E.J. Brill, 1970), p. 4, finds the "unifying principle" in Calvin's theology to be "the absolute correlation of the Spirit and the Word," order ensuing when the Word expresses himself and is worked upon by the Spirit.

2. Hermann Bauke, *Die Probleme der Theologie Calvins* (Leipzig: Verlag der J. C. Hinrichs'schen Buchhandlung, 1922), pp. 11-19. Bauke believes that in Calvin "the particular fundamentals of dogmatics stand alongside each other and are dialectically bound to each other, but not deductively derived from one or two fundamental principles" (p. 32). Cf. Wendel, *Calvin*, p. 357.

3. Warfield, *op. cit.*, pp. 22f.

4. Josef Bohatec, *Calvin und das Recht* (Feudingen in Westfalen: Buchdruckerei u. Verlagsanstalt GmbH, 1934), p. 62.

5. Warfield, *op. cit.*, p. 107.

6. E.g., Werner Krusche, *Das Wirken des Heiligen Geistes nach Calvin* (Göttingen: Vandenhoeck & Ruprecht, 1957); Simon Vander Linde, *De Leer van den Heiligen Geest bij Calvijn* (Wageningen: H. Veenman & Zonen, 1943); H.J.J.T. Quistorp, "Calvins Lehre vom Heiligen Geist," in *De Spiritu Sancto* (Utrecht: Kemink en Zoon N.V., 1964), p. 109.

7. Milner, *op. cit.*; I. John Hesselink, *Calvin's Concept and Use of Law* (unpublished dissertation, Basel, 1961), Ch. VIII; Lucien Joseph Richard, *The Spirituality of John Calvin* (Atlanta: John Knox, 1974), pp. 97-166.

8. Cf. Cochrane, *Christianity and Classical Culture*, pp. 165f., and Chs. X, XI; Josef Bohatec, *Budé und Calvin* (Graz: Verlag Hermann Böhlaus, 1950); Quirinus Breen, *John Calvin: A Study in French Humanism* (Grand Rapids: Eerdmans, 1931); Wendel, *Calvin*, pp. 27-37.

9. The expression is from Flückiger, *Geschichte des Naturrechts* (Zurich, 1954), quoted by David Little, *Religion, Order, and Law: A Study in Pre-Revolutionary England* (New York: Harper & Row, 1969), p. 36.

10. *Op. cit.*, p. 166.

11. Little, *op. cit.*, pp. 36f.

12. Comm. on Lam. 3:37f.; cf. Comm. on Lev. 26:26; *Inst.*, I, xvii, 12. In *Calvin's Doctrine of the Church*, pp. 13-16, Milner calls attention to the distinction in Calvin between "order" and "ordinance."

13. Cf. the chapters in the *Inst.* on predestination (III, xxi-xxiii) and providence (I, xvi, xvii); also Comm. on Jonah 1:4; Acts 28:1.

14. Milner, *op. cit.*, p. 164.

15. Cf. A.A. van Ruler, *De Vervulling van de Wet* (Nijkerk: Callenbach, 1947), pp. 185, 152.

16. Cf. Milner, *op. cit.*, pp. 191f.; Krusche, *op. cit.*, pp. 5-12; I.J. Hesselink, *op. cit.*, VIII, 8, 20.

17. See this emphasis in Van Ruler, *op. cit.*, pp. 174-79.

18. Milner, *op. cit.*, p. 164; cf. p. 138.

19. Cf. Alexandre Ganoczy, *Calvin: Theologien de L'Église et du Ministère* (Paris: Editions du Cerf, 1964), p. 12; A.M. Fairbairn: "Calvin was greater as a legislator than a theologian. ... His polity is a more perfect

expression of the man than his theology." *The Cambridge Modern History*
(Cambridge: The University Press, 1934), II, 364.

20. Ganoczy, *Calvin*, p. 13; cf. p. 275 and all of Ch. IV; see also Wendel, *Calvin*, pp. 302f.

21. *Inst.*, IV, iv, 2-4; cf. J. Pannier, *Calvin et l'épiscopat* (Paris/Strasbourg: Cahiers de la RHPR, 1927). In his letter to the King of Poland of Dec. 5, 1554, Calvin approves bishops while criticizing the papacy. About bishops he writes, in part: ". . . as if, at the present day, one archbishop should have a certain pre-eminence in the illustrious kingdom of Poland, not to lord it over the others, nor arrogate to himself a right of which they were forcibly deprived, but for the sake of order to occupy the first place in synods, and cherish a holy unity between his colleagues and brethren. Then there might be either provincial or urban bishops, whose functions should be particularly directed to the preservation of order." *Letters of John Calvin*, III, 104 (CO, XV, 333).

22. Cf. W.P. Stephens, *The Holy Spirit in the Theology of Martin Bucer* (Cambridge: The University Press, 1970), p. 270 n. 4.

23. Wendel, *Calvin*, p. 71.

24. CO, X/1, 15-17.

25. Cf. Ganoczy, *Calvin*, p. 300.

26. *Ibid.*, p. 366. In the Comm. on Eph. 4:11 Calvin calls teachers a "distinct class . . . who preside both in the education of pastors and in the instruction of the whole church."

27. Ganoczy, *Calvin*, p. 384.

28. Milner, *op. cit.*, pp. 152f.

29. Comm. on Mal. 2:4, quoted by Milner, *op. cit.* I am indebted to Milner for his excellent exposition.

30. John T. McNeill, "John Calvin on Civil Government," in *Calvinism and the Political Order*, ed. George L. Hunt (Philadelphia: Westminster, 1965), p. 24.

31. A.M. Fairbairn, in *The Cambridge Modern History*, II, 366.

32. Little, *op. cit.*, p. 45.

33. William A. Mueller, *Church and State in Luther and Calvin* (Nashville: Broadman, 1954), p. 129.

34. Josef Bohatec, *Calvins Lehre von Staat und Kirche* (Breslau: M. u.H. Marcus, 1937), p. 171;cf. Mueller, *op. cit.*, p. 128.

35. Mueller, *op. cit.*, p. 129.

36. Marc-Edouard Cheneviere, *La Pensée Politique de Calvin* (Geneva: Labor, 1937), p. 123.

37. In Hunt, *loc. cit.*, p. 34.

38. *Ibid.*, p. 37.

39. *Ibid.*

40. Ronald S. Wallace, *Calvin's Doctrine of the Christian Life* (Grand Rapids: Eerdmans, 1959), p. 215.

41. M. Eugene Osterhaven, *The Spirit of the Reformed Tradition* (Grand Rapids: Eerdmans, 1971), pp. 88-94. Luther held a similar position; see J.T. Bakker, *Coram Deo: Bijdrage tot het Onderzoek naar de Structuur van Luthers Theologie* (Kampen: Kok, 1956).

42. Hesselink, *op. cit.*, Ch. VI, p. 6.

43. *Ibid.*, Ch. VIII, p. 84.

44. *Ibid.*, Ch. VIII, p. 2.
45. *Ibid.*, Ch. VI, p. 10.
46. *Ibid.*, Ch. VI, p. 4.
47. *Ibid.*, Ch. VI, pp. 11f.; VIII, pp. 49-54.
48. A. Dakin, *Calvinism* (Philadelphia: Westminster, 1946), p. 198.
49. Richard, *The Spirituality of John Calvin*, p. 112.
50. James I. Packer, "Calvin the Theologian," in *John Calvin*, ed. G.E. Duffield (Grand Rapids: Eerdmans, 1966), pp. 167f. Doumergue called Calvin the "great systematic thinker of the Reformation." *Jean Calvin*, IV, 476.
51. John Dillenberger, "An Introduction to John Calvin," in *John Calvin: Selections from His Writings* (Garden City, N.Y.: Doubleday, 1971), p. 18.

Notes to Chapter 15

1. Morton S. Kelsey, in a lecture at Western Theological Seminary on "The Reality of the Spiritual World," March 14, 1979.
2. Descartes assumed that the mind can cut itself off from the rest of experience to construct a system of thought. William Temple says that the day Descartes sat by the stove and hit upon this method was the "most disastrous moment in the history of Europe." *Nature, Man and God* (London: Macmillan, 1951), p. 57.
3. Robert Middlekauff, *The Mathers: Three Generations of Puritan Intellectuals, 1596-1728* (New York: Oxford U.P., 1971), p. 314.
4. On this so-called "practical syllogism," see J. Steven O'Malley, *Pilgrimage of Faith: The Legacy of the Otterbeins* (Metuchen, N.J.: The Scarecrow Press, 1973), p. 151.
5. Barrett Wendell, *Cotton Mather* (New York: Dodd, Mead, 1891), p. 9. The words are those of John Cotton, the maternal grandfather of Cotton Mather; but the grandson held the same position. Middlekauff's claim that three generations of Mathers held a "traditional Calvinist theology with experimentalism" (*op. cit.*, p. 315) is true of Cotton Mather in particular.
6. F. Ernest Stoeffler, *The Rise of Evangelical Pietism* (Leiden: E.J. Brill, 1965), p. 124.
7. S. van der Linde, *Opgang en Voortgang der Reformatie* (Amsterdam: Ton Bolland, 1976), pp. 160-65.
8. Quoted by James R. Tanis, *Dutch Calvinistic Pietism in the Middle Colonies* (The Hague: Martinus Nijhoff, 1967), p. 104.
9. William Ames, *The Marrow of Theology*, tr. and ed. John Dykstra Eusden (Boston: Pilgrim Press, 1968), I, I, 1.
10. *Ibid.*, I, I, 3.
11. *Ibid.*, I, XXVI, 14, 19; XXIX, 1-4, 8.
12. *Ibid.*, I, III, 1.
13. *Ibid.*, I, III, 2-4, 22.
14. *Ibid.*, I, I, 9.
15. *Ibid.*, I, XXVI, 25; XXIX, 11; II, I, 35, 20.
16. *Ibid.*, II, VII, 13, 17.
17. Among questions in the Heidelberg Catechism that ask what "advantage," "benefit," "comfort," "help," or "assurance" comes from faith are

Qq. 1, 28, 36, 43, 45, 51, 52, 57, 58, 59. Most answers are framed to express the practicality and usefulness of faith. Cf. G. Voetius, *De Uitnemdheid van de leer der Gereformeerde Kerk* (Rotterdam: De Banier, 1936). Voetius held that "all theology that follows Scripture or is based upon it" is practical theology. *Selectae Disputationes Theologicae*, I, I; quoted in *Reformed Dogmatics*, ed. John W. Beardslee III (New York: Oxford U.P., 1965), p. 265.

18. Cf. Leonard J. Trinterud, *The Forming of an American Tradition* (Philadelphia: Westminster, 1949), pp. 53-195; Tanis, *op. cit., passim.*

19. Cf. James C. Livingston, *Modern Christian Thought* (New York: Macmillan, 1971), p. 91.

20. Ames, *op. cit.*, I, I, 10.

21. Richard R. Niebuhr, *Experiential Religion* (New York: Harper & Row, 1972), p. 113.

22. *Ibid.*, p. 140.

Notes to Chapter 16

1. See especially Karl Barth, *The Epistle to the Romans*, tr. Edwyn C. Hoskyns (New York: Oxford U.P., 1933).

2. Herman Ridderbos, *The Coming of the Kingdom*, tr. H. de Jongste (Philadelphia: Presbyterian and Reformed, 1962), p. 19. Ridderbos should be read for a complete discussion of this subject.

3. *Ibid.*, p. 27.

4. *Ibid.*, pp. 352-54; cf. Geerhardus Vos, *The Teaching of Jesus Concerning the Kingdom and the Church* (Grand Rapids: Eerdmans, 1951), pp. 77-90; Richard C. Oudersluys, "Eschatology and the Church," *The Reformed Review*, XIV/4 (May 1963).

5. Cf. Oscar Cullmann, *Christ and Time*, pp. 144-74. This is a major theme in A.A. van Ruler, *De Vervulling van de Wet*, and in Jürgen Moltmann and Wolfhart Pannenberg, who have been influenced by Van Ruler.

6. Cullmann, *op. cit.*, p. 140.

7. Ridderbos, *op. cit.*, p. 55.

8. Cullmann, *op. cit.*, pp. 145f.

9. Van Ruler, *op. cit.*, pp. 40, 48.

10. *Ibid.*, p. 26.

11. A.A. van Ruler, *Droom en Gestalte* (Amsterdam: Uitgeversmaatschappij te Amsterdam, 1947), p. 200.

12. A.A. van Ruler, *Religie en Politiek* (Nijkerk: Callenbach, 1945), p. 44.

13. *Ibid.*, p. 48.

14. Van Ruler, *De Vervulling van de Wet*, pp. 185, 152.

15. *Ibid.*, pp. 200, 185.

16. A.A. van Ruler, *Theologie van het Apostolaat* (Nijkerk: Callenbach, 1954), p. 20.

17. A.A. van Ruler, *Het Apostolaat der Kerk en het ontwerp-Kerkorde* (Nijkerk: Callenbach, 1948), p. 68.

18. *Ibid.*, pp. 69f.; cf. *Droom en Gestalte*, p. 201.

19. Cf. *De Vervulling van de Wet*, pp. 49, 353.

20. Van Ruler affirms that the Synod of Dordt (1618-19) was "the only church gathering in the whole, worldwide history of the church in which the

truth of predestination has been fully confessed and declared." *Het Aposto-laat der Kerk*, p. 66.

21. W. Pannenberg, *Basic Questions in Theology* (Philadelphia: Fortress, 1970), I, 74.

22. W. Pannenberg, *Jesus — God and Man* (Philadelphia: Westminster, 1968), p. 388.

23. *Ibid.*, p. 38.

24. *Ibid.*, p. 224.

25. W. Pannenberg, *Theology and the Kingdom of God* (Philadelphia: Westminster, 1969), p. 56.

26. W. Pannenberg, *Basic Questions in Theology*, II, 242.

27. Pannenberg claims that God is the origin of all *(Basic Questions*, II, 138); that he is transcendent Lord *(ibid.*, pp. 154f.); that he "remains distinct" from history *(ibid.*, I, 158); and that "from eternity to eternity" he is God *(ibid.*, pp. 216, 236).

28. E. Frank Tupper, *The Theology of Wolfhart Pannenberg* (Philadelphia: Westminster, 1973), p. 299.

29. Charles Hartshorne, "Process Philosophy as a Resource for Christian Thought," in Perry LeFevre, *Philosophical Resources for Theology* (Nashville: Abingdon, 1968), p. 45. Cf. Hartshorne's essay "Philosophical and Religious Uses of 'God', " in Ewert H. Cousins, *Process Theology: Basic Writings* (New York: Newman, 1971), pp. 115ff.

30. Hartshorne, in LeFevre, *loc. cit.*, p. 47.

31. *Ibid.*, p. 52.

32. *Ibid.*

33. *Ibid.*, p. 59.

34. *Ibid.*, p. 60.

35. Cf. Whitehead, *Process and Reality* (New York: Macmillan, 1929), p. 528.

36. William Beardslee, *A House for Hope* (Philadelphia: Westminster, 1972), p. 58.

37. Cf. Arnold Bittlinger, *Gifts and Graces* and *Gifts and Ministries* (Grand Rapids: Eerdmans, 1968 and 1973).

38. Cf. Harry R. Boer, *Pentecost and Missions* (Grand Rapids: Eerdmans, 1964); John H. Piet, *The Road Ahead* (Grand Rapids: Eerdmans, 1974).

39. Cf. Ronald C. White, Jr., and C. Howard Hopkins, *The Social Gospel* (Philadelphia: Temple U.P., 1976).

Notes to Chapter 17

1. Herman Dooyeweerd, *Transcendental Problems of Philosophic Thought* (Grand Rapids: Eerdmans, 1948); cf. his *A New Critique of Theoretical Thought*, tr. David H. Freeman and William S. Young (Philadelphia: Presbyterian and Reformed, 1953), I, 68ff.; and *Roots of Western Culture: Pagan, Secular and Christian Options*, tr. John Kraay (Toronto: Wedge, 1979).

2. G.W.F. Hegel, *Lectures on the Philosophy of History*, tr. J. Sibree (London: Henry G. Bohm, 1957), pp. 40ff.

3. Charles Norris Cochrane, *Christianity and Classical Culture*, pp. 500f.

4. Walter Lippmann, *A Preface to Morals* (New York: Macmillan, 1931), p. 330.

5. From a 1940 address to the American Association for the Advancement of Science; quoted by Ordway Tead, in *Toward First Principles in Higher Education: A Dynamic Quest for Unity*, The Hazen Pamphlets, No. 19.

6. Quoted by Tead, *ibid.*, p. 5.

7. Cf. Hugh T. Kerr, "Time for a Critical Theology," in *Theology Today*, XX/4, 461ff.

8. Quoted in Herbert Hartwell, *The Theology of Karl Barth* (Philadelphia: Westminster, 1964), p. 7.

9. J.L. Hromadka, *Thoughts of a Czech Pastor* (London: SCM Press, 1970), pp. 96f.

10. Cochrane, *Christianity and Classical Culture*, p. 221.

11. *Ibid.*, pp. 214, 508.

12. *Basic Questions of Theology*, I, 199-202.

13. *Ibid.*, pp. 199f.

14. André Biéler, *La pensée économique et sociale de Calvin* (Geneva: Librairie de l'Université, 1959), p. 520.

15. André Biéler, *The Social Humanism of Calvin*, tr. Paul T. Fuhrmann (Richmond: John Knox, 1964), p. 15.

Index